THE ROBBER'S DOG

Over 30 years of blood, sweat, tears and emotion

D. LAURENCE

For the quiet times!
Best wishes
Dave Laurence Ellen
25th September
2005

Note for Librarians: a cataloguing record for this book that includes Dewey Decimal Classification and US Library of Congress numbers is available from the Library and Archives of Canada. The complete cataloguing record can be obtained from their online database at:
www.collectionscanada.ca/amicus/index-e.html
ISBN 1-4120-5513-X

Printed in Victoria, BC, Canada

 Printed on paper with minimum 30% recycled fibre. Trafford's print shop runs on "green energy" from solar, wind and other environmentally-friendly power sources.

TRAFFORD *Offices in Canada, USA, Ireland and UK*

This book was published *on-demand* in cooperation with Trafford Publishing. On-demand publishing is a unique process and service of making a book available for retail sale to the public taking advantage of on-demand manufacturing and Internet marketing. On-demand publishing includes promotions, retail sales, manufacturing, order fulfilment, accounting and collecting royalties on behalf of the author.

Book sales for North America and international:
Trafford Publishing, 6E–2333 Government St.,
Victoria, BC v8t 4p4 CANADA
phone 250 383 6864 (toll-free 1 888 232 4444)
fax 250 383 6804; email to orders@trafford.com

Book sales in Europe:
Trafford Publishing (uk) Ltd., Enterprise House, Wistaston Road Business Centre,
Wistaston Road, Crewe, Cheshire cw2 7rp UNITED KINGDOM
phone 01270 251 396 (local rate 0845 230 9601)
facsimile 01270 254 983; orders.uk@trafford.com
Order online at:
trafford.com/05-0411

10   9   8   7   6   5   4   3   2

ACKNOWLEDGEMENTS

Special thanks to both my Son and my Daughter for giving me the positive encouragement and total belief that helped me through the long hours needed to write this book.

I would also like to say a big thank you to the following for giving me the strength to complete the last 18 months, without their help and support I doubt I would be here today to recount this story:

Mrs P O'Shea, Diane Smith, Ms L Lawson, Ms Allen, Mr. Ballard, Tony 'Full Blown' Russell, Charlotte Hadley, Annette & Sean, Basingstoke Police – Child Protection Team, Basingstoke Social Service – Children and Families, The Guinness Trust, Rt Hon Sir George Young, Malcolm 'Killer' Davis & Joy, Rt Hon Sir Andrew Hunter, Steve 'The Dog' Hale & Tasha, Tresa, Ellen and Freddie Allabush, and the tribe, Bob 'The Daddy' Knott, Julie & Steve Amey, Ian & Maureen Ellery, Pete & Carole Parker, Mr J. Martin, Ms Bhanu, Ms Trow, Ms Thomas, Mick Aubrey, Shana, Katie & Arthur, Clair & Justin Smith, Cathy Watson and the tribe, Maz and the tribe, Kell Hickman, Karen & Mark Copeland, Spencer, all the crew down at the 'Priory' in Basingstoke, Sue Towndrow, Graeme McPherson, Robert Pulson, Sam Axton, Mark Weller, Jonathon 'Whoosh' Armstrong, Oscar, all the mums at both schools who have taken the time to take care of me and last, but defiantly not least, is the person who gave me unquestioned support both emotionally and also financially – my mum Carole.

CONTENTS

Introduction

This book is dedicated to both Tori and Nathan, 2 people who have brightened up my life in so many ways.

And also to the memory of the following, who for various reasons couldn't complete the journey - Martin Hale, Adrian Payne, Mick Fry, Jamie Saul, Pete James, Paul Hutton, Alan Carter, Paul Watmore, Dave 'Wink' Watson, Mick Richardson

And Brian Jolly

There are some things which cannot be learned quickly, and time, which is all we have, must be paid heavily for thus acquiring. They are the very simplest things and because it takes a man's lifetime to know them, the little new that each man gets from life is very costly indeed, and the only heritage that he has.

INTRODUCTION

I am going to tell you about the worst thing that has ever happened to me. I don't really want to tell you, because at the time it was too terrible for me to recall, but after careful thought I felt that I had to tell you. I think it's important that you know, and I feel it's the only way I will ever be able to get it out of my heart.

I've survived some awful moments during the last 30 years and each time I believed that someone, somewhere was trying to break me, but now looking back I think that those events occurred just to make me stronger – to prepare me for what was to come. My world fell apart on 11th July 2003, but if you are to fully understand why this event had such a drastic effect on me, then I think I need to take you right back to the beginning.

I'm not ashamed to admit that somehow I managed to loose my way along the 'path of life' for a while – in fact I take strength from the fact that I managed to survive, and in the end I am proud to say that I managed to turn many negatives in my life into positives.

What follows is a long hard look at the life of a man who has been to the bottom of the 'pit' – treading among the vomit and piss in one of her majesty's Prisons. The same man who ten years earlier had only just left a private boy's prep school. Marching around on his last day with his chest out, his blazer on and his cap seated firmly on his head, proudly showing off his school's coat of arms, and beneath it the immortal words 'Be strong and of a good courage'. Well guess what, I did just that, so thanks to Bury's Court boy's prep school in Reigate, Surrey for giving me the strength to survive and the heart to continue.

In later years I then had to fight, not only for my very existence, but also that of my children. I doubt that I will ever be able to convey the true trauma and emotion that we, as a family, had to endure between July 2003 and August 2005. I've thought long and hard about how to get my message across and each time I just seem to come up with a different answer. In the end I decided that the best way would be to tell you the whole story, warts and all. I also decided that I wasn't going to spend hundreds, or even thousands of pounds, enlisting a group of boffins that would only insist that I change almost everything. I wasn't going to spend hours, days or even weeks sitting in a chair with a microphone stuffed under my nose, giving quotes to some sad individual who had little interest in me harping on about how hard life has been to me. In the end I decided that the best way would be to just go ahead and 'write it as I see it'. So far this journey has already lasted for over 37 years, and now I have decided that it would be as good a time as any to 'stop the bus' and have a good long look at my life, to try and work out once and for all where it is that I am heading.

Due to circumstances beyond my control, and after seeking legal advice on the matter, some of the names in this book have been changed in order to protect the identity of those involved.

All of the following is based on fact. So here it is…my story.

CHAPTER 1

KENYA/AFRICA

The story begins on 27th October 1966, when I was born in Nairobi hospital, East Africa – the son of a British diplomat. My parents had been on a 2-year overseas posting there with the Royal Air Force, based at R.A.F. Eastleigh in Kenya. My arrival was duly registered at the British High Commission in Nairobi.

Although I didn't know it at the time, life for me was going to start within the relative safety of the British Embassy. From now on, and for the next fourteen years, I would be protected by diplomatic immunity, surrounded by people who not only thought that they were better than everyone else on the other side of the 'wall', but as I got older I could see that they actually believed that they were. Having said that it's also true that if I had been able to choose my own place of birth, I think that I would have been hard pushed to have chosen a more beautiful place anywhere in the world than Africa.

Although it's fair to say that Africa is generally thought of as the home of the big cats, in reality it's so much more than that. Most of the people that I have met in England over the last 20 years or so only have the documentaries that are force fed to them weekly through the television to base their assumptions on. Even more so now with all of the 'sky' channels available to us, images of cuddly lion cubs and eagles soaring high over elegant tree-tops are an everyday occurrence to our generation of children. But to actually set foot on the open plains of Africa and to touch the orange dust that blows gently over your feet, really is an experience that you would be unlikely to forget.

It is fair to say that I cannot recall anything at all about the first two years of my life that were spent there, although I was fortunate enough to return and spend three whole weeks on safari in East Africa in 1999. Starting in Nairobi, I then headed out over the plains, north toward Sambaru, stopping overnight at local campsites which had been built around the traditional water holes that had been used by the local wildlife for many generations. Our evenings were spent huddled together in make shift 'hides', watching various magnificent beasts from only a few feet away. Families of elephants would come and go. The cheeky brown hyena would lurk in the dark shadows – and trust me you don't need to get to close to appreciate the power of this magnificent beast. The best way to describe them is one big walking muscle with jaws to match, capable of crushing bone with no effort at all. The occasional solitary leopard would suddenly appear from nowhere for a quick drink and then head off back into the night. In between all of this the impala would spend hours trying to get a taste of the murky water, hoping that the other animals were only interested in quenching their thirst and wouldn't decide to take them as an easy meal while they drank.Every morning we were up at 5am to continue our push North, towards Lake Nukuru, which is famous for its unrivalled number of flamingoes – if you have ever seen a post card with a sea of pink flamingoes, then it was probably taken at Lake Nukuru. God only knows how many birds there are on the lake, it's as if the water is totally pink. One can only sit in awe and watch what I can only describe as one of the most amazing scenes that I have ever been fortunate enough to see.

Once again it was back in the jeep to continue our journey northwards, and up onto the Mara – the world famous northern plains of Africa, and home of the Masai tribesmen. These traditional warriors still marched around with their rawhide shields and hand sharpened spears, although today it's generally for the benefit of the tourists.

As I sat there it crossed my mind more than once what a lonely place this would be if you were to be stuck out there alone at night with lions strolling freely around as your neighbours. A daunting thought isn't it, and yet these remarkable people had managed to do just that for many generations – it really was quite a humbling experience and one that I will never forget. The only shame was the fact that now their warrior paint and the dried goat's blood in their hair was applied mainly for the benefit of the fat middle-aged tourists, the men and women who had flocked there just to be able to say that they had seen a leopard, or touched a real life Masai warrior.

In the evenings they crowded round the camp-fires hoping to be the one chosen to join in the festivities that had so conveniently been laid on for their amusement, just so they could return home to their safe little lives with a photo to show their friends back home. Every night they were there, these sad little individuals who cared nothing for either Africa or its people – the funny thing was, little did they know but what they were actually volunteering to do was the traditional dance performed over many generations to celebrate circumcision. I'll leave you to work out who was actually having the most fun and who was humouring who!

I feel that it would be unfair on the people who live there if I did not mention that although many western people go there to live out their dreams and fantasies, I also saw poverty and heartache on a massive scale. Children under ten walk the streets of Nairobi dependent on various solvents. Nearly all are homeless orphans, drifting in the breeze of life. Life can be hard under the sun, very hard. In Africa there is no welfare state, so if you do end up on your dream holiday strutting your stuff under the burning sun, stop and spare a thought for those less fortunate than you and if nothing else give them 5 minutes of your time – the results can be very rewarding.

It's interesting to note that all of the politicians in the western world have spent the last few years telling us how Africa has been mistreated, and what a bad deal they have had from the rest of us over the last 50 years. They will tell anyone who will listen, how they feel it's time to give the country back to the people, and that all the suffering must end. I haven't heard too many of them mentioning the fact that between all of us we have stripped this once noble land of its diamonds and just about anything else of any value. It's ironic that they have chosen to preach such good thoughts now that there's nothing left to give back.You now have to look deep into your conscience and ask yourself why the western machine has decided to steam roller itself across the Middle East, now that they have finished with the African nations. I wonder, could it be that the beast needs to feed again just to sustain its growth, or do you believe that Sadam did actually have weapons of mass destruction as they told you. I sit here and I believe that even Stevie Wonder can see that it's all about greed and oil, and yet they have managed to convince quite a few people in England that poor Sadam could have been a threat to them.

Although this book is not about politics or war, I feel that I should just say that when the recent Iraq/America war started, I was in South East Asia sunning myself amongst various nationalities including the Dutch, German, Swiss, French and the good old Danes - and not one of them thought that either Sadam was dangerous or that the war was justified. But then they didn't have the benefit of good old-fashioned British/American propaganda did they! I guess I'm moving away from the point now, but it needed to be said because history looks very likely to repeat itself from where I'm sitting. I guess that in about 50 years or so my children will have to listen to the politicians waffling on about how hard done by the Middle East is, and that it's time to give it back – minus a few hundred million barrels of oil.

Back to the story and although I cannot recall anything at all about the first two years of my life that were spent in Nairobi, I am still proud to say that I was born in Africa and one day I hope to return to the land of my creation, because for me the magic and sparkle of Africa will never fade.

All too soon it was time to pack our bags and head off to our next posting, which was to be in Lima, Peru. For those like me that are not to hot on geography, Lima is in South America.

CHAPTER 2

PERU/SOUTH AMERICA

We arrived in Lima, Peru – the traditional home of the Red Indian and blowpipes, sometime early in 1969, and I would have been just over two years old. Once again we would be protected by diplomatic immunity and our new home was again to be within the relative safety of the British Embassy. I use the word 'safety' because it's worth remembering that in 1969 when we were there, there were still more than a couple of places in the Amazon that were unlikely to welcome western visitors complete with denim jeans and sunglasses. If you were to think that you were Indiana Jones and go wondering about in the 'bush', then there was a real probability that you would end up cooked and eaten by the locals. My memories of this period in my life are vague to say the least. I suppose many scientists have spent hours pondering the big question of; How far back into our childhood can we actually remember? The way I see it, sat here trying to write a book, is that the further you try to go back – the fewer memories we are obviously able to recall. But there must be a point where it is difficult to distinguish fact from fiction. What I'm actually trying to say is that before I started writing, I wondered what if anything I would be able to recall about the first five or so years of my life. You would have had quite a job on your hands trying to convince me that you could recall exact details of something that happened to you before your fifth birthday. And yet now that I have started to write, I have found that if you trawl deep enough into the depths of your mind then you may well surprise yourself as to how much detail you can actually unlock. It's all in there after all because you were definitely there; you just need the right code to unlock your memory. And so, although I cannot explain how, I do now seem to be able to recall events that had previously been unknown to me or at the very least, had lay buried so deep in my memory that I had long since forgotten all about them.

One of the strangest early memories that I can recall is having conversations with a woman that I could not identify, in a language that I did not understand. Although I have been aware of this fact for many years, I couldn't explain it either to myself or to anyone else. In the end I had just put it down to some sort of childhood dream, or to be honest I had just blocked it out as it didn't seem that important. It was only recently while researching for this book, I mentioned it to my mother and she laughed for a couple of minutes and then informed me that indeed it was true and that she could make sense of it, if only I had bothered to ask. She explained to me that in the British Embassy it was standard practice for everyone to have a housemaid who would do the washing, ironing and a few bits and pieces around the house, including taking care of any children that happened to be lying around. She also explained that while in South America she had learnt Spanish, as this was the local language used out side of the compound, and that if you wanted to get anything at all from the locals then you had better learn Spanish pretty quickly. Well due to my age when we arrived, coupled with the fact that the maids doubled up as a nanny for convenience, I had indeed learnt Spanish very quickly, so quickly in fact that it had become my first language by the time we left some three years later. All of my day-to-day conversations took place in Spanish, due purely to the fact that I spent most of my time with someone who couldn't speak any English.

All of a sudden these strange conversations with a strange women started to make sense. My mother was astounded that I could recall this in such detail some thirty years later, and for me it solved a mystery that had been bubbling about in my head for over three decades.

I'm finding it hard to explain, but when I sit here and try to recall our house in Peru, I'm definitely getting a very negative feeling. The picture in my head is one of sadness. Although it was obviously a long time ago, I really am struggling to reach deep into my mind and recall anything positive at all, strange though it may seem. I can distinctly remember that my mother would go out during the evening, and I can clearly remember something about books. I have a picture in my head of big white books, in the centre of the cover is a small picture, I think it's a picture of some fruit or some sort of flowers. My judgement is that she may have had an evening job packing or sorting these books.

This would tie in with another strong memory that I have from this period. I can remember spending a lot of time hiding under my bed. I'm not sure what I was hiding from but the memories are clear, so it will have to be said that for some reason I was regularly scared and alone, under my bed, waiting for my mother to come home. My elder sister would have been there around this time and yet I cannot recall her being with me. I can also recall a strong memory of hiding under the covers in my bed, but being unable to get out. It's as though someone has come along and made the bed with me in it, leaving me in a position where I cannot get out. Sitting here writing, some thirty odd years later, it's still giving me a very uncomfortable feeling.

I can hear the psychologists and the sociologists shouting at the top of their voices *"I'm telling you, he's mad, he's fucked up – and it's all there in his childhood. Can't get himself out of bed, hiding under his bed – it's simple and it's straightforward – the boy simply isn't wired right and he never was"*. Well I don't agree. Many lesser men have just had to except comments like that, many men were never in a position to defend themselves with a worthy response, through no fault of their own and often due solely to a lack of education. Not me, I don't believe that any of the above is relative to the path that I chose to follow through life. It would be all too easy to blame things on everyone else but I'm not looking for excuses, I just want to write this book to let people know how things were, based purely on fact. It may well be the case that some of these things contributed to what I became as an adult – I don't know for sure, but I have to say that I doubt it very much. Anything that I have ever done, or have been responsible for, was done with a clear and conscious mind. And in my opinion it would be simplifying things a little too much for me to just say that a few bad experiences as a child could be responsible for much of what I have been through.

One of the most important lessons I have learnt over the last few years is that we must, as adults take responsibility for our actions, good or bad – therefore I am not seeking to offer any excuses and I say these things purely as a statement of the facts.

Another memory that is very clear from this time is that one night I can clearly remember being woken up by the sound of shouting coming from downstairs. Again I can only write it how I remember it. What I recall is being woken up one night to the sound of a very serious argument. As I crept out of my bedroom, and made my way along the hall to the top of the stairs, the shouting was getting louder and louder. I carefully peered around the corner where I saw our housemaid struggling with a man in the hallway. He was dragging her around by the hair and she was shouting and screaming. It was a really serious argument although I'm not quite sure who the man was. He could have been her husband, boyfriend or some unwanted guest, either way I'm not sure – but what was obvious to me was that she didn't want to talk to him and that she was screaming for help. Things then get a bit blurred, I must have been spotted because the next thing I know my mother appeared and escorted me back to my room. The only other thing I can recall about that night was that before I was ushered back to my room, my father had appeared holding a golf club and shouting at the top of his voice. The next thing I know, I'm back in my bedroom and it all goes eerily quiet. At this point I cannot recall anything at all, so I guess I fell asleep. It really is a strange feeling putting these thoughts onto paper some thirty years later, but then I knew that there would be difficult parts while writing this book so I'm not surprised, in fact it's a relief to get it of my chest. And anyway I don't think that there's much harm in a bit of self-counseling do you?

In total we were to spend the best part of 3 years living in Lima. Then in April 1972 my parents received the news that our time in South America would be coming to an end, and that they would be returning to an R.A.F base in Aylesbury/ England, to await their next posting, and also for the birth of their new baby, which was due in mid August 1972. For my parents it was to be a time of great celebration, as they would be returning home to see their families for the first time in about six years. For my elder sister and me it would be our first glimpse of England. Of course it didn't quite have the same exciting effect on us, as 'home' was something that we would be leaving in South America. I'd love to say more about my time spent in Lima but unfortunately I just cannot remember anything else of any significance, and anyway I'm convinced that if I could the results would only be more of the same. Whatever the reason, even now I cannot recall anything positive at all from those early years. It could just be that I was too young; it could be a mixture of things so I guess we may never know.

I did however make an enquiry with regard to places to stay in Peru, late in 2001, with a view to going backpacking there for six weeks. Unfortunately I found that it would be a hard place to travel alone and it also became very clear that before you could head to that part of the world you would be well advised to polish up on your Spanish, which is something that I have long forgotten.

CHAPTER 3

AYLESBURY/ENGLAND

We arrived at Heathrow airport sometime around May 1972 and waiting to meet us were members of our immediate family, on my Mothers side. I can remember this row of little white faces with big smiles standing in a line. As it turned out they were my grandmother and her husband, together with my mother's sister Maureen and her husband George. They were standing proudly next to their three daughters – Marie, Sharon and Faye.

As we made our way to the car two things really stood out to me above everything else. The first was the weather - it was so cold. I hadn't realized that this new place that was to be our home was going to be cold. All I'd ever known in my lifetime was bright sunshine, and here I was all excited and shivering.

The other thing that stood out was the fact that everyone was white; sure I had seen lots of white people before, after all I was British. It's just that they had always lived inside the compound and generally walked around as if they owned the place, and now here they were everywhere and to my amazement, some were actually serving food and moping the floor – now that is something that I had never seen. Imagine being me at that point – just about everything that I had come to believe in as 'normal' had just been reversed, and it didn't seem to be bothering anyone around me. I was so confused and yet all around me people were smiling and hugging as if nothing had changed. We walked along with the adults chatting away and eventually we arrived at the car, paid for our ticket and then drove out of the airport car park and headed north. From the conversation I quickly realized that we would be staying at the home of my auntie Maureen and my Uncle George for the next few months. During the journey my father explained that he was expecting to get news of his next overseas posting some time around the end of the year.

As we drove I couldn't help noticing how green everything was; we passed field after field of grass, and various other crops that the local farmers had chosen to grow. This was a totally different world to the scorched landscapes that I was used to, and unlike anything that I had seen before, and the cows – well they all seemed over sized to me. If you've never seen a South American cow to compare with an English one then it would be difficult to explain, but let's just say that to me these cows that were passing before my eyes looked so fat that they were ready to explode. Of course now that I'm older I realize that the African and South American cows were under nourished, but at the time I just couldn't work it out. As we drove along I was also amazed to see such beautiful gardens full of flowers. The only time I had ever seen flowers before was inside our compound, the people outside didn't have gardens, flowers or grass, just scorched earth – where I came from this was a privilege reserved only for the so-called elite.

After a couple of hours in the car we arrived at their house and arrangements were made to help us settle in. I have to say that my mother's sister and all of her immediate family made us very welcome; to this day they have always had a smile and a hug for me whenever and wherever we have met. My Uncle George was the type of guy that was always building things in his shed at the top of the garden and I can still remember the times that he would encourage me to build something out of his old scraps of wood. He was always saying to me, *"go on then boy, build something out of that then"*, as he pointed to a pile of scrap wood laying in the corner - and he never complained no matter how much mess I would make, and as I'm sure you're aware a six-year-old can make a hell of a lot of mess!

I can still remember the day that my cousin Sharon arrived home from school and announced that she wanted to take me 'banking'. With great expectation I was handed some old clothes and a set of oversized Wellington boots that seem to be standard issue to children. We set off over the fields that backed onto their garden and walked for what seemed like hours, although I expect we only travelled a mile or so. We then arrived at the river Trent, I say river, but it was a small section of the river that was only a few inches deep - I started to get the feeling that whatever we were about to do, one thing was certain; I was going to enjoy it. As we sat there by the river, Sharon carefully explained the rules of 'banking' to me. It involved slowly making our way along the riverbank inch by inch holding onto the roots of the bushes and shrubs that had formed all along the sides of the river over the past few centuries, and that had become exposed over time by the constant flow of the water moving downstream. The sides of the river were vertical making it quite a challenge for a six year old; although to be fair the sides were only about 6' high. We spent the next few hours slowly making our way upstream, doing our very best not to loose our grip and end up falling backwards into the ice cold water below. Every now and again one of us would slip and the splash would be drowned out by the fits of laughter that rang out from the other members of the group as we giggled our way upstream. After a few hundred yards and what seemed like an eternity, Sharon announced that the time had come for us to start making our way back as it was getting late. The return journey was great because we were all so confident as we had obviously only just covered this particular stretch of water, and were now familiar with the hand and foot holds required to negotiate our way home. Of course we all made the mistake of thinking that we could go faster and faster as our confidence was now high, needless to say we all got a hell of a lot wetter on the return journey and duly arrived back at their house freezing cold and soaking wet – a good day out was had by all. Writing about it now it seems to have lost a lot of its fascination, but at the time it really did fill my world with wonder. If only adults could be pleased so easily. Over the following few weeks I spent as much of my time as possible hounding my cousins and begging them to take me back to the river 'just one more time'.

Another adventure that I can recall was the day that we had spent playing about on the canal. If I remember correctly we had been spending the weekend at my Grandmother's caravan, I don't recall where it was, but I believe that it was about an hour's drive from Burton on Trent. On this particular day there was my cousins Marie and Sharon together with my elder sister and me. We were walking along the canal in the sunshine, generally larking about, as children do. All along the banks of the canal there were boats of all shapes and sizes, people's weekend crafts all neatly tied to their individual posts, red ones, blue ones, and green ones – you name it and there was probably one there.

As we walked along in the sunshine, the further we went, the less crowded it became. We passed fewer and fewer boats, and then suddenly a small craft that was moored on an extremely short rope caught our attention. It looked like a mini speedboat complete with a small cabin at the front and it was light blue and white in colour. I'm not sure if it was the boat that attracted us so much, or the fact that because it was so near to the bank it meant that with little effort we could board it. Within a few minutes we were all aboard and having the time of our lives. We fiddled with all the controls and sat in the driving chair. For an hour or so we felt like lords of the ocean. Suddenly someone shouted that the boat was moving and panic set in. Our fun adventure suddenly turned into mayhem, as I scrambled over the side and back to dry land. As I turned round to look, my heart pounding with a mixture of panic and fear, I noticed that the rope that held the vessel to the bank had worked itself loose and the craft was now starting to drift away from its mooring and the safety of the canal bank. As I stood there shaking I realized that my sister and Marie were lying at the front end of the boat, doing a spot of sunbathing, and they hadn't heard the call to abandon ship. I started screaming at the top of my voice to my sister, to get off quickly, but being the eldest pair that were there, they coolly ambled to the back of the boat, doing their very best not to show any fear. The problem was that by this time the boat was a good eight to ten feet from the bank and it was impossible for them to disembark without getting wet. Well by now I was screaming my head off, believing that I was going to lose my big sister forever. Panic had really set in and I can still remember being absolutely terrified at the time.

Suddenly as if by magic, a middle-aged man appeared, he'd heard our screams and had come to our aid. He quickly assessed the problem and then casually picked up the mooring rope, which still lay at our feet, although in the panic none of us had noticed it.

He wrapped it around the old oak post that had previously been used to tie up the boat and began to pull the craft back to the bank, with very little effort. My sister and Marie climbed of the boat a little red face as the old sea dog told them that they should have known better than to be playing about with boats. He then sat us all down and proceeded to give us a half-hour lecture on the dangers of the canal and the surrounding area. Now in my later years I have to say fair play to that man because he didn't shout at us, but instead made it very clear that we were very lucky and he went on to explain that not everyone was as kind hearted as he was and that we were very lucky not to end up with a bill for the recovery of the boat. He then sent us on our way with a flea in our ear, having made us all promise that we would not fool about on boats for as long as we lived. I guess he achieved his aim, because I have had the greatest respect for canals ever since.

I can also recall spending hours on our bike's riding around the local area. Having been confined to such a small space inside the embassy, both in Nairobi and in Lima, I was now determined to enjoy my new found freedom. I remember the feeling of being so free, with the wind blowing in my hair, furiously peddling after my cousins. One of my favorite places was an old chalk pit. It seems now, in later life, that just about every town that I have ever visited in England seems to have a chalk pit! This one was absolutely massive and you could ride up and down the sides doing jumps on your bike. We'd spend hours up there chasing each other all over the place.

Even at that age I was starting to see how so called 'normal' people would amuse themselves without spending any money and they were genuinely having fun, it was written all over their faces. Whereas my friends from the Embassy seemed to have a lot of money spent on them - but never seemed to be having any real fun at all. Everything was so controlled in their lives. When you went round to their house there were so many rules, don't touch this and don't touch that, even as young as I was it used to get on my nerves.

One of the biggest nightmares that I had to face around this time was going to school with my cousins Marie and Sharon. Both of them tried their best to get the local kids to except us but to be honest it was still very hard as we were very much a novelty everywhere we went. The main thing was that we both spoke very differently, so it was difficult to hide. I could hold a conversation in English but my preferred language was definitely Spanish at that point, and here I was in Burton on Trent! At least I didn't have to put up with it for long, as we were only staying for a few months, and the summer holidays were coming and that would use up some valuable time for me. It was still a constant battle because I didn't understand any of the work as the schools that I had attended in South America had been working to a completely different syllabus to the schools in England; looking back I had absolutely no chance of success.

I struggled through and did actually manage to make a couple of friends – although once again it would only be a matter of time before I would have to leave them all behind. A familiar pattern was already starting to form in my life, even at that young age I was starting to notice that anyone and everyone that I ever got attached to would desert me in the end for one reason or another. Sure I agree that it often wasn't their fault but whichever way you look at it, the result was always the same.

Some time around July 1972 my mother was admitted to the hospital, the baby's birth was obviously imminent. She must have been in there for a while because I can recall spending quite a few of my evenings being dragged from pub to pub and being force fed salt and vinegar crisps and coke, by my father and my grandfather. I guess that was their idea of fun but to tell you the truth both my sister and I were bored out of our heads, and to this day I don't like salt and vinegar crisps or coke!

It must have been around this time that I first met my relative's on my father's side of the family. First there was his mother whose name I cannot recall, and his stepfather who was known to me as 'Sandy'. My father also had one sister whom we called Auntie Anne and her husband Uncle John – they in turn had one daughter called Debbie. Now this lot really were a strange bunch and for some reason, which was never explained to me, they had never accepted my mother into the 'fold' as it were – I honestly have no idea why this was the case. I've met some strange people over the years but I can honestly say that my father's family ranked as the strangest. They seemed to be stuck in a time warp, some would call it old fashioned – maybe it was just my interpretation, maybe it was just the difference between one generation and another – but I have to say I don't think so, I truly believe that they were strange. They lived in a big posh house in Ealing/London and always gave me the impression that I wasn't fit to be in their presence. I can't recall very much about them, mainly because I didn't see very much of them and when we did I always got the impression that we were all in the way. Their house wasn't designed with children in mind and we were forbidden to touch anything at all whenever we visited. Now I'm not saying that children should be allowed to run riot in other people's homes, but I definitely got the feeling that, if my mother wasn't around, then this lot would have taken great pleasure in dishing out some serious punishment for really minor crimes and I'm sure they would have really enjoyed doing it too – maybe that's what they didn't like about my mother, in their eyes she was probably too good to us and I bet they hated it, they really hated it.

I often wondered what it was that kept Anne and John so close to my father's parents because it was obvious that anyone with even the smallest brain would have moved as far away from them as possible at the first opportunity, and yet in all the years I have known them they have always lived within shouting distance of each other. I don't believe that anyone in their right mind would volunteer to live near that lot because they really were genuinely evil people who seemed to thrive on other people's misfortune – at least they were up front and honest about it and never made any effort to cover up that fact. In later life I found out that what made them stay so close was that special thing that makes people do, and put up with the strangest things – money. In short, I haven't got much else to say with regard to my relations on that side of my family. All my life they have shown absolutely no interest at all in me, so now I guess it's my turn to show no interest in them. In fact I wouldn't have bothered using the ink to write the last couple of pages if it wasn't for the fact that I just wanted to say that my cousin Debbie and I have always got on fine with each other on the few occasions that we have met over the years, and on more that one occasion we had quite a laugh at her parents expense. I'm sure that life couldn't have been easy for her growing up with that lot for support, so wherever you are Debbie you know that my thoughts are with you mate.

Eventually my mother returned home with my new baby brother. He was born on 18th August 1972 at the Royal Air Force hospital in Aylesbury/Buckinghamshire. The following weeks quickly passed and it wasn't long before we received the news that our next posting was going to be abroad again, at first we weren't sure exactly where, but we were told that it would definitely be abroad.

To be totally honest, apart from my relations on my mother's side of the family, I wasn't really very impressed with what I had found in England. I hadn't enjoyed my time spent at school at all and I hadn't enjoyed the weather, all in all it really was a total let down from my point of view and I couldn't wait to get out of there and head back to the sunshine once again.

Eventually the news filtered through and I can still remember the excitement that filled the air as my mother and father called me in one day and announced that we would be moving to Jeddah in Saudi Arabia, for the next three years.

CHAPTER 4

JEDDAH/SAUDI ARABIA

We arrived at Jeddah international airport sometime during November 1972. As we taxied along the runway to our allocated position, I looked out of the window and I was glad to see the familiar glow as the burning sun hit the tarmac. As we left the plane and made our way towards customs and immigration, three things really stood out.

The first was that all the men seemed to be wearing dresses. I'd seen some strange garments of cloth in my time but nothing had prepared me for this. The second thing was the heat; it really does hit you full in the face. The third thing that I noticed was the fact that there were no women at the airport, although it was 1972, I doubt very much if that fact has changed in the last thirty odd years.

We passed through customs and immigration very quickly, considering the chaos that appeared to be going on all around us. For those you haven't had any experience with Arab's, all I can say is that two words, 'organized' and 'chaos' spring to mind. God only knows how they get anything done, but they do. This was when I first really noticed that we were different as wherever we went, there was always someone there to meet us, collect us and deliver us to wherever we wanted to go.

Over the next few years I was to get to fully understand the importance of the diplomatic plates that would once again be permanently attached to our vehicle and the diplomatic immunity that came with them. At the time diplomatic immunity didn't seem such a big deal as it was something that had been protecting me since I had been born. The full impact of what it was didn't actually hit home until I was living in England years later, when a young policewomen by the name of Yvonne Fletcher was shot dead in London in 1984, outside the Libyan embassy, in broad daylight and in full view of passers by. In fact its twenty years this week since she died and still no one has been arrested over her murder. Britain has recently re-opened diplomatic relations with Libya and there is talk that maybe someone may be bought to justice in the near future as part of the deal – but for now we will have to wait and see, rumour has it that the foreign office has a good idea who was responsible so you never know.At the time the whole country was in uproar and it was all over the national press for a couple of weeks, as the politicians publicly discussed how such a terrible thing could have happened. Talk about double standards and politicians being two-faced, because every one of them already knew that the man responsible could not, and would not be arrested because he was a serving diplomat and he had already claimed diplomatic immunity from prosecution – and I was quick to learn that it meant that any individual working on behalf of their government in another country, was immune to prosecution in that country, irrelevant of what offence they had committed. Obviously this case was an isolated incident and I do not want to imply that people from all over the world can come here and shoot who they like and get away with it, although I have to be honest and say that if you were a serving diplomat you could in effect do as you please until such time as the British government would formally request to your embassy that you were removed from office.

To cut a long story short, when those politicians were discussing the incident with such a caring attitude in public, they were indeed only humoring the public because like I have said, they all knew full well that they were unable to arrest anyone with regard to the shooting as soon as the shot was fired, and that the whole media event was done purely to subdue the masses. You should ask yourself whether or not it was worth the eventual cost of a human life just so that a few toffee nosed fools could live a permanent holiday abroad on your behalf and come to think of it, on your tax – personally I think not, but then again it's easy for me to say because I have of course already been there.

Back to the story - we made our way to the car, which incidentally was right outside the front door of the arrival's lounge. The Embassy chauffeur that had been dispatched to collect us got in, and we headed out into the desert towards the British Embassy in Jeddah, which was to be our home for at least the next couple of years.

The landscape is pretty much as you would imagine it to be, sand, sand and more sand, with not much else in between. As we drove along I couldn't help noticing that each time we came to a junction, there was always one or more wrecked vehicles abandoned by the side of the road, and I do mean wrecked. From what I was seeing, the drivers of these small vehicles would have been seriously injured at best or more often that not it was obvious that they would have been killed by the impact required to create such carnage. Over the next few years I was to witness many of these accidents which, as it turned out, were caused by the large 20 ton sand Lorries that relentlessly shifted sand from one town to another 24 hours a day, 6 days a week. These Lorries and their drivers hadn't quite got the hang of the Highway Code, and as a result still operated on the old fashioned theory of *'If I'm bigger than you, then you had better move out of my way'.* It always amazed me how this practice just seemed to be accepted out there, and although it resulted in total carnage on Saudi roads, not once in all the years that I was there did I see any effort at all being made to stop it happening. There really didn't seem to be any 'rules' of the road at all – except one, and that was that women were not allowed to drive at all under any circumstances. It was quite comical really when you witnessed the destruction that the men were causing, and yet someone somewhere actually believed that women might actually be a danger to others on the road. I would honestly rather drive 10 miles in Ibiza at 3 o'clock in the morning, rather than 1 mile on a Saudi road having to chance my luck with those lorries.

In 1972 the British Embassy was situated literally in the middle of nowhere, surrounded by desert on all four sides and Jeddah was nothing more that a market town. As we approached in the car I noticed some large wooden boxes that had been placed adjacent to the road but were set back about 20 feet, so that they sat neatly under the shade from the palm trees that lined the side of the road. When I asked what the boxes were for, the chauffeur told me that the boxes had come from inside the embassy and that they were identical to the ones that would soon arrive for us from England carrying our household equipment, he added that it was the 'done thing' for families to offer their empty boxes to the locals when they had unpacked, so that the locals could use them to live in. I learnt a lot that day about those who 'have' and those who 'have not' – it really stuck in my mind that people would want or need to live in something that we would throw away. Seeing such poverty I must admit that I was beginning to wonder what we had let ourselves in for.

I can also remember seeing children playing 'rounders' - or as the Americans would call it baseball, just outside the main entrance to the compound. The compound was exactly that - a secure area in the middle of the desert, and I do mean secure. On all Four Corners and midway along each side there were small century boxes. The funny thing was that the only time I had seen these boxes before was in my comics about the Second World War – but what was within them was no laughing matter. Inside each one were hand picked soldiers from the Saudi army, and each carried a clearly visible Uzi sub machine gun, which was loaded at all times.

As we approached the entrance, the guards obviously recognized the car and our chauffeur and duly lifted the barrier that was blocking our path. Inside was a whole different world, considering that we had just driven for an hour and a half looking only at sand, what now lay before me took some believing. All around me were beautiful flowers, trees and shrubs. The only way I can really describe it was like driving into a garden centre. I'm not surprised that they have so many droughts over there because it looked like half the national water supply was being used to sustain not only the British Ambassador's garden but as it turned out our new garden, along with the gardens of another twenty five properties that formed the compound. It was so strange because within a stones throw, on the other side of the wall, there were signs of severe poverty and yet here I was looking at such riches. Surely in a fair world, there has to be a strong argument to knock down the dividing wall and let both families share the wealth between them – but if you were to say that 'they' would call you a communist and probably arrest you and then charge you with treason, because they are so terrified that their sons and daughters would lose the perks of the job, like the lifetime on holiday thinly disguised as work.

As we drove in, directly in front of us was the main building of the Embassy – the place where all the important work was done, and high above shimmering in the afternoon breeze I could see the Union Jack flying proudly. Directly on our right stood a smaller building, which turned out to be a couple of squash courts for the use of the families who lived there. We followed the road round to the right and past what I later found out to be the communal rubbish dump. This was quite a large area and it was separated from the rest of the compound by an eight-foot high, concrete block wall.

A couple of years later I was playing in this rubbish dump with a young Scottish friend called Angus, who's father if my memory serves me well was the British Consul at the time. We were doing what young boys do best – mucking about. We were in there playing, probably because it was just about the only place that we weren't allowed to play. Strange how it works isn't it, but you know how it is when you are young, one of the only rules of life is that you have to play in the one place that you're not allowed don't you! Well there were two mischievous little boys, a box of matches and 500 tons of very dry rubbish and I think it's fair to say that this particular adventure was only ever going to end in tears – and it did! We started by lighting one small piece of paper, then we took it in turns to run about 10 feet to the rickety old tap that was bolted to the nearby wall. The idea was to collect some water and then run back and put the fire out. It sounds so easy sitting here now all these years later but at the time it felt like quite a challenge.

The first problem that we encountered was that the old tap hardly worked, the second was that when we got there we realized that we didn't have any sort of container to help us carry the water back to fight the fire - and so the old fashion method of cupping ones hands together was used with limited effect. This lasted for about half an hour, and yes as you've probably guessed, the small piece of paper turned into 2 small pieces of paper and the walk to the rickety old tap turned into a brisk walk. Then it was 3 pieces of paper and a run to the tap, and so on and so on. Of course it had to happen in the end, with that burning sun above us making the whole area so dry and crisp, and sure enough it did, all of a sudden the whole place was alight. We ran and ran with our hands outstretched trying to carry enough water to put out the blaze, but we didn't stand a chance. Luckily we hadn't ventured very far in when we first started playing in there, so when the adults saw the black smoke billowing a couple of hundred feet into the desert sky and came running to see what was happening, they quickly found two soot covered boys standing by the entrance trying to look as innocent as possible - but without success.

We were given a major telling off, not only for playing with matches, which was bad enough. But can you imagine the shock on people's faces, I don't think that poor old wing commander this and squadron leader that had ever been so shocked in all their lives. You simply didn't do that sort of thing when your next-door neighbour is the British Ambassador. As far as I can recall there was nothing that anyone could do as there was just too much rubbish piled up and it was all so very dry and crisp. Just to make matters even worse for us, the whole compound had to watch it burn for about 2 days.

I can still hear the old cheese and wine brigade grizzling

about how the smoke had ruined their dinner jackets that had been hanging out to dry, and how it had singed their lawns. Looking back it was hilarious and it probably made me a legend. I'd bet good money on the fact that the ambassador at the time still uses that story for his after dinner speeches, if he's still out there driveling on!

Back to the story, and the first day that we arrived. We continued in the car past the two green steel gates that formed the entrance to the dump. These were now directly behind us as we turned sharply to the left and made our way past a large communal swimming pool, complete with a sun shade roof made from traditional palm tree leaves. This was for the sole use of the families within the compound, and it was a place where I spent much of my spare time over the next few years.

Another 80 yards or so down the winding road and we pulled up outside our new home. I remember thinking how handy it was being so near to the swimming pool. All of the properties within the compound were bungalows and all came complete with a fully planted garden.

No sooner had the car stopped when a plump little man with a well tanned, rounded face appeared, and in the best queen's English announced that he was Squadron Leader something or other and that we were most welcome. Although all of our neighbours were 'good eggs', to be honest I can only remember the names of a few of them from our time in Saudi, so I guess that the following must have made an impact on me.

The first name that springs to mind is Innes Rae, the father of Shona and Angus, and an old drinking partner of my late father. Innes was a single parent bringing up two young children in a foreign country in the 1970's – god knows what he was doing out there with two small children but he was, and he seemed to be doing alright as well. As the name suggests he was from Glasgow, and very proud of it. Angus and I shared some brilliant moments together as we grew up, and the way I remember Shona is that she was the best swimmer that I've ever met.

Next there was Phil and Liz Robinson, both are still involved in Embassy life and have kept in touch. Both have been friends with my family for over thirty years now. At the time of writing this book they are on an overseas posting in the British Embassy in China. Phil's claim to fame is that he taught me to dive; all of us were excellent swimmers due to the fact that we had a swimming pool so close to the house and as kids we spent a large part of our time in it!

Next up was another friend of my parents, and his name was Dave King. I've no idea where he is now. I remember him because he owned a bright orange lotus kit car that he built himself, and he was crazy enough to drive it from Saudi Arabia to England and back again. I remember him as a quiet, likeable man. I've no idea what actually possessed him to make such an incredible journey. You have to remember that this was over 30 years ago now, and it really was quite an achievement at the time. A couple of years later he talked my father into doing the same journey, which he completed twice with my mother and my younger brother. I have no idea how long it actually took Dave King to make the journey but I do recall having a conversation with my father about it and he told me that it had taken him about 10 days to get from Jeddah to Burton on Trent in England.

A family that lived a couple of doors away from us in the Embassy were the Quinlans. They had three daughters and the middle one was about 15 months older than I was. In later years when I returned from boarding school we would 'hang out' together. She was tall and slim with beautiful dark hair. Well she grew up to be even more beautiful and she went on to marry one of England's true sporting heroes - a man called Daley Thompson. He really was a true legend when it came to athletics; I think most will remember him for his heroics in the decathlon during the eighties. If I remember rightly they met at university and I believe that they are still happily married today.

We soon settled in, although anyone who has emigrated to another country will tell you that for various reasons the first couple of months can be quite hard. It usually takes about 8 to 10 weeks for your furniture and other major household items to arrive – if you're lucky!

Within days I had managed to burn my forearms due to a major lack of sun cream. I'm not quite sure how I managed it, as we were all familiar with the problems caused by the sun. I guess I was busy running around exploring new places of interest and not keeping an eye on things, before I knew it I was burnt to a crisp. I can still remember the blisters that covered my forearms all those years ago. I still bear the scares of those first few days under the Saudi sun some 30 years later, although in my late teens I made great efforts to cover my scarred forearms with a couple of tattoo's, much to the annoyance of my parents.

Just like in Lima we also had a maid that took care of the everyday things around the house, I remember that she used to like making bread – whenever I used to go out the back door I would always see a loaf that she had put outside in the sun to 'rise' before baking it. I can't recall her name although I can remember that she was a quiet person and that she didn't speak much English at all.

As both myself and my sister were getting older now, we weren't confined to the house so much and we actually spent a great deal of our time at the swimming pool, with other members of the embassy clan, or learning to play tennis on the tennis courts that were right next to the pool.

Life generally was excellent in Saudi. Imagine being a little boy and having all that sand to play in, although it did have its drawbacks sometimes. At dusk you had to be very careful due to scorpions and various other things that were wandering about – walking about without shoes was definitely not advised. Our weekends, which in Muslim counties are on a Thursday and Friday, were often spent camping in the desert. I can remember many visits to places like Yambu and Taif with friends from the Embassy. My father would pack the long wheelbase land rover full of camping equipment and off we would go into the desert for an adventure. Lawrence of Arabia was big box office at the time and I guess all the dad's felt obliged to act the part.

Food would be either a barbecue or those dreaded Army ration packs, which were standard issue at the time. If you have never seen one you're not missing much, they are very basic and the idea is that they feed 10 men for 1 day, or 1 man for 10 days – the only drawback was that the packs only contained dried or tinned food. This is fine for the kids as just about everything looked and tasted like a biscuit, but not so much fun for the adults!

One of the most amazing things about the desert is that no matter where you go or how far you travel, you can guarantee that, when you least expect it, an Arab will pop up from nowhere. You would be amazed how far those people can travel without a car or a camel; it really does take some believing. Often we would go camping and you could hear the adults talking in the front, chatting about how secluded this place was and that 'No-one could be out here this time' – and sure enough before you had erected a tent, an Arab would appear as if by magic.

Another amazing feature of the desert is what is known as a 'mirage', and no it's not a French fighter plane! I'm not too sure about the technical aspect, or the 'science' involved – but in layman's terms, a mirage is when you see something in the desert that isn't actually there. The most common type of mirage that occurs in the desert is the one where you will see water a few hundred yards ahead of you, but no matter how far you travel, you never seem to get any closer to it. Coupled with the hallucinations that can accompany heatstroke, many men have perished trying to reach a water source that never actually existed.

The moral of the story is treat the desert with the utmost respect and never think of going anywhere in the desert without water – take as much as your circumstances will allow. The bottom line is that in the desert, water = life – it's as simple as that.

Jeddah is situated right next to the Red sea, so it made sense that a large part of our life would involve either being on or in the sea itself. To be honest it really was just like having an aquatic paradise on your doorstep, some people spend thousands of pounds every year traveling around the world looking for the best places to dive with the most varied assortment of fish and coral – and here we were, living right next to it. My younger brother is now a very keen diver himself and he spends large quantities of cash every year taking himself and his wife to exotic places to dive – I'm quite sure that this habit stems from his childhood because he was swimming amongst some of the strangest fish in the world by the time he was about four years old.

I remember the time that my late father acquired a 'mirror dingy' that was in need of some minor repair work. For those who don't know, I think that the best way to describe a 'mirror dingy' is to say that it looks like a small rowing boat with seating for 2 adults or 1 adult and 2 small children. The main feature that distinguishes it from other sea faring vessels is that it has a 'flat' shaped front end, as apposed to a point like most small boats. It also has the addition of a small sail rising from the centre. Just about anyone who was anyone in Saudi Arabia had one of these boats in the 70's and I believe that I am correct when I say that they are strongly recommended as an ideal first boat for anyone who wishes to learn how to sail. We had hours and hours of harmless fun with it once my father had repaired it and I lost count of the times that we ended up in the water when my father attempted a 180 degree turn without success, for some reason he just never quite got the hang of it.

As well as the mirror dingy we also had the alternative choice of booking the 'royal launch' for the weekend, from the embassy. I'm not quite sure why they needed this type of equipment or how exactly someone had managed to justify and acquire it on our behalf but somehow they had managed it, after all I suppose that one couldn't be seen to be representing ones country abroad without a suitable craft to travel in now could one!

To be fair I should add that over the 7 years that I eventually ended up staying in Jeddah, we did have a couple of royal visits to the embassy from people like the duke and duchess of Gloucester and the duke and duchess of Kent, and I have to admit to being the proud owner of some rather nice photographs from those memorable days with me stood proudly shaking hands with both couples. I suppose that one reason that they would need a royal launch would be in case such people were to ask to be taken out for the day to the seaside! Looking back it seems quite comical and we must have looked like a right bunch of fools as we boarded the launch, complete with union jack flying proudly on the front, and proceeded to sail out of Jeddah harbour. It would have been just like a scene from the 'African Queen' and it's making me chuckle even now sat here writing about it all these years later.

It just goes to show how much my life has changed since those days because I just couldn't imagine doing it now and to be honest if I ever saw such a sight I would be more inclined to try to sink them than to wave at them as they passed. I don't mean to be rude it's just that it seems a world away from where my life is now.

Back to the story, we would often be taken out with other families for a day trip on the royal launch. I'm sure most of it was for show but nonetheless we did enjoy some memorable days out, there were quite a few small islands within an hour or so from the harbour and they were easily reached by such a small craft. Looking back we really were living the high life, a holiday doing all of the above would cost you thousands of pounds today, and yet here we were doing this every other weekend when we felt like it because it was our way of life – our reality.

Although our initial posting had only been for three years, we did in fact end up staying in Jeddah for almost seven years. I look around today and many of my friends have never even left England for a holiday and it really does make me realize just how lucky I was to have spent those years growing up under the Saudi sun.

Without exception all of the children in the embassy went to private school, usually at about eight to ten years of age and then on to university. I guess that although I didn't know it, my school life had already been mapped out for me. If you were too young to go to private school then you only had two choices: the first was obviously the Arabic speaking Muslim schools, which to be honest would have been impossible for many reasons. The only other choice available at the time was a school called Jeddah Prep. This was an American run school that had been established in the late sixties in the centre of Jeddah and it was just like the high school in the film 'Grease'. There was a strong American force in the Middle East in those days and as always the yanks liked to do things their own way, so I guess that it was no surprise to anyone that they had bought a school with them!

Things for me personally seemed to be going from bad to worse, a few months earlier I had been trying to learn to speak English with a northern accent and now here I was trying to learn English with an American accent, looking back it was hardly surprising that my school days always seemed to be a bit of a struggle.

And so once again I was the 'new boy' and I had to start all over again making new friends. I guess that I should point out that as a child I was very small for my age, not only in height but also in general build, even now at 37 I only weigh in at about 67kg, and I'm six foot tall, with my dark brown hair I suppose that I resemble a pencil when viewed from the side.

I managed to survive Jeddah Prep for about 3 years, the first two years I was lucky enough to have the company of my elder sister but then the day came when it was time for her to move on and start her private education. The decision was made that she would be going to a convent in England, and she was duly enrolled at Notre Dame Convent in East Grinstead, which was in Southern England. Just about the only thing that I can actually remember about it is that it was built right next to a horse-racing track. There's not much more to say about this except that I'm sure she would have her own stories to tell.

While I'm on the subject of schools it's probably worth mentioning that as you can see there were many positive things about embassy life, but as I've always said 'everything comes at a cost', and one of the 'costs' was that I was made to attend Sunday school every weekend – the strange thing was that the Muslim weekend was on a Thursday and Friday and I've always wondered why we didn't call it 'Friday school' during our time in Jeddah.

In and around the town of Jeddah there was a lot of Turkish influence that dated back to the wars between the two countries that had raged years earlier. Many of the buildings were covered in beautiful wooden carvings which had been left behind by the Turkish invaders.

We would often take a trip into the beautiful market town on a Thursday morning to buy odds and ends. The traditional name for an Arab market is a 'Souk' – pronounced 'Sook'. Now this is where the action is to be found, because the Souk is the centre of Arab life. Every Thursday people from all walks of life would travel great distances to the local souk to buy or sell their wares. One of the things that I found most fascinating as a young boy was how they got round the problem of keeping the chicken's fresh at the market. Just about every Souk that I visited in the Middle East had a chicken stall. Each one had metal crates with folding lids stacked as high as it was physically possible, and each crate was full of live chickens – all of which were white in colour. At the front of the stall stood a large stone wheel, attached to the wheel was a drive belt that led to another larger wheel which in turn was attached to a bicycle frame, complete with a seat and a set of pedals. As you sat on the seat and started to pedal the drive belt would start to turn and as a result of the motion the front wheel would start to rotate at quite an alarming speed, causing an instant stir of excitement.

The general idea was that you approached the stall and selected your live chicken from the crates; usually all you would have to do was point at it. The head of the stall would then leap into action. Quick as a flash your chicken would be hauled from the safety of its cage, and with a lightening flick of the wrist, the chicken's neck would be broken right there before your eyes. He would then bark the order to start peddling at his 'boy' who would be sat in the saddle eagerly waiting for the command. The large wheel at the front would pick up speed and then your chicken, which up until a few moments ago was so full of life, would be pressed eagerly against it sending feathers flying in all directions. Within a couple of minutes your chicken would be completely featherless and you would be presented with it as though it was a work of art – and I suppose in a way it was. It's definitely something that you have to see to believe. I have to be honest and say that the sight of the Saudi chicken stall and the smell that always accompanied it will probably be with me until the day I die!

Something else that's very likely to stay in my memory are the markets that were totally dedicated to gold. Here you could buy just about anything, and I do mean anything. Over the last few years many friends have asked me about the gold markets of the Middle East. Many of them had heard or read stories and had always believed that it was just a myth. So for the benefit of those people and all the others who are still wondering if it's true, then I can tell you without doubt that it is true and I have seen it with my own eyes. I have walked through them many times, in fact when I was young one of the highlights of my weekend was to go down to the local gold Souk and practice my bartering with all the salesman. Unlike in England, none of the gold was hall marked, therefore lowering the value; nevertheless it was an amazing sight. Imagine for one moment actually walking amongst a whole market full of gold – awesome!

While I'm on the subject, many people around the world have asked me if it's true that the streets of London are paved with gold. Well my friends I've been there as well. I've walked through Camden market and I'm afraid that I didn't see any gold on the floor, in fact as true as I'm sat here writing, the only thing that covers the pavement in Camden market in dog shit. So I'm very sorry to have to disappoint you, but the latter is definitely not true!

Back to the Saudi market, as I've said this is the centre of the local community. Believe it or not, many of the films made in western countries, such as Monty Python's 'The Life of Brian'; although being an obvious piss take, when you strip away the humour they do actually portray life in the Middle East very accurately indeed. Punishments like public floggings were routinely carried out in and around the market square. Who can forget when the Saudi's actually flogged one of their royal princesses at a public market in the early 1980's. Can you imagine going shopping one weekend in London, turning a corner and seeing Princess Anne being flogged. I'm sure you might be able to recall that there was a huge public outcry from all around the world, any yet the Saudi's didn't bat an eyelid. In fact quite the opposite as they couldn't understand what all the fuss was about – under the law's laid down in their country, if you broke the rules then you paid for it and it didn't matter who you were – even royalty. I can remember at the time how often people who knew that I had lived out there asked me if she really was a princess, as they didn't believe for one minute that she was and they truly believed that it was some sort of publicity stunt. The answer without doubt was of course she was, and not only was she a princess but she was also a highly respected one as well. She was the 'real deal', but out there it makes absolutely no difference at all - she broke the rules and she got flogged, it's as simple as that. If only our laws were so straightforward here in England, then I think most would agree that life would be a lot simpler – and safer.

Well to be honest there are a thousand memories that I could share with you about my years spent in Saudi Arabia but maybe now isn't the time for all of them, but it's fair to say that I have no regrets about those years spent in the desert. There are definitely days when I miss it and would gladly turn back the clock if I could, so that I could sit on the banks of the Red Sea just once more – unfortunately Saudi Arabia doesn't have any tourism and as far as I'm aware, you can only enter the country to work or to visit someone who already works there – so there are no package deals to Jeddah I'm afraid.

Before I knew it the years had ticked by and suddenly it was my turn to head off to a private boarding school. I've no idea how my parents came to choose this particular school, but I can remember the day that they announced that I would be going to Bury's Court Boy's Prep School in Reigate/ England. They also told me that I would be staying there during the school term and that I would then fly home to Saudi for the school holidays, like all the other children in the Embassy.

And so at the beginning of September 1977 I said my goodbyes, but at least this time I knew at the back of my mind that I would return in a few months. We packed a few items that I thought I would need to help me settle on my new adventure, based on the recommendation of friends who were already at boarding school, and we headed to Jeddah international airport. The next thing that I knew, I had boarded a plane along with my mother, father, elder sister and my younger brother and we were heading to England once again. The plan was to drop my sister back to her convent in East Grinstead and then to head across to Reigate to try to find my new boarding school.

CHAPTER 5

BURY'S COURT BOYS PREP SCHOOL

As we drove down the winding lane, I really was beginning to wonder if we would ever find it, the last building that I could remember seeing was the 'Black Horse' pub, and now that was at least a couple of miles behind us. All of a sudden there it was, right in front of us – a large dark blue sign approximately 2m x 2m and written neatly on it in lovely gold lettering were the words 'Bury's Court Boys Prep School', and underneath was the address which read Leigh, Reigate, Surrey, and the school motto in Latin, which when translated meant 'Be strong and of a good Courage'.

We crossed the cattle grid that defined the boundary and made our way steadily down the driveway, you could feel the apprehension in the car as we all eagerly gazed forward wondering what we would find. Eventually we pulled up and came to a stop outside what I could only describe as a stately home. We got out of the car and were swiftly greeted by a gentleman who introduced himself as Mr Donald White - the head master. We briefly introduced ourselves and then it was straight down to business.

It turned out that the school was run by Mr. White, with the help of his mother and father; he explained to us that in order to 'keep things simple', the easiest thing to do would be to call his mother and father Mr and Mrs White and address the headmaster as Mr Donald. Mr. Donald was about 40 when I arrived and had been handed control of the school sometime over the last few years.

I looked around and could see about a dozen boys playing on the large green behind us at the front of the school, and in the background I could hear a dog barking. Mr. Donald turned and led us towards the main school entrance. The doors were solid oak, trimmed with black hammered steel fittings and they were absolutely enormous, the only comparison that springs to mind is that of a castle. The entrance hall was open planned and lined with oak, to my right was a full size snooker table with a couple of boys quietly playing happily together, like a couple of experts. We walked round to the right, past the snooker table and through a doorway in the corner of the hall, this turned out to be the main school office. Over the next 4 years some of the most important decisions about my well-being and also my future were to be made in this small room.

A prefect was summoned and I listened intently as the head master told him to take me to the school matron, so that I may be kitted out in the school uniform, plus anything else that I would require for my stay.

I collected my suitcase, which had been left in the entrance hall and I followed the prefect across the hallway and up the stairs. As we walked my new guide explained to me that this would be the last time that I would use this staircase for at least the next 3 years – the next time I would walk down these stairs I would be either a prefect myself or I would be leaving the school, having passed my common entrance exam. All the boys were expected to use the stairs at the rear of the building so as to cut down on the wear and tear of the main stairs.

At the top of the stairs was the dreaded 'sickbay'; a small room not much bigger than a cupboard, and in it were two beds, one of which was occupied by an unfortunate soul. As soon as we appeared a voice bellowed, 'Name', there was silence as we looked at each other, and then the voice boomed again, 'Name, I haven't got all day' – it was at that point that I realized that she was in fact speaking to me – this was my first introduction to the dreaded school matron. I gave my name and was ordered to follow her; she then led the pair of us down a dark, narrow corridor that was lined on both sides by what seemed like a thousand drawers. As we made our way along she kept looking me up and down, measuring me for size with her eyes – she suddenly stopped and started to pull open various drawers and presented me with 2 pairs of Navy blue corduroy shorts, 2 shirts, one school tie – complete with the school motto, 2 pairs of socks, 2 pairs of pants, 1 Navy blue school blazer + a navy blue peaked cap to match and finally one bath towel. I followed her back to the sick bay where she stopped, reached up to another set of drawers and handed me 2 sheets, a blanket and 2 pillowcases. We then headed back along the corridor to find my allocated bed. Looking back it was like a scene from Oliver Twist, with me cast in the role of Oliver – here I was 7000 miles from home and just about to be left alone to start a new life, and it was supposed to be good for me!

As we walked, I noticed that each dormitory had a wooden plaque hung above the doorway and each one, in gold lettering was named after a famous ship. We came to a halt outside the 'Cutty Sark' and as we entered the room I realized that this was going to be my new home for the foreseeable future. I looked around and could see that there were 2 bunk beds in the room, I was informed that mine was going to be the bottom bunk, behind the door – in all honesty, had I been given the choice I would have chosen that one anyway. Next to my bed was a wooden 'tuck box' which was approximately 2 foot long, 18 inches deep and about 18 inches high, and on the front of it my name had been written in large black letters. It turned out that every boy at the school had his own 'tuck box', and in it we had to keep anything that we wished to use during the term time – I learnt from a very young age that to survive in the big world one didn't actually need many things at all, as most of our possessions are there purely to fuel our own greed or to massage our egos. Even today, some thirty years later, I still find that I could pack my little wooden box and lead a happy existence just about anywhere in the world, should the need arise.

I was left to change while the school matron wandered off clutching my suitcase. When I asked where it was going, I was told that she would sort through it and return anything that I would need, anything else would be boxed up and handed back to me at the end of term. She announced before she left that when I was changed I was to report back to her at the sick bay.

After about 20 minutes I appeared. Matron then explained to me that from now on I would be addressed as 'Laurence' at all times. Just for the record, if there was more than one boy from a particular family, then the oldest would be known as 'Laurence Major', the next one down would be 'Laurence Minor' and finally the youngest would be known as 'Laurence Minimus'. I never saw an instance when there were four boys from one family, but I was assured that if there ever was, then the youngest would be known as 'Laurence Mini-Minimus'.

Another prefect was summoned to escort me to the other end of the building and back to the school office, only this time via the 'back' stairs. These were made from stone and were very tight and steep; I guess that in years gone by this would have been the servant's entrance/exit. We made our way back to the headmaster's office to the usual bullshit sounds of *'oh doesn't he look smart'*. Looking back I guess that my parents had been signing the relevant paperwork and getting the final 'sales pitch' about what a good decision they had made for their son by sending him to 'Bury's Court'. As we stood there it suddenly dawned on me for the first time that they were about to leave.

We made our way back out to the parking area and headed towards the car. Mr. Donald then summoned one of the boys that had been playing on the green adjacent to the car park; he then turned to me and suggested I go with him to join in. Without thinking I followed the boy onto the green and over to his group of friends, as I turned I just managed to catch a glimpse of our car as it disappeared back down the drive towards the exit, and I suddenly realized that I was all alone – it would be three and a half months before I would see any of my family again, for a young boy under 10 years of age it was a very emotional time.

And so just like that I began the next phase of my education. I was to spend the next 4 years learning how to be an upstanding member of the community, not only was I there to get an outstanding education but I was also there to learn how to behave, to learn right from wrong, so that I could develop into the perfect young male that I guess all parents want their son's to be. Everything was set to a routine, all you had to do is follow the instructions that were given and life would be simple and straight forward. Everything was done to the sound of and old church bell, when it rang you quickly realized that you should be somewhere amongst a line of little boys, all lined up in total silence waiting for the next instruction to be given. The first rule of Bury's Court was that there was to be no running within the school building for any reason.

There was 106 boys at Bury's Court during my stay, of which approximately 40 were full time 'boarders' – in other words they spent the whole term time living there and only returned home during the school holidays. Generally the parents of those boys that 'lived in' were abroad on various postings with the armed forces just like my parents, although there was the odd doctor's or lawyer's son mixed among us. There were 17 boys in my class and due to such small classes it was very difficult to hide during a lesson – anything you did in that classroom was spotted by the teacher. The other thing worth noting is that during my entire 4 year stay, I had the same desk in the same classroom. At the end of each lesson a bell would sound and this was the signal for the teacher to pack his things and move to the next classroom, all I had to do was open my desk, put my books away and replace them with the books required for the next lesson – so there was no disappearing between classes and no getting lost in the corridors, we were there to learn and learn is what we were going to do. At the change of each lesson, as the next teacher approached the classroom, we would always hear him or her coming before we ever caught sight of them. If we were about to have a math's lesson all you would hear was *'one four is four, two fours are eight, three fours are twelve'* and so on – by the time the teacher reached the classroom door, they would be welcomed with a chorus of boys eagerly repeating the chosen times table back to them. The same applied to all other lessons, in science we would recite the chemical formulas that we were working on at the time. For example I can still recall the hours spent repeating formulas such as $D = M$ divided by V, or for those that don't know: Density equals Mass divided by Volume. We would also have to recite the densities of various items from a homework list, such as the density of gold, lead, water and so on.

When the bell sounded for meal times we would all make our way towards the school dinning room and line up in an orderly fashion, single file in total silence. On the right hand side of the corridor, just outside the entrance to the dining room was the school 'notice board'. Every morning all the boys would line up for breakfast with their eyes transfixed on the notice board, as it was here that you would find any mail from overseas that had been delivered to the school. I remember eagerly looking for a letter every single morning during my four years there.

While we silently queued for our meals the duty teacher would pace up and down the corridor seeking out anyone who would be silly enough to be chatting away. If you were caught you would be removed from the queue, marched to the nearby entrance hall and made to 'stand in the corner', in full view of everyone and right outside the headmaster's office. Now there was only one way to end up with your nose 6" from the old oak panels, and that was to have broken one of the rules – although the punishment wasn't harsh it did have the desired effect. As you had been removed from the safety of the crowd and placed alone against a wall then everyone who walked past, teachers and children alike knew that you had misbehaved. You couldn't hide it and every teacher that passed by while you were there would give you a stern look or a brief lecture on the need to follow rules in society – and every child would pass you doing his best to snigger at your misfortune while making sure that he wasn't noticed, or he too would end up stood next to you staring at the oak. To be honest the shame alone was enough to keep everyone in order – they had obviously learnt that if you use violence and aggravation to control people, all you do is create more violence and aggravation – definitely a lesson to be learnt there.

Once we were all in a nice, silent, straight line, the first group of twenty or so boys would be ordered to make their way inside the hall. Inside there were neat rows of tables with seats bolted onto the sides – the same type that years later I was to find in every pub garden in England. Each table would seat 9 boys – 4 on each side and at one end the teachers had added a chair for the head of the table, which if you were lucky would be a prefect or if you were unlucky – the duty teacher. The meal would be then be bought to your table by the nominated prefects and served to each individual by the head of each table. When everyone had their serving of food the head of each table would say the immortal words, which were to be repeated by all - *"For what we about to receive, may the lord make us truly thankful"*. You would then hear the clattering of cutlery as over 100 boys tucked into their meal that they had been waiting what seemed like an eternity to eat. We were allowed to chat to each other but as always behaviour had to be of the highest standard. You would of course occasionally be hit in the back of the head by a flying pea or a piece of sweet corn, hurled by some brave soul – strange isn't it that even under the strictest of conditions, children will still be children.

Evening meals were the best mainly due to the fact that when someone had a birthday, the resident cooks would bake a birthday cake – now this was no ordinary cake, this was a work of art. We didn't get many sweet things as sweets were banned unless they were given out by the school, so the sight of a cake being paraded in front of us was definitely a highlight!

When it was your birthday you would be called up to the front of the hall, you would then be asked to choose your three best friends and they would be summoned to assist you in the job of handing out your birthday cake to all the other boys. The cake would always be the same, a light sponge, covered in icing, approx

12″ by 12″ and about 6″ high; this would then be divided between over 100 boys! You can imagine how small each piece was by the time it arrived on your plate – and yet we were so pleased to see it arrive.The chosen 'three' would walk round the room delivering the pieces of cake, and for their efforts they would be rewarded with a double sized portion – this had the effect of making you feel on top of the world as you made your way back to your seat, making sure everyone in the room was aware that you had been chosen as a 'best friend' for the evening.

Every day was the same, the only exception being that during the summer term, if the weather was good, the lunchtime meal would be served outside on picnic tables. Although it doesn't sound like this minor detail would have much effect, in reality it did, as to a 9 year old this turned another boring meal time into a mini adventure.

After the break for our evening meal, which lasted for 45 minutes, a bell would sound and we would then make our way to our classrooms to collect our books in order to do our 'homework'. Homework was done under the supervision of the duty teacher. When the bell sounded all the boys who 'lived in' at the school would make their way to the attic, which was on the forth floor. Up on the forth floor there were 5 classrooms, a school library and an area allocated to the storage of the dreaded 'tuck boxes'. We would all choose one of the five classrooms in which to do our homework. All five classrooms were under the supervision of a prefect and the duty teacher would patrol between the rooms, looking for anyone who was misbehaving and disrupting all the people who wished to do their work.

Anyone caught misbehaving would be given 100 'lines' to do on top of their homework that had been set for that particular evening. You would be given a piece of paper and written neatly at the top would be the words that you would have to write out 100 times i.e. '*I must not misbehave during homework*'. Each line would have to be written neatly so the duty teacher could actually read it! If they couldn't then you would be handed it straight back and you would have to start all over again. Along with being made to stand in a corner this was the punishment handed out for almost all offences committed at Bury's Court. It's quite strange but it worked, bad behaviour was very rare in my boarding school, we were all taught to respect each other and also each others belongings and property. During the next hour we would quietly sit revising for our next exam or just going over some Latin vocabulary that we would be working on that week. The evening homework class lasted between 6pm and 7pm every week day without fail.

At 7pm the bell would sound again and we would gather our stuff and return to our desks to put everything away for the night. We now had half an hour to watch TV in the common room or to quickly grab a couple of games of chess. Then at 7.30pm the bell sounded and it was off to the dormitory to collect our pajamas and head of down to the showers. The showers were in the cellar of the school and so it was really spooky down there, you defiantly didn't want to be first to head down the old stone stairwell into the dark abyss. The cellar consisted of our changing rooms for P.E, the showers and also an area that was used to store our football boots and Wellington boots when they were not in use. At the far end was a large room that was used for our 'hobbies' on a Wednesday afternoon.

We would all form an orderly queue for the showers, which held about 10 boys at a time. Once a week the dreaded 'Vosene' shampoo was handed out and we had to wash our hair. I don't know if they still make 'Vosene' now, but every time I think back to the 70's it's the first thing that pops into my mind – that dreaded green slime and that horrible medical smell. Once showered it was back to the dormitory to wait while all the other boys got showered. While you were waiting for the others to finish you would be expected to climb into bed and sit there reading or doing some revision. At about 8.30pm Mr. Donald's head would appear at the door saying the immortal words *'Good night, god bless you all'* - then it was off to sleep.

Within minutes of the head master disappearing down the corridor the gentle whispering would start, usually if you had a decent dormitory captain he would instigate the conversation. As he was responsible for the running of the dormitory; this meant that he was also held responsible if the duty teacher heard any noise or misadventure coming from the room. If he was a decent fellow, as most of them were (although just as in the real world there was the occasional 'jobs worth' who would report you in the morning for the smallest of offences) – he would offer to tell a 'bedtime story'. Although it sounds like fun, not everyone in the room always appreciated it! The stories told involved the usual stories that children will always tell each other when they are left to sleep in a group. They always seemed to be set in a forest, in the pitch black and generally involved a large dog or some sort of creature that was bound to cause some sort of mayhem. Generally the idea was to scare the hell out of the younger boys without actually pushing them to the limit upon which they would run out of the room screaming and everyone would be in big trouble in the morning.

If you had a really good dormitory captain it had been known for pillow fights to break out, which were always great fun – the only problem was that unfortunately little boys the world over have never grasped the fact that they are extremely noisy when it comes to a pillow fight. In most cases we would all end up with a hundred lines in the morning. The strange thing was we never did work out how the duty teacher always managed to catch us right in the middle of it.

There were four boys in my dormitory, the dormitory captain was always a prefect and would have been 13 years of age. The other three were made up of various aged individuals and I'm sure that at least a small amount of thought went into deciding who was in the room with who as we always seemed to get along together without any problems. Just for the record there were 8 dormitories in total at Bury's Court and they all held between 4 and 12 boys. Only one, named after 'HMS Hood' held 12 boys, the rest had four, five or six.

Wednesday afternoons were set aside so that the boys could enjoy a selection of 'hobbies'. Usually this involved building Air fix models – these were available in an assortment of themes. You could buy both first and Second World War airplanes in a plastic kit, various tanks or armored vehicles, formula one cars etc.

You could also buy model airplanes in kit form that were made from balsa wood. These required a lot more time and effort to build as you would have to do things like building the mainframe of the wings, using a technical drawing.

If we were really lucky, during the summer months Mr. Donald would organize a trip to 'Biggin Hill' so that we could enjoy the delights of flying our home built model planes. We would spend an afternoon up there, until one by one the boys would damage their planes and then it would be back to the Wednesday hobbies club to carry out the repairs required before the next flight. Although I made various aircraft during my time there using the air fix plastic kits, I never got round to attempting the more advanced method of balsa wood.

During my stay I also joined a couple of other clubs that were available on Wednesday afternoons. One of these was the stamp collecting club and in time I became an avid philatelist. I still have a collection of first day covers from 1977 to 1980 that were bought by me, after standing in the queue outside Mr. Donald's office on a Monday evening

Another was the chess club. Chess was something that was always encouraged at Bury's Court and boys could always be found sitting quietly in dark corners enjoying a game of chess. This was introduced to our Wednesday afternoon activities and so I joined the chess club at about 10 years of age. I still enjoy playing the game even today – during recent trips to southeast Asia, the first thing that I packed was my travel chess board – it really is a powerful tool as you can pull up a chair anywhere in the world, get your chess board out and someone will soon approach you and strike up a conversation. I know it's true as I've done just that, I've played a game of chess with a Dutch hippy in Malaysia and I've also played chess with a Swiss psychologist in Bangkok in recent years – both interesting stories and one day I may well write about both of them.

Any equipment that you would require for your 'hobbies' could be ordered on a Monday evening after dinner, and before the homework session was due to start. You could only order items if your behaviour during the previous week was acceptable. If you felt that you qualified you would queue outside the headmaster's office after dinner and wait for your turn to be called in to place your order. Money to pay for these items was supplied each term by your parents and all the relevant information regarding your individual wealth was kept in a records book. On entering the room you would be asked what you would like to order, the details were recorded in the order book and the headmaster would inform you that Mrs. White would do her best to purchase your selected items during her weekly journey into Reigate every Tuesday morning. You would queue again the following evening to collect your order, and while you were in the office you would have to sign the order book to say that you had received the items and the total spent would be deducted from your account

And so it was that Wednesday afternoons were enjoyed by everyone in the school as it meant no lessons, the only exception being that at the end of each term, Wednesday afternoons were used for doing our mock exams. Questions would be based upon whatever we had been working on during lessons for that particular term. The standard was very high and generally if you didn't achieve at least 60% in the exam, you would be asked to do extra revision and then on the following Wednesday afternoon, when all the boys were doing their hobbies, you would have to take the exam again. Now we did 15 or so subjects and that's a lot of one hour exams to re-do if you failed them all. We all hated these exams with a vengeance as you really did have to work hard to pass each one. I don't remember many occasions when a pupil passed all of them – sometimes it just felt like you were just destined to fail them because it was uncanny how often we would score 58% or 59% - but it made no difference, *'an inch is as good as a mile'*, the teachers would say, and the following Wednesday you would have to do the whole thing again under exam conditions.

Every Sunday morning I had to sit down for an hour with all the other boys in the school, to write a letter home. I then had to queue up outside the head master's office where I had to wait until it was my turn to be summoned inside while my letter home was read and checked for grammar. It if was neat enough I would be allowed to go and watch TV while the others finished writing theirs, if not I was sent back to the classroom to write it again. I would then have to return to the back of the queue and re-enter the office for another inspection until I got it right.

The effort that was put in to make our education as complete as possible had to be seen to be believed. The teachers worked tirelessly non stop in their efforts to help us to become perfect little members of society. The amazing thing was that they always worked wearing a smile therefore the atmosphere was calm and controlled – both things that in my opinion are missing in many areas of society today. I really don't have anything negative to say about Bury's Court or any member of its staff. Every single day that I spent there was enjoyable in its own way. The teachers couldn't have done any more for us and although I cannot recall many of their names, I salute them all as individuals.

One name that does stay in my memory for various reasons is my old physics teacher Mr. Whymess, a man who was a true gentleman and I'm sure if I was to see him today the first thing he would say would be *'Laurence, What's the density of air?'* – well Mr. Whymess believe it or not I can still remember, along with all the other snippets of information that I was forced to digest during your lessons – therefore as those things have now stayed with me for over 30 years we would have to say that his system worked.

Another useful thing that I picked up at boarding school was an interest in building things. In the school grounds there was an old barn that had been renovated, and in it would be held the woodwork classes. I can't recall the name of the old boy who taught me but I do still have a wooden stool that I made in that old shack back in 1978, I also have an egg rack complete with mortise and tennon joints that still hangs proudly on the wall of my kitchen that I made when I was 12 years old. In edition to both of those old antiques I have a desk that I made in 1979 complete with beautiful dove tails. – Again over 30 years later it is still in once piece, not even the hinges have been replaced - Woodwork classes were happy days.

Whenever I stop and think about Bury's Court, one things always springs to the front of my mind, and that's the fact that whatever we did, everything was geared towards giving each boy the best education possible. The hours we used to spend doing mock exams were unbelievable. Every term time a large amount of time would be allocated to revision and doing mock exams over and over again, to ensure that everything that had been taught in the classroom had in deed penetrated the brain of each individual without exception. There was no hiding place at Bury's Court.

Speaking of hiding places, the school was built it approximately 60 acres of woodland, so there were many places for the boys to build 'camps' and 'dens' during the summer months. To be honest you couldn't ask for much more – we had what seemed like the perfect place for a child to grow up.

In one part of the grounds, near the main entrance, was a small stream. I do mean small, even during the winter months it would only get about 4 or 5 inches deep – and yet that stream has occupied the young boys from Bury's Court for years with hours and hours of endless fun. We would get out there at every opportunity and build dams and all sorts of other contraptions, designed to stop the natural flow of the water downstream.

Surrounding the school were numerous types of trees which were perfect for building various 'dens' for the boys. We would select a small group of trees and then spend hours building barricades between them until we had blocked all four sides, leaving just a small entrance that could be guarded by one individual – usually the youngest boy in the group! The good thing was that it was very unlikely that anyone would come along and wreck your base as everyone got on so well, we all just played together – fights or disagreements were very rare.

Other outdoor activities in the summer included cricket – a game that I still hate today. Maybe it was all those hours spent sat watching cricket at boarding school, where each boy that wasn't playing in the match had to fill in an official score card. The only problem was that a cricket match takes so long – I can assure you that you soon get fed up sat there in the cold waiting for someone to actually hit the ball, so that you could jot down the runs.

We also had a tennis coach who came in the summer to teach us how to play. Now this is something that I really enjoyed, I went on to become reasonably good at tennis and I have to say that I used to get a lot of pleasure from the game and I used to play whenever I could at school and also when I had travelled home for the school holidays. I would play under the burning sun in Jeddah with anyone who volunteered to give me a game.

The only down side to the summer term at boarding school that I can remember, was the fact that at that time of year, every Sunday morning we would all have to get our clean uniform on – including blazers and cap, and walk the mile and a half down to the local church for a service. It makes me cringe even now. We walked single file along the lanes like little soldiers, all identical in our uniform. The locals in their passing cars probably laughed their heads off every time they saw us trundling down the road. As though that wasn't bad enough, afterwards we would all line up and walk the same journey back to school. I don't think anyone enjoyed it and every week there would be the usual complaints about blisters and or sprained ankles.

Something else that had started to develop during my early years was an interest in Martial Arts – I was lucky enough to start learning Judo when I was about 8 years old. I really enjoyed it and I can still recall the hours spent on the matt learning how to roll from one corner to the other. This is so important as any Martial artist will tell you, the first thing you need in a combat situation is the ability to fall over properly in order to enable you to get back on your feet as quickly as possible in a controlled manner.

As a young boy I would spend hours in the woods going over and over the different punch combinations that we were taught, often adding more and more complex moves to the routine. Maybe this was an early sign of an addictive personality because I do mean that I spent hours and hours practicing those punches, I was small with long arms and legs and believe me those punches got faster and faster over the years. I guess that starting at such a young age helped because by the time I left I could easily through over a hundred punches a minute and not even break a sweat doing it. I'd realized that I was built for speed and all the other boys were amazed when I stood there in my own little world, counting the punches in my head and just letting my hands go. Looking back the strange thing was that I had absolutely no aggression in me at all at that point; the object was not to hit anyone, but to just get the punches going faster and faster, while paying great attention to ensuring that the punch was executed correctly. In order to effectively throw any punch or kick you need two things – power and velocity – and I was working on the both big time.

At the time I guess that the strangest thing that I had to do at boarding school was to learn Latin. When you are 10 years old, you don't quite understand the concept of why you would need to learn a language that had been used by people that had been dead for a couple of thousand years – Latin hadn't done the Romans much good and I therefore failed to see how it could possibly bring any joy or fulfillment to my life – how wrong I was, and I guess I was just showing my ignorance because in fact now, thirty years later I can honestly say that the best and most useful tool that

I had acquired during my time at boarding school was without doubt Latin – those endless hours spent chanting 'Ammo, Ammas, Ammat' that had seemed so pointless at the time, have indeed proved to be the greatest of all the gifts that I was given as a child. My understanding of both the English and French languages was without doubt helped by my understanding and grounding of the dreaded Latin. And so I guess a big thank you is due to my old Latin teacher Mr Fishbourne, who I suspect is no longer with us – mainly due to the fact that back in the seventies when he taught me, he must have been well into his 60's – Mr Fishbourne I salute you, your legend lives on.

As my parents were on an overseas posting I had to fly back to Saudi Arabia at the end of each term. The travel arrangements would be sorted out between Mr. Donald and my parents, and when the time arrived I would be delivered to Heathrow airport by a chauffeur, where I would be met by the British airways staff. They would then collect all of the children together ready to board the plane.

As we were travelling alone at such a young age we would get really pampered by the aircrew. We would be given a British airways travel pack that contained various pens and pencils, along with colouring books to entertain us during the flight. Inside this travel kit their was also a white tin which was always popular, as it was the free tin of sweets that we would be given to enjoy during the journey. We also always carried our flight 'logbook'; this was used to record your journeys around the world. During the flight we would be taken in pairs to see the cockpit of the aircraft where the captain would fill in the flight details and sign your book to show how far we had flown, and where we were heading. It shows how much the world has changed since those innocent years in the 70's as now it would be unthinkable to request a visit to the cockpit of an aircraft due to the recent bombings at the world trade centre in New York a couple of years ago.

Sometimes my flight home was scheduled a couple of days after the end of term and I would then be allowed to help with some of the general maintenance that was carried out during the school holidays. In the summer you could help mow the school lawns by driving the school sit on mini tractor all over the place, it had a mini trailer that came with it and was great fun. I think Mr. Donald was just grateful that he had a volunteer to help him mow the lawns as I'm sure he had a thousand other more important things to do. The mini tractor only did 7mph and yet I felt on top of the world and so important driving up and down – pity all the other boys had gone home and were unable to see it as they would have been green with envy.

The school would close for a week during half term and again all the boys would disappear back to their families. Unfortunately it wasn't possible to fly all the way to Saudi Arabia for a week, so I would be left to help out around the school again or if I was really lucky, one of the boys whose family lived locally would offer to take me home to stay at their house for the week. One such boy was Stuart Gregory. He would often invite me to stay at his house over the half term period and his family always made me feel very welcome. It was always nice to get some home cooking and taste the comforts of family life. I cannot recall the names of either of his parents but I do remember that his father was the drill sergeant at Sand Hurst, the army training base for officers in the south of England. I can still remember his father taking us up to the barracks on a Saturday, where we would be taken up to the firing range and given private instruction on how to fire the popular 'SLR' rifle, which was standard army issue at the time. For a young boy who's life existed within such a controlled environment for most of the time, this was like a dream come true for me and I have to say that I loved every minute of it.

In my later years at boarding school I did actually do rather well, and during my last year I became a prefect and as such I walked along the queue at meal times and removed any boys that were misbehaving, I took my turn standing in the corner and now it was time for my payback! I also sat at the head of the table at meal times and served the food. I went on to become dormitory captain of HMS Cutty Sark, and as such it was I who was now responsible for the bedtime horror stories and pillow fights during 1979.

I also went on to become captain of swimming which was a very honoured position, as you would have to represent the school when we had swimming competitions against other schools, such as 'The Gordon Boys School' in Woking. I also held the school record for the 100m breast stroke during my last year. I was always a half decent swimmer mainly due to the fact that we had always had a swimming pool in the garden. There was a pool inside the embassy in Lima, Nairobi and also in Jeddah, so it was no big surprise that myself and my brother and sister were all very strong swimmers.

Also during my last school year at boarding school my fathers posting in Jeddah was coming to an end, and so was his time in the R.A.F, he was due to finish in the summer of 1979 having completed 22 years of loyal service. My mother and father made the decision to buy a home somewhere in England so that they could finally come home after many years abroad. After speaking with two very good friends from the embassy called Phil and Liz, they settled on the idea of buying a bungalow in a small village in Hampshire, in the south of England, and so in the summer of 1979 my family home moved from Jeddah in Saudi Arabia to a lovely Hampshire village called Sherborne St John – 18 Manor Road to be precise. I had continued to stay at school while the big move took place.

It was clear the whole boarding school system was designed to gear us towards the main exams that we would be required to take during our last year at Bury's Court. These exams were known as the dreaded 'Common Entrance' – they were very important as they would determine which school you went to from the age of 13 to 17. Each school had its own set of requirements that you would have to achieve in order to attend that particular school. My chosen school was Ardingly College – famous the world over for holding the annual 'Horse of the year Show'. The standard for Ardingly was exceedingly high and I can still recall the pressure and the build up to taking my common entrance in the summer of 1980. The pressure was unbelievable, so much money had been invested into each individual at the school – it was clear from the outset that each boy was expected to pass his exams into his chosen school no matter what. The word failure didn't exist at Bury's Court. Over and over again we would go through our exercise books trying to absorb as much information as we could to prepare ourselves for the exams. You had to take an exam in each subject so that it really did give a clear indication of your knowledge 'across the board' so to speak.

The actual exams were taken in the school gymnasium – the teacher sat at the front and on his desk was a stopwatch and a small handheld bell. Our tables and chairs were neatly spread out in little rows, just like in any other exam hall in the world. The little bell would sound and then the exam would start. There was total silence in the room as all the boys racked their brains trying to dig out the answer from the depths of their memory. After what seemed like an eternity the bell would sound again and the teacher would walk round and collect of the exam papers.

Once this was done we would be instructed to stand up one row at a time and leave the room in an orderly fashion. We had nearly 3 weeks of exams and it was just such a relief to get the last one completed.

Then the long wait began for the results to arrive. The papers had been sent off to be marked by the examination board and so it was generally about 6 weeks or so before the news spread around the school that the results were back. Panic spread through the ranks as we all knew that this was make or break time. No excuses, this was it – results time!

I can still recall standing in the queue outside Mr. Donald's office for the biggest day in my life so far – you had to pass, it was as simple as that. The expectations were so high; all I could think about was what would happen if I should fail. We lined up in alphabetical order outside the office and I was shaking with apprehension as I neared the front of the queue.

Before I knew it my turn arrived and I crept into the office like a lamb to the slaughter. I was handed a small brown envelope which contained my results, I looked at Mr. Donald but he just gave me a look a professional poker player would have been proud of, I guess he'd done this a thousand times by now and he knew not to give anything away! I opened the envelope and inside was a little white piece of paper giving the details and percentage of all my exams. I glanced down to the bottom and read the immortal word 'PASSED' in big blue letters – I'd only bloody passed! I felt like jumping in the air and doing a cartwheel at the same time. Everything I'd worked for during the last 4 years had been worthwhile, I honestly felt 10 feet tall at that point – I was going to Ardingly College and it was now official. I can remember thinking to myself that I had better get used to horses and flowers. While my head was still floating round the room I was bought back down to earth by the voice of Mr. Donald who congratulated me and announced that I had better ring my parents and give them the good news. He dialed the number for me and handed me the phone. With tears in my eyes I explained to my mother that I had passed and she said she was so proud of me, I guess she would spend the next few days calling all the relatives to tell them that *'David was going to Ardingly'*.

By the summer of 1980 it was time for me to pack my bags and say farewell. I had a thousand fond memories of my time at boarding school flooding through my mind as I made my way round all my friends to say goodbye. The school had done well with me. To this day my name is etched in gold letters on the 'prefect board' in the school hall for eternity and I'd passed my exams with flying colours, I also spoke the queen's English just about as well as the queen. My record for the hundred metre's breaststroke has surely long been beaten but it's still nice to know that the immortal words 'DAVID LAURENCE' stand proudly on the wall looking down on this years boys as they take their first steps inside Bury's Court. In a strange way that made it all worth while, it meant something and to me that's important as I sit here now. I can't think of much else they could have done for me to prepare me for life at Ardingly. I guess there must have been a little sadness at the time but it's also fair to say that I was just looking forward to seeing the new home that my mother and father had moved into. That said I have to say that I'll always look back on the place with the greatest affection.

When the day arrived for me to leave, I shook the headmaster's hand and walked out to the air conditioned chauffer driven car that had been ordered to take me home. I stood there for a moment, right next to the car and as I looked around for the last time, I knew in my heart that I would miss Bury's Court. This place had been my life for the last 4 years and it held so many special memories for me. I climbed into the car and as we drove out of the school grounds I glanced over my shoulder and with a heavy heart I waved goodbye, as the driver headed for my new home in Sherborne St John/Hampshire. I had achieved everything that I should have done during my time spent there and so it's fair to say that another success story had just left Bury's Court.

CHAPTER 6

SHERBOURNE St JOHN – HAMPSHIRE

I arrived at 18 Manor Road, Sherborne St John, during the height of summer in 1980. Our new home was a beautiful little bungalow, set in a quiet cul-de-sac, deep in rural Hampshire. For the first time in my life I found that I wasn't living within the confines of an embassy compound – no armed guards and no 8 foot wall keeping me closed in. I was 13 years old and had never spent a single day of my life in the 'real' world. I guess looking back that being the son of a diplomat had its advantages, but it also had its disadvantages and the main one was freedom of movement. For the first time I could go where I wanted and do what I wanted, but this new found freedom was going to take some getting used to. Looking back I guess I should have seen the major life change coming, all I knew at that point in my life was armed guards and diplomatic immunity.

Instead of the barren landscape of Saudi Arabia and South America, now I surrounded by open fields and woodland. I'd experienced similar at boarding school but life there was so restricted that sometimes it was hard to appreciate such beauty.

Now at long last I was free to enjoy the fresh air that comes with living in the countryside.

The village itself is quite small, with only 2 roads passing through it. The Swan Public House is still there, although it's had a couple of major overhauls since back then. Like most country pubs today it now caters for both food and drink and so gone is the old public bar with the traditional open fire and in its place now stands a 100 seat restaurant – I guess that's just a sign of the times.

There is a place within the village that over the years has become a particular place of solitude for me - the recreation ground. As a young man I would spend hours up there at the rec, either playing football or tennis – both of which I have played in the local league with Sherborne St John teams. I spent many years playing football either for or against them in the Saturday league. I also spent a few years playing tennis for them in the winter league back in the late 80's.

In the summer you could walk across the fields from the recreation ground all the way down to Popley, which is a big estate within Basingstoke. Or if you chose to follow the road past the recreation ground it would lead you to the historical 'Vyne House' situated between Sherborne St John and the next village – Bramley. The house itself attracts many visitors every year. People come from far and wide to view this national treasure and to sample the legendary cream tea's while they are there. The house itself is set in lovely woodland on all sides and English heritage have maintained some lovely walks along the river which runs straight through the grounds. At the weekends the woodland becomes alive with like minded people out enjoying the fresh air with their pets.

All in all it was a nice place to live and we quickly settled into village life. I remember my first trip into the local town centre on a bus with my elder sister; we walked to the bus stop at the bottom of manor road and caught the old 118 bus into Basingstoke. I'd only ever been shopping at the local 'souk' in Saudi where you had to haggle for anything that you wished to buy – here everything was in posh shops and the prices were all pre-set. I'd also never seen so much concrete and brickwork. In the middle east they just set up their stall on whatever was available, pretty much like a market – everything was mobile and people would walk miles in the desert heat to sell their wares.

On the bus home from town that day I was to meet the girl who would later become my wife – Kate. Unfortunately for legal reasons I cannot give her real name. Kate lived with her mother, father, brother and sister in the village. Even on that simple bus journey it soon became apparent that Kate had lived a very restricted existence. She was quick to point out that her mother was very protective and that she wasn't allowed to play outside in the village. She was extremely worried that she might be spotted on the bus 'chatting up' the boys. It was obvious even then that her mother was very controlling.

Over the next few months I managed to make friends with some of the local kids, and although I had a posh accent they excepted me with open arms, after all I was well brought up and you could take to anywhere and I would be very unlikely to offend anyone – all the parents liked me as I was so polite. I used to walk round to spring close, which was only a couple of hundred yards away to play football. Anyone who remembers me from that age would tell you that I always wore a tracksuit and had a football permanently attached to my feet. I'd spend hours round there enjoying the freedom and fresh air with the lads - Ian Crammer, Andy Coles, Russell Booth, Simon Nash, Paul Lumm,

Clive Hooey – I wonder where you all are now.

Things settled quite quickly at this time and I spent the next couple of weeks trying to adjust to my new found freedom. I spent a fair amount of time with my old friend Paul Lumm, and so it wasn't long until we got round to talking about schools. I explained that I would be going away again in September to Ardingly College but that I would be back for the school holidays. He said he was already at a local school about a mile away and that it was great and he loved it there. He told me that it was a comprehensive school and that everyone he knew went to one of these.

I can still remember the look of horror on my parents face when I came home and announced that I thought it would be a good idea for me to go to the local comprehensive with all my new friends, after all Paul went there and he was happy. My parents always had time for Paul as he was a good kid, he always said please and thank you and even took his shoes off when he came in the house. After a week of 'discussion' it was decided that I could attend school with Paul and I was over the moon, I couldn't wait to tell him the good news. I jumped on my bike and cycled round to see him. His parents were lovely and always made me welcome, they explained that Paul had to ride to school on his bike and it that I took about 20 minutes or so. I couldn't believe my ears; this adventure was getting better and better. A couple of months ago I was confined to an all boys boarding school and now, here I was, planning to go to school on my bike.

We spent the rest of the summer holidays just doing the things kids do. We had a good group of us in those days and I don't ever remember any aggravation – life was fun and it seemed that my parents had chosen a really good place to make their new home. To anyone who hasn't been to Sherborne St John, all I can say is that it was a beautiful place to live with a really friendly atmosphere. To this day I still drive up to the old recreation ground and sit there in the car whenever I need to 'think' about anything.

As September approached, we headed into town to buy my new school uniform. It was such a nice feeling to know that I wouldn't have to wear a blazer or a cap any more and also that I would never have to walk down those dreaded lanes to the church ever again.

Soon the big day arrived and Paul and I jumped on our bikes and headed down the country lane to my new school – I felt so free with just the wind in my hair bombing along on my bike without a care in the world.

I doubt I will ever get over the shock of my first day at John Hunt. I never realized that there would be girls there, and that was a massive shock to the system. The other thing that stood out was that there were just so many children. They came from every direction like ants heading to a nest. Paul was a year older than me and therefore he was a year above me at school. I was now joining the comprehensive system in what was known as the old year 3 – today it is now known as year 9 for some strange reason.

As soon as I walked through the school gates I felt totally lost, but luckily I was soon spotted by a member of staff and pointed in the right direction. I made my way to my new tutor group, introduced myself and I was shown to my seat. To be honest the only word I can use to describe the scene was mayhem. I was used to doing as I was told and speaking when I was spoken to, now I was in a room where everyone seemed to be doing exactly what they liked. Don't get me wrong, there was order in the room and I'm not trying to suggest that I was in the middle of a battle field, as that would be unfair on the staff and pupils of John Hunt at the time. It's just that I was now seeing a different version of 'order'

– to my mind it was unorganized order that was bordering on chaos! It was the little things that made a difference. Someone would grab another pupil's book for instance and run around the class with it, while being chased by the owner who would be letting go a whole load of expletives as they clattered round the room knocking tables and chairs all over the place. They whole day was a complete nightmare.

The lessons were also much shorter than I was used to and every time the bell sounded everyone would jump up and run out of the door to head to the next lesson. My old school had all been in one big building and I'd never moved classrooms between lessons in my life. The teacher always came to me, now suddenly I was expected to find my way around a school that was spread between 6 or 7 buildings, and just to make the challenge a little bit harder, I had to do it trying to dodge between over 1000 children to achieve it. That first day was a nightmare it really was, I couldn't wait for the bell to sound so that I could climb on my bike and cycle back to the safety of my house with Paul.

Inevitably I soon developed a reputation for being late to my classes. As the teachers had never had a pupil straight from public school, I think that they just thought that I was taking the piss every day. Although to be fair, I am aware that the whole situation was a little alien to them as well. It would also be fair to say that they just didn't realize that the whole comprehensive system was alien to me. The first time in each lesson I was given the benefit of the doubt but it didn't take long for me to start acquiring after school detentions for being late to my classes: It was hopeless and for months I just couldn't get the hang of it.

It didn't take long for me to realize that most of the stuff they were trying to teach me, I had already done at boarding school. The difference was that I had covered their whole syllabus and in much greater detail, when I was 9 years old – now I was sat there approaching my 14 birthday re-doing the same things again. Well to me that was one big joke I have to say. I guess I pretty much lost total interest within a couple of weeks. It all became one big laugh, and when the teachers seemed powerless to take any worthwhile action I just played up and became a disruptive influence.

During the 3 years that I spent at John Hunt I was eventually sent to see the school psychologist. In total a group of 8 people were summoned, of which I was one - so that this rocket scientist that the school had hired could try and asses each of us individually, and as a group, to try and understand why we behaved the way we did during our lessons.

The 7 other members of that group had been assembled together as they had been deemed to be the most disruptive individuals in our school year. I was there simply because the teaching staff couldn't work out how I always managed to score highly in any tests that were set. I also always scored highly in any school exams that were set, and yet at the same time I never bothered to do any of my school homework. Apparently I showed a total lack of interest during lessons. Now I'm not sure what the local council had paid for the services of this individual, but when the report was finally completed and presented to the school, I was called to see my year head. His assessment was honestly the biggest load of bollox that I'd ever heard. In his opinion I was deemed to be uninterested and bored because I had an absent father, therefore there must be lack of parental control in my household. Twenty grand a year and that's what they came up with, it's hardly surprising that the situation was rapidly turning into a mess. I guess that all of that was a bigger insult to my mother and father than it was for me. The staff at John Hunt hadn't even managed to get my family background matched to my name. It was so comical as I had to sit through this character assassination, and yet in my head, I had already realized that the fool talking to me was reading a load of nonsense about someone else's family background – and politicians try to tell us that there is no difference between a private education and a comprehensive one! I suppose they think that they can get away with it as no one in their right mind would go to a public school and then change to a comprehensive. I guess there is always an exception to the rule – and this time I'm the exception.

Having seen both sides of the coin I feel that I have the relevant insight to be able to comment, and believe me there is no comparison between the two. So now the secret is officially out – if you pay for your education you will have a much greater chance of long term success in the workplace than if you do not – simple as that, no matter who tries to tell you otherwise.

Over a period of time things did settle and somehow I managed to adjust to the comprehensive system, although to be fair I never did adjust to the slow pace of the lessons and the total lack of any interest shown by the teaching staff. One thing that was memorable about my time spent at John Hunt was the French exchange trip that I went on in October 1980. All the children on the trip had spent the previous year writing letters to their French pen pals, during the build up to the annual school trip to Soissons. As I had only just joined the school and was therefore a late edition to the event, there wasn't time to arrange a pen pal for me, and so it was decided that as I was such an upstanding member of the community, it would be suitable for me to stay at the headmaster's son's house from the school that we were exchanging with.

To be honest I had a great time. The best part was the fact that 'Bertrand', my French partner for the week, had an older brother who was about 17 years of age. Now in France the law states that at 14 years old you can ride a 50cc motorbike. Due to this the whole of France in the 80's was alive with teenagers riding various versions of a moped. The French had mastered the art of converting a standard bicycle into a moped. They did this by simply attaching a small engine onto the front handlebars of the bike, adding a hand clutch and away you went. Bertrand's brother had one such article and I spent every opportunity during that week pestering him for another go round the school grounds on his moped. His brother didn't seem to mind as long as I kept putting the petrol in daily; he was well chuffed just to be given free fuel for the week.

By the time I came to leave school in the summer of 1983, I had managed to achieve o'levels in six subjects: English Language, English Literature, Math's, History, French and Physics. That was pretty impressive for a comprehensive in the 80's – until you realized that 3 years earlier I had been in a position to have taken the same exams and passed them all with flying colours. I have to say that taking my common entrance exam at 13 years of age was far more daunting and much more difficult than any of the o'levels that I took in the summer of 1983.

When I left John Hunt I managed to get myself a job on a local farm while I was waiting to go to Queen Mary's College in Basingstoke, at the start of the September term. The farm produced lettuce and potatoes and my job was to be on the lettuce side of things. I used to walk along in front of a moving 'rig', cutting the lettuce in the field as we went along and handing them to one of the crew behind me, who would proceed to wrap it in its official wrapper for either Marks and Spencer's or Sainsbury's – depending which order we were working on that day. The lettuce would then be boxed and stored at the back of the 'rig' to await transportation from the field back to the farm yard, where they would be freeze dried, and then refrigerated ready to be shipped out over night to the shops ready for sale in the morning.

I remember my fist pay packet that was for about forty pounds – I felt like I'd won the pools. All in all it was a very efficient system and once again I have nothing but found memories from those days that I spent with the other members of the Sherborne St John lettuce crew. As everything must, it came to an end a couple of months later, and I was off to start at Queen Mary's college.

I spent one school year at QMC, as it was generally known. I guess I had nowhere else to go so I ended up trying to improve my results by staying in 'school' for another year. My parents had always wanted me to go to college so it was by mutual agreement that I went. I really enjoyed my time there and the best thing about the place was all the *'free'* periods that you get. Now these are supposed to be spent doing revision or home work that had been set, but I'm afraid that I spent most of mine with a couple of mates playing football.

At the end of the school year I returned to work at the lettuce farm, only this time I moved up the ladder so to speak. I now had the job of driving a tractor and trailer down to the field, where I would pull up along side the lettuce rig while they loaded all the boxed lettuce onto the trailer ready to be freeze dried back at the farm.

Things were going reasonable well, although I didn't seem to have any real direction in my life at that point. There had been so many dreams and expectations in the past and now I was back on the lettuce farm a year older and apparently no wiser.

I worked most of the second season at the farm and then one day while I was in the local village shop in Sherborne St John, I was informed that 2 young men from Oxford were going to open a bakery in the back of the shop and that they were looking for a young man from the village who they could train up to be a baker. The shop owner asked me what I was doing and I said I was up at the farm but the season was coming to an end. They gave me all the details and asked me to think about it and to let them know what my intentions were, so that they could arrange an informal chat with the two bakers - Simon and Dale.

I hurried home with the news and I think my parents were just very relieved that I had come up with something to do to earn a living. To cut a long story short, I worked a couple more weeks at the farm and then joined the bakery. What I hadn't realized at the time is that it would be night work. Now I can tell you from experience that there are three things that don't go together, and they are: Night work, alcohol and young adolescent males. I was a young adolescent male at this point and I was about to start night work and unfortunately I was just about to discover alcohol, now we had a full house and it was only going to be a matter of time before problems began to appear in my life.

Due to the usual problems associated with having teenage children in the family home, I had moved out of my parent's house by this time, thinking I was big enough to look after myself, I think we've all been there!

My problem was I hadn't even arranged anywhere to live at that point. I had been left home a couple of hours and I was wondering through the corridors of Basingstoke hospital when I bumped into my sister. She had moved out a year earlier and was living in the town centre; she went on to say that I could stay at her place for a while. This meant that I was living in the town centre; I was 18 and I could start using the pubs.

By this time I also had my first serious girlfriend in tow and her name was Tamara. Meanwhile Kate had gone on holiday to Ibiza with her parents and had refused to come home at the end of the holiday. She ended up staying there for the whole holiday season. Years later when we were married I asked her what had eventually made her come home, her family, the weather or just missing home and she said none of those things. She said she'd been driving a car and that she had crashed it - Interpol were looking for her, so she just flew home. I guess Interpol must have hundreds of similar unsolved crashes every year caused by people on holiday. I think that in this case, Kate has no intention of going back to Spain just in case. Speaking of crashes – in June of the same year I managed to pass my driving test at the first attempt.

After a few weeks at the bakery, it was suggested by both Simon and Dale that, as things were going quite well, maybe it would be a good idea if I went on a day release bakery course at one of the local colleges. Enquiries were made and it was decided that I would go to Reading Technical College in September. I duly enrolled and took my place amongst the other students at Reading Teck; I was on a 2 year course in 'Bakery and Cake Decorating'.

Meanwhile I continued to work nights at the shop in Sherborne St John and as I was now mobile, I started to spend more and more time in the town centre socializing with friends. Back in 1986 when I was 18 and allowed into the pubs for the first time, they were only open from 11am to 2pm, they would then shut for lunch and a quick tidy up before re-opening for the evening trade at 5pm till 11pm. I would work my night shift of midnight through to 7am, quickly grab a couple of hours sleep then get up to be at my mate's house by 10.30am, so that we could drive to town and be waiting outside for the pub to open at 11am. We would then spend the next 3 hours drinking in the town centre and we would wander between The Feathers, The Bass House and The Nightjar. At 2pm it was back round my mate's house to grab another couple of hours sleep before heading back into town to the pub again at

5pm for the evening session. I was still only about 19 years old so all this alcohol, coupled with being up all night working, was never going to be a very successful way to approach life and it wasn't long before I started to have some major problems in my life.

Within a year it all became too much for me and I dropped out of Reading Teck without taking the exams at the end of the year. Everything that I had been bought up to believe in had been turned on its head. All the dreams and expectation of going to Ardingly had vanished a few years before and now it felt like I was just wandering through life in a daze. Gone were the sandy beaches and weekends on the royal launch in Jeddah and here I was pissed up and extremely tired, stuck in rain drenched Basingstoke. I'm not looking to make excuses or pass the blame over to anyone or anything else; I just want to tell it how it was. In just under a year I had gone from being a well bought up son, that any parent would have been proud of, to a tired, touchy, drunk 20 year old – it wasn't rocket science to figure out that without the controlling influence from members of my immediate family, a young male like myself out in society and now full of alcohol was always going to struggle.

A few weeks later I quit my job at the Bakery as I just couldn't cope with the night work, and I moved out of my sisters house and into lodgings – although the offer was there for me to move back to my parents house, I guess that not for the first time, I just had too much pride inside me and felt that I could find my own way in the world.

CHAPTER 7

THE REAL WORLD

My new home was now going to be on one of the estates that surround the town of Basingstoke, and during the summer of 1986, together with Tamara, I duly moved into a rented room on Wilmot Way, on the outskirts of the Winklebury estate.

Looking back it's hard to see where the problems started but its fair to say that at least some of the events of the last few years must have contributed in some way. I was still growing and yet my body was so tired that it ached all over. It just wasn't possible to work those hours and live the high life, it was always going to end in tears. I was living away from the security of home and I'd spent so many years being told what I could and couldn't do, now I was enjoying my new found freedom, in fact I was out of control. My mind was so mixed up, yes I knew right from wrong but life had turned into a dead end and nothing seemed to make much sense. I wasn't sitting on the banks of the Red Sea now, I wasn't out sailing with my father: the real world had arrived - big time.

I bobbled along in a daze until in May 1986, after a night out with the lads, I found myself arrested after a minor incident in what was the old 'Wimpy', situated next to the Basingstoke sports centre. After being held in the police station cell for a few hours, I was taken into a side room to be interviewed about the incident. Shortly after that I was bailed to appear at Basingstoke magistrate's court on a charge of criminal damage. There had been some damage caused to the entrance door and also some minor damage to half a dozen polystyrene roof tiles inside the Wimpy. I was fined ten pounds but also had to pay compensation of one hundred and nineteen pounds to the manager of the Wimpy. It had been an expensive night out and I was now seeing life from a totally different angle compared to the past.

That night spent pissed out of my head in the cells at Basingstoke police station should have given me a wake up call, the strange thing was that it didn't. I stumbled along until mid November 1986, when I was arrested again on the way home from a drunken night out and charged with causing ABH – or in layman's terms – Actual Bodily Harm. Generally speaking this means that you caused another person to sustain a reasonably serious cut or bruise: for example a broken or bloody nose or a black eye. I was also charged with assaulting a police office with intent to resist arrest. I appeared again at Basingstoke Magistrates Court and was fined fifty pounds for my part in the fracas and seventy pounds for assaulting the police officer. I was also ordered to pay twenty pounds towards the cost of the court fees. Things were definitely heading in the wrong direction for me now and yet at the time I didn't really notice, or maybe I just didn't want to.

Shortly after the court appearance I was offered the chance to start work for a company that built swimming pools. I decided to take the job, and as it turned out I started work as a labourer on the same day as another young lad and he was to become a long term friend of mine. His name was Carl Vernon. Now I can't mention

Carl without somehow squeezing in the name of his brother, as he would never forgive me – big up to my old friend Andy Vernon. I was now earning more money that ever before and I felt it was a good time to put the past behind me and make a fresh start.

The following year passed quite quickly and without incident. Then one day, while talking to my mother, she explained that she felt it would be a good idea for me to move back home, so that together we could start to build on the progress that I had made over the previous year. Although I hadn't been in any trouble for a while I still felt that if I was to move back home and start again, then Tamara would have to go. It just seemed that whenever we went out together then there was usually some form of problem during the evening. I split up with Tamara in mid 1987 and moved back to my parent's house in Sherborne St John, the reconnaissance mission into the real world had ended in total disaster.

Meanwhile Kate had finally returned from her adventures in Ibiza. I bumped into her a few times in the village, we got chatting and as we had always got on well together we started a relationship. It wasn't long before her erratic behaviour stated to show itself. She was obsessed with wanting to know where I was at all hours of the day and night, and I lost count of the times that my parents warned me that her controlling behaviour just wasn't normal. It was difficult to know what to think at the time. She felt that her actions were reasonable and if I'm honest I would have to admit that Kate had been raised in a very controlled and selfish environment, so it was hardly surprising really that she exhibited such traits herself as she approached adulthood. That said I have to say that I often found her mother's actions beyond comprehension. For example, although we lived in a village with no street lights, Kate's mum would never drop her off or pick her up in the car from my house – of course in my house it caused some concern because we all felt that no-one in their right mind would let their teenage daughter walk home late at night, especially as there were no street lights in the village and especially as they had a car available, sitting on the drive. On the two occasions that I can recall that Kate was collected from my house, she later told me that her mother had charged her a couple of pounds for the petrol. Something else I found a bit weird was the fact that she wasn't ever allowed to use the washing machine at home under any circumstances – that was for her mother's sole use.

There are good arguments for and against such actions by a parent and I don't want to be a judge, but I should point out that in this case there was a feeling that it was done just to be cruel and controlling. Kate's mother was the most selfish person that I've ever met and I think most level headed people would agree that for a mother not to allow her adult daughter to use a washing machine just because *'it is mine'* was definitely bordering on obsessive and controlling behaviour.

After Christmas in 1988, Kate and I decided to buy our first house as I was enjoying building the swimming pools, and it paid extremely well. Kate had also got herself a job at a local communications company and so it seemed the logical thing to do. We decided on a one bedroom luxury maisionette that had just been built in Chineham, on the outskirts of Basingstoke.

We moved in and to be honest things were great. The following year passed without any major problems and we settled down to enjoy our new beginning. Kate had wanted a cat for her birthday and so we bought a British Shorthair, blue and cream Persian cat – we now had our first family member and her name was Yasmin.

In November 1989, I was arrested again after a night out, but this time it was a little more serious. After another night in the cells I was charged with ABH again, and also possession of an offensive weapon in a public place. Off I went again to Basingstoke Magistrates Court and this time I was fined ninety pounds for possession of the offensive weapon, with another fifty pound fine for the ABH, I also had to pay ten pounds towards the court costs. It had been another expensive night out.

As we rolled into 1990 things were about to get ten times worse. I was still trying to make sense of a lot of things that were going on in my life. In general I felt a lot better in myself as I wasn't working those dreaded nights anymore and yet I still managed to get myself into difficult situations every now and again.

The year started really well, in the March of 1990 Kate realized that she was pregnant - we were going to have a baby. The news spread like wildfire and the excitement started to build. We had all the usual chats from family members about responsibility and so on.

The good news didn't last long as I was again arrested a couple of weeks later for ABH. But this time when we got to Basingstoke Magistrates Court they said that the assault was too serious for them to deal with and that they felt that I should be dealt with at the local Crown Court, which in this case was to be in Winchester. My case was put on a waiting list and for a couple of months I waited for notification as to when I would have to appear at the court. And then on June 14th 1990 the phone rang and it was an official from the court. Unbeknown to me this phone call was to start a chain of events that were to change my life forever. He said that there had been a cancellation of another case and that it had been decided that my case would be scheduled for the next day. He also told me that he was not from Winchester Crown Court but from Southampton Crown Court. He then proceeded to give me the address of the court, adding that I was to be there by 10am, and with a quick goodbye he was gone.

As I had never been to Southampton before I decided that the best way to get there would be on the train, and so the following morning I caught the 8am train from Basingstoke to Southampton and headed for the Crown Court. I arrived at the Courthouse and as I stood in the open courtyard at the front of the building, it dawned on me that this wasn't going to be a place of fun for the next 2 days. It really was absolutely enormous and extremely daunting – I guess that's exactly what it was supposed to be, after all this was the place that enforced the law of the land – the so called *'will of the people'*. The court had originally set aside 2 days to hear my case, but after seeing the evidence against me my solicitor advised me to plead 'guilty' to the charge, so as to avoid wasting the court's time. He advised me that if I was to plead *'Not guilty'* and then go on to be found *'Guilty'*, the court would feel obliged to impose a harsher sentence due to the fact that I had refused to accept my guilt.

And so it came to be that I found myself standing in the dock at Southampton Crown Court, after entering my plea of *'Guilty'* and confirming my name and address, the court officials got on with the business of hearing what the prosecution had to say. The strange thing was that as the evidence unfolded before my eyes, it seemed as though everyone was talking about another event. All the details were blown out of all proportion and enhanced to make it sound like an absolute bloodbath had taken place. By the time they had finished, even I was beginning to wonder if I was safe to be on the streets. When all the gory details had been heard the judge announced that the court would adjourn for 20 minutes, so that he could have a quick cup of tea while having a think about what sentence he was going to impose.

Upon his return I was asked to stand and face the judge. He looked down at me from his big legal desk like some sort of sacred figure and after lecturing me about the rules of society, he explained to me that I was a very lucky young man, because as my girlfriend was now pregnant he would impose a shorter sentence than he had initially planned to ensure that I returned from prison before the birth of our expected baby, at the end of October 1990. When he had finished his lecture he looked at me and sternly announced that I was to be imprisoned for a period of 4 months – and then I heard him mutter the immortal words which stay long in the memory with any human being that has been sent to prison – *'Take him down'.*

With those words still ringing in my ears I was escorted out of a side entrance of the courtroom, down a narrow corridor followed by a steep set of stone steps that led down to the cellar where the holding cells were. I was booked in by the duty officer and informed that I could make one phone call to let someone know what had happened. I was also told that in a couple of hours, when all the cases due that day had been heard, we would be leaving for Winchester prison.

It suddenly dawned on me that no one knew where I was as I hadn't told any members of my family, and Kate had gone to work that morning as usual. Isn't it strange how quickly reality always hits home when it's too late. I was off to Winchester prison and I'd better get used to that fact, and quick. As I sat there I couldn't help wondering how things had come to this. A few years earlier I had the world at my feet and now here I was starting a prison sentence. I have to say that I don't feel that I was in any way a bad individual, just a very confused young man.

CHAPTER 8

HMP WINCHESTER

I arrived at HMP Winchester at about 5pm on 15th June 1990 and I was immediately escorted through to the area where the prison officers booked us in. There were three of us who had been convicted that day at Southampton Crown Court and as I sat there waiting for my turn to be called, I can still remember that deep rooted feeling of being isolated and alone – reality hits home big time the first time you enter that room. All the laughter and joking that you had enjoyed with your mates while committing the offence soon wears off when you are sat in that small room at the mercy of the 'system'.

Now I'm not a big one for giving advice but if you did ask for my opinion then I would say that before you decide to swan around acting the big man, I would recommend that you sit down and think very seriously as to whether or not your balls are big enough to sit on the hard wooden bench of a prison waiting room, because believe me when you eventually get there you will find out if you really are as tough mentally and physically as you think you are.

I'm not nieve enough to believe that I can give you a full insight into the English prison system just by writing a chapter in a book. To truly feel the suffering and violence that goes on within those huge walls you would have to go and spend a small amount of your life living under those extreme conditions yourself. In this chapter my only hope is that you get a brief feel, at the very least, of what it's like to be confined at her majesty's pleasure.

The first thing that you need to realize about the prison population in general is that it is made up by very *'severe'* people. By that I mean severely violent, severely dangerous, severely cunning, severely stupid and occasionally even severely intelligent. As any prison officer will tell you, each and every one of them should have a public warning written on their forehead – the bottom line is when you are dealing with prison inmates you must at all times *'handle with care'* or very quickly things can go horribly wrong, due to all the tension that just seems to go hand in hand with such an establishment.

The British prison system has two things in common with all the other prison systems around the world. One of them is that within it, wherever in the world you look, you will find the lowest of the low from society. The drug dealers are there, the fraudsters are there, the car thieves are there, the rapists are there, the con men are in there, the violent offenders are there and the murderers are there.

The other thing that you will find in any prison in the world, is that mixed amongst this potential backdrop of extreme violence, there are quite a few mentally ill people who for one reason or another have been missed by the medical system and they end up serving long sentences, when in fact what they really need is help. That may also entail secure accommodation, but surely a prison isn't the place to put them as to be honest most of them don't even realize what it was that they did wrong to end up there in the first place. You see prison is a very violent place to spend your time and so it isn't rocket science to realize that the quickest way to stand out in the system is to dish out some serious violence to get yourself noticed and in turn, hopefully you would then be left alone to carry out your sentence in peace. Now that's all well and good in theory but in reality what actually happens is that the stronger inmates dominate the place, while the weak and some of the mentally ill become the victims whenever someone decides to prove a point and dish out some instant justice.

I guess the moral of the story is that if you have to go to prison, at least go for committing a violent offence, that way you will get a decent start to your time *'inside'*. Go in for rape, child abuse, theft, or fraud and you will have lost the respect of the prison population before you have even started your sentence. Believe me no matter how tough you think you are it is a fact that if you commit any offence to either women or children then your life will become a living hell once you enter the prison system.

I was booked in and given my prison number; XCO 755 – then I was issued with the clothes that all inmates have to wear while 'inside', a pair of Blue jeans, Blue/White stripped shirt, Blue Rugby top and a pair each of underpants, socks and shoes. The strange thing about the uniform is the amount of starch that was still in the clothes when they came back from the launderette. These garments were rigid, and I'm not joking. Weapons were obviously banned in prison but I'm sure that at some point in the past someone somewhere must have been injured by a garment of rock hard prison clothing. Once I had everything we all headed off to our new home which for me was on going to be on 'B' Wing.

Winchester prison is a very old building and so in the late eighties and early nineties it was only used as a *'Holding prison'*.

This meant that all the permanent inmates usually only had a sentence of 18 months or less to serve. Although you would get all the other variations passing through as they were moved around in the system, which happens quite a lot. If you caused any problems you could expect to be shipped out the following morning and moved to another area of the country – generally further away to make it more difficult for your family and friends to visit. In my opinion this was done purely out of spite, but then I guess you can just do that to prison inmates as no one really gives a fuck about them anyway do they. Maybe there's a lesson for society there but that's another story altogether.

The prison itself had a centre 'hub', within which is the main entrance, office and all the other relevant things needed to run a full time prison. It also had 4 'wings' fanning out from the centre, within which all the inmates were housed.

One wing was allocated to the 'young offenders', or YP's as they are known. All the inmates on this wing were under 21 years of age. The majority of the day to day problems and incidents within the prison usually occurred on the YP's wing. All night and all day you could hear them shouting and swearing at each other. No matter where you went within the building you could hear the bloody YP's.

Another was allocated to the prisoners who were 'on remand'. This meant that they were in prison awaiting trial for something, but that they hadn't actually been found guilty yet of committing any offence. They had their own wing and a lot of the rules were slightly different for them, although it still didn't make that wing a fun place to be – prison is prison no matter what wing you are on.

A third wing was allocated to the inmates held under what is known as 'rule 43' within the system. This was the protection wing; all inmates were on this wing because they would not be safe within the main prison system. These included people who owed money within prison and also all the oddballs of society like rapists, child abusers or anyone whose crime would be frowned upon in any normal society - within the prison system they are know as 'nonce's' or 'beasts'.

Last but not least was the wing that held all the convicted males that were over the age of 21. This was the wing that I would spend my entire spell in Winchester on – and it was known as 'B Wing'. I never did figure out which letter of the alphabet related to each of the other wings – I guess it doesn't matter now.

As we were escorted through the prison we had to pass through a series of locked metal gates, each with solid bars built from steel an inch thick, just like in the movies. As you entered 'B' Wing you were faced with 2 rows of cells, parallel to each other, and each row was 3 storeys high. The ground floor was known as the 2's, the 1st floor was known as the 3's and the 2nd floor was known as the 4's. Between each level, stretched from all four sides was a wire netting, positioned to catch anyone who either jumped from the 3's or 4's or was unfortunate enough to be given a helping hand over the guard rails that ran the length of each landing.

Half way along each landing on both sides and on all levels were the communal sink and toilet. There were a couple of hundred inmates on 'B' Wing and only 6 toilets, I guess that should give you an idea about the stench inside a prison, as soon as you walk inside your lungs fill with air polluted by vomit and piss. In the end you don't even notice it anymore as it becomes so unimportant compared to all the other things that you witness daily within the confines of those walls.

My new home was going to be B16, so therefore I was on the wing that held all male prisoners that were over 21, that had actually been convicted of a crime. I was up on the 3's which seemed a good place to be, after all I wasn't on the bottom level and neither was I on the top level, I was right in the middle, which is a place that life has taught me is a good place to start anything that you are not sure about. Take the 'middle road' and you shouldn't go far wrong – or so the theory goes.

To enter each individual cell, first you had to pass through the four inch solid steel door, which was fitted with an enormous lock just like in the films. I'd always wondered if the cell keys really were as big as people make out in the movies, well I now know that they are, although unfortunately I'd had to go right to the bottom of the pit of society to find out – to be honest it wasn't worth it.

Once inside the cell you were faced with 2 beds, one behind the door and the other situated diagonally opposite the first to utilize all the space available in the cell. The room measured approximately twelve feet long and about nine feet wide. Also in the room we had two very basic tables that were just large enough to put a few personnel possessions on, and an old tin bucket to use as a toilet during the night. The walls and floor were painted in a thick coat of a very basic grey with a smooth finish, spill any water on the floor and the place became a death trap.

I began to get myself sorted out and settled down for my first night behind bars. I had no idea what to expect and my head was still spinning from my day in court. There had been so much technical information read out during the day, and as the accused you tend to filter every single word that you hear, thus resulting in the mother of all headaches by the end of it – to be honest I just wanted to get into bed and go to sleep, maybe it would all go away!

I hadn't been lying there long when the cell door suddenly

burst open and in charged 3 inmates, the commotion was enough to make me jump out of bed and stand bolt upright with my fists up and ready to start throwing punches. Suddenly one of the three men shouted *"fuck it Jack, wrong cell"*, and as quick as they came in they were gone. As my head cleared I wondered what all that had been about, it didn't make much sense to me but then that night nothing seemed to be making much sense.

Over the next few days things settled down quite quickly. I later learnt that during my trial, unbeknown to me there had been a *'court orderly'* sat at the back of the court listening to the evidence. He was a trusted inmate from the prison and his job was to go with the prison officers to the court and make them their cups of tea during the day. He also had another function in life. It was his job each evening to report back to the wing all the relevant information regarding the new arrivals for that day. He had heard all the evidence in my case and duly reported back that I was in for a fight and had received 4 months. He also reported back on the other two, one of which was a scout leader who had been convicted of molesting some of the scouts in his care. It turned out that the three men who had stormed into my cell on the first night, had in fact been looking for the scout leader to give him a proper introduction to the prison system, but they had come into the wrong cell. I was later told that they did find him that night, and when I saw him a few days later he was absolutely black and blue. He had boot marks all over his neck and face. Believe me he got some instant justice that night and also at every available opportunity during his stay there. Thank god that the court orderly hadn't had bad eyesight that day and thank god that the three stooges had realized that they were in the wrong cell and left.

Within a couple of days of my arrival I was asked if I wanted a job while I was in there, or did I just want to go *'on the dole'*. I had to laugh, a lot of what I saw in prison I was expecting to see but never in my wildest dreams did it ever occur to me that I might be able to *'go on the dole'* while inside. I was tempted, as up to that point in my life I had never been unemployed so maybe it was a good time to try it. After careful thought I decided against it and took the job. The dole paid you one pound fifty pence per week, but as I had shown commitment to the cause by taking a job, I was to be rewarded with an extra ten pence per week, and if that wasn't enough to get you doing cartwheels then how about this then – I was also going to be entitled to a pay rise of ten pence per week so long as I worked a full five days in that week.I think I was supposed to be ecstatic at this point or at the very least overjoyed, *"you jammy git"* they said *'you've landed right on your feet with a job in the stores'* – somehow I must have missed the point as I don't remember feeling overjoyed at all, I wanted to work just to get out of my cell for a few hours. The riots at the famous Strangeways prison had only happened about 2 months before the start of my sentence and because of that the whole prison system was on a *'lockdown'*. This meant that unless the inmates had to be anywhere in particular, then they had to stay locked in their cells for 23 hours a day.

I think most sane minded people would agree with me when I say that prison is supposed to be about reforming people ready to re-enter society. I fail to see how you can improve someone's mental state of mind when they are locked in a small cell with plain grey walls to look at for that length of time. You can make your own judgment about it but I've been there and believe me all you actually achieve is to breed boredom, which in turn leads to resentment and hate. Human beings don't just sit there sulking, thinking about how naughty they have been. They sit there resenting their predicament and planning how to get revenge on the person or the system that put them there in the first place. You see the thing you have to realize about the prison population is that for one reason or another most of the inmates don't believe that they have done anything wrong. Now I know that we can't have that sort of attitude in our society and I only say it as a fact, but ignoring that fact won't make it disappear. I therefore believe we need to face it and address it if we want make ridiculous claims such as, prison is about reforming people. Maybe I'm wrong and I'm willing to except that, but what I do know is that simply locking people up in a cell for 23 hours a day definitely doesn't work and I doubt it ever will.

Back to my new job – I worked in the main stores of the prison. I was collected from my cell after breakfast and would go to work for a couple of hours, then back to my cell for lunch. Again a little while after lunch I would be collected and escorted back to work for another couple of hours. There was nothing strict about working within a prison; I wouldn't want to give the impression of a labour camp. We had good times at work and everything was done at a leisurely pace – after all none of us were rushing to get anywhere in particular, we all knew where we would be tomorrow, and the day after. Everything that came in through those big wooden gates came through our department and was then sorted out and moved on to its final destination. Food to the kitchen, laundry to the washhouse and so on. There were 4 of us in the group and we were accompanied by a civilian escort everywhere we went. We also handled all the prison clothes, including the officer's uniform as it returned from the launderette. This meant that not only could I help myself to clean clothes every day unlike the others who only got clean clothes once a week, but I could also get a clean shirt or trousers to 'trade' with other inmates. This enabled me to get things like extra sugar from the kitchen or varnish from the workshop whenever I needed it. It might not sound much but within an environment where everything had been taken away from you, these are the things that become very important. If you could supply something like a clean shirt when somebody wanted one, then you were definitely *'somebody'* within the prison system. I have to say that working with the lads in the stores made all the difference to me, they were a good bunch and it definitely helped to make the days go by quite quickly.

When I wasn't at work the majority of my time was spent *'banged up'* in my cell. Now a prison cell is a strange place, so grey, dull and boring. There is only so much you can do within such a small room. Even against all the odds I feel that I managed to do quite well; first I was lucky enough to get a decent cell-mate. As you can imagine it's pot luck who you end up sharing a room with, with the short list running from psychotic to someone who would rob his own mother.

My cell mate was a thirty year old Sikh from Southampton who was doing a couple of years for *'attempting to supply a class a drug'* – it turned out to be heroin. Like all the good business men that I've met over the years he was very aware of the first rule of business which is; don't ever use your own products. He never touched the stuff, not only did he not use heroin but he didn't look like he used it either and so as I always do, I took him as he was and it never crossed my mind to judge him in any other way what so ever. He was a top bloke and a good friend and wherever he is in the world I can honestly say that if I saw him I'd gladly shake his hand and wish him well. His first name was Ammeric, but it would be unfair to give his surname. Most of the lads couldn't cope with the name Ammeric and his surname was even longer so we decided to shorten it for him. He quickly became known affectionately as Micky Sing.

Micky Sing was an honest, straight forward, hard working guy who had just come unstuck. He never made out that he hadn't done anything wrong, he accepted his fate and was just looking forward to getting back to his family. For a brief spell fate had decided that our paths must cross, it was also his first time inside. He'd lend you anything and always thought of others before himself, I sit here wondering sometimes why people like him are in prison, but deep down I know that only people who have served a prison sentence would even begin to understand what I'm trying to say, so I guess I'd better save that story for another day.

Once I got started at work and received my first weeks pay, the following Tuesday I joined the queue at the 'canteen'. The canteen was the place where you could buy various items that were allowed within the prison like toiletries, biscuits, tea bags, tobacco, matches etc. While standing in the queue listening to the other inmates, I quickly realized that I had a problem. The bastards had got one over on me, as it turned out that my first week's wages wasn't quite enough to buy ½ oz of tobacco, a packet of cigarette papers and a box of matches – I was 4p short that first week. It may not sound a lot but when absolutely everything has been taken off you, and there is no way in the world that you are going to get another 4p from anywhere, suddenly that 4p becomes very, very important. In some ways prison really puts things into perspective for you, I had never before been in a position where 4p could make such a difference and yet there I was standing in a corridor in Winchester and that miserly 4p was making a real difference to my life. I'd always been bought up to believe that life was tough at the top, but I learnt that day that it is even tougher at the bottom!

Sure enough my good friend Micky Sing was able to come to the rescue as he didn't smoke and therefore he didn't have the problem with the tobacco that I was facing, he was there to buy extra goodies for the cell. Having overcome the problem of paying for my smokes I now realized that I had the additional problem of making one box of matches last a whole week. I'd heard the rumours that once inside the cons used to split their matches lengthways, right down the middle, in order to double the amount of matches they had, but never in my wildest dreams did I think that they were serious! How wrong I was, and I duly spent the next hour in my cell splitting my matches in half just to make them last. Again it may seem odd but at least it was something to do to relieve the boredom. After a week I got my 10 pence pay rise and the problem was solved, to this day I'm sure they set the wages 4p short just to let me know who was in charge.

As you can imagine, once you were banged up for the night one of the most common problems that you would encounter is that you would run out of cigarette papers or matches. You could ring the emergency alarm in your cell as much as you like but you would quickly realize that no-one is coming to answer the call. I guess that explains why so many unfortunate souls have burnt to death in their cells after starting a fire as one last cry for help. Ringing the alarm bell thinking that someone would come running to your assistance can be a very expensive mistake to make while you are in prison. Of course people will argue all day long that things like that never happen and all I would say to you is, take your blinkers off, there is a generation of forgotten people in our prison system and they routinely have to deal with all sorts of emergencies – you think its not happening just because you don't see it or hear about it. Well I can tell you that it happens more often than any of us would like to admit and I'm so glad that

I'm not so wrapped up in my own self pity to be able to sit hear and speak for some of those people, because they are humans just the same as me and you and they don't deserve to die such an appalling death just because someone cannot be bothered to do their job and answer the alarm.

I think it's fair to say that we are all aware that people will always find a way to adapt and overcome, no matter what the problem, one could usually find a solution given enough time, and we had time in abundance. In this case the communication problem was overcome by getting the blanket off your bed and unstitching a couple of the green woolen strands. These would then be tied together to make a longer piece of 'string'. On one end you would make a loop to wrap around your hand and on the other end you would tie a blue, standard issue prison plastic mug that was to be found in every cell, to aid in the traditional English pastime of drinking tea.

Once you had made your *'communications rig'* the fun really started. Each cell had a tiny window on the outside wall. The window was only about 8 inches wide and about 24 inches high, now that doesn't sound too bad so far does it. The problem was that the outside wall was about 15 inches thick and on the inside there were extremely thick steel bars running vertically down the opening. This almost perfect design meant that you had to stretch your arm out with your face squashed against the inside bars just to open the window.

Once you had achieved this, the idea was that you would write down whatever it was that you needed, for example some cigarette papers, and place the note in the cup. You then had to hold the string and cup in your outstretched arm and begin a pendulum motion, swinging the cup from side to side building up some momentum. Meanwhile your cellmate would knock on the side wall of your cell to attract the attention of the poor soul next door. He would then hopefully realize that someone wanted him and would open his window and stretch his arm out as far as he could in order to try and catch the cup. Unfortunately catching the string line proved to be much harder than swinging it, as you were literally holding your hand out into the darkness and you just had to wait and hope that the guy next door could get enough motion going for the cup to reach you and make a connection with your outstretched hand. Even if you succeeded there was no guarantee that the bloke next door either had any cigarette papers or even if he did, then there was always the chance that he didn't want to part with them. All communication after the hours of darkness within the prison was done by using this method. If you all got on well enough you could get something delivered from 4 or 5 cells down the line, all it took was a lot of patience and plenty of time. We had the time, after all no-one was going anywhere in a hurry, but the patience bit often got stretched to the limit. It could be so frustrating swinging that bloody cup, but also very rewarding if you persevered.

The prison system itself is like a merry-go-round at the fair, inmates are always coming and going. New arrivals from the court pour in daily, as do many inmates that are just being moved about within the system for various reasons. What I'm trying to say is that it wasn't uncommon to be moved without notice and as the moves took place early in the morning before breakfast, it wasn't uncommon to wake up to find that you had new neighbour.

I'd only been inside a week or so, when one night there was a knock on the left hand wall in my cell. I climbed up to open the window and stretched out my arm. After some time I duly managed to catch the cup from next door and inside was a note asking for some *'skins'* (cigarette papers). Not being one to turn away a man in need, I placed half a dozen cigarette papers inside the cup and then stuffed the cup full of Micky Sing's best toilet roll to stop the papers from falling out on the return journey. I gently let go of the cup sending it back on its merry way. With a job well done Micky and myself settled down for the rest of the night.

Before going to sleep we used to spend hours doing all sorts of isometric exercises that Micky had stored in his brain. The best thing was all you needed was your own bodyweight, and so using his system you could have a workout anywhere in the world using even the smallest amount of space. This proved to be a handy way of keeping fit in such a small room.

In the morning when the cell door opened there was a sixty year old man stood there waiting for us to come out. As I approached him I was greeted with a warm smile as he offered his outstretched hand and announced that his name was Eddie. We shook hands and as I gave my name. He thanked me for the skins, adding that he really appreciated the cigarette papers. He added that he'd had a really bad day yesterday and that he had been desperate for a roll-up. We chatted for a couple of minutes then decided to head off down to the kitchen to get our breakfast. He was a likable fellow and very easy to get along with, I guess the warm smile helped as first impressions can mean so much. When we returned to our cells, we said our goodbyes and agreed to have a game of chess later in the day. Shortly after this, Micky returned with his breakfast and his daily copy of the news paper. It certainly had its advantaged sharing a cell with a non smoker. Micky could buy all sorts of strange things with his wages as he didn't smoke, believe me it was a big thing to have a copy of the daily paper in your cell, as it said to all the other inmates that you had money to burn – or that's how a lot of cons used to interpret it, to get a daily paper was defiantly a luxury in HMP Winchester. Sure you could get an old copy of one for a few roll-ups but we had one daily and therefore Micky was '*The man*'.

When Micky handed me the newspaper I nearly fell over, right there on the front page was my new neighbour, and the headline stated that yesterday he'd been given 20 years for importing and handling cocaine. He sure wasn't joking when he said that he'd had a bad day was he. Sit there and think about it for a couple of minutes – 20 years, not 20 minutes or 20 days or even 20 months – 20 bloody years and he was already about sixty. The man who had greeted me with such friendliness early that morning, had only hours before learnt that he was now never going to be a free man again. He was never going to do the things with his family that so many of you take for granted. The rest of his days would now be spent at the mercy of her majesty's prison system.

I can hear you all shouting that maybe he should have thought about that before starting out on his life of crime, well I can tell you that he was proud and he wasn't complaining. I could see that he had spirit and he stood out from the crowd, it was obvious that he was no ordinary person. How do you think you would feel if you were unlucky enough to find yourself in his predicament? Could you walk about hours later as though nothing had happened, I don't think I could. No, this man was special and as I read down the page I soon realized that I had been in the presence of a legend - his name was Eddie Richardson, the same Eddie Richardson who along with his younger brother Charlie had been accused of various acts of violence in the now famous 'Torture gang trials' in the 60's. If you believe everything that the papers say then the word was that they had also enjoyed a fierce rivalry either side of the river in London over many years with the Kray twins. In previous years I had read quite a few books about both sets of infamous brothers, including Charlie's Richardson's biography 'My Manor', which ironically I actually read while I was in the cells during my trial that year.

You can think what you like about such individuals as I'm too long in the tooth to believe that I'm going to change your views, but for the record, my view is that I take everyone as I find them, and as such to me he was just another poor soul just trying to do his time, the only difference being that he was now very unlikely to be going home again. With your hand on your heart what do you honestly think you would say to a man in such a predicament? 20 years – if the idea had been to break that mans spirit then the system had failed big time, so to be honest I really couldn't see the point of giving any man that amount of time to do. I hope you can appreciate what it would feel like to be given such a sentence but to be honest I know deep down that you would have to have spent some time behind bars to ever begin to truly understand.

Eddie was next door for a week before his was shipped out to another prison to continue his sentence. So much has been written about the Richardson's over the years, most of it by people who have never even met them, and yet they claim to be so called experts on the subject, that I feel that there would be little point in writing any more, other than to say that I enjoyed Eddie's company immensely, especially the deep and meaningful games of chess that we played together. All I can say is that I found him to be a warm, honest and caring man with a great sense of humour.

I also had two good friends from Basingstoke in Winchester prison with me at this time. The first was my old buddy who we are going to call 'Tex', and he was serving just over 5 years for a fight that had taken place at his house. There's only really one thing that you need to know about Tex and that is; you don't go to Tex's house to pick a fight with him. I'm not joking when I say that he is the 'real deal' when it comes to a punch up. He's a 17 stone powerhouse and the story goes that three men had gone round to his house to 'sort him out'. They were armed with baseball bats and an axe and were intending to dish out some instant justice for one reason or another. Unfortunately one of the men made the mistake of walking up to Tex's lounge window in the dark, cupping his hands firmly against the glass in the process, in order to get a better view inside the lounge. Tex was watching TV when he first notice this complete amateur peering into his lounge, he got up from his chair and walked over to the lounge window and I guess the dreaded 'red mist' must have descended upon him because he punched both his arms through the window and grabbed his would be attacker by the face. He then proceeded to pull his would be assailant through the window and into the lounge, ripping wounds in his own forearms that required dozens of stitches in the process.

Apparently all hell broke loose in the house with his girlfriend and young children screaming and taking cover as he pounded his victim unconscious on the lounge floor; meanwhile another fool was giving it large with an axe chopping the hell out of Tex's front door. I bet he wishes he hadn't bothered now! After Tex had immobilized the guy in the lounge he turned his attention to the man trying to chop his way through the front door. Tex helped him with his task by opening the door from the inside and duly firing a 10 inch crossbow bolt into his attacker's chest. The third assailant decided to leave his mates to it and ran off into the night – I guess we could say he was the smartest one of the bunch. In short both attackers were in a serious state in hospital, Tex was also in there having some stitches put into both his lower forearms, and before the anesthetic had worn off he was arrested for 2 counts of wounding with intent to endanger life, for which he got the 5 year sentence that had put him with me in Winchester. I don't think many people would look forward to seeing Tex, but I can tell you that when I first walked onto 'B' wing and heard a shout coming from the 4's saying *'Laurence you wanker'*, his ugly face had been a very welcome sight and I was well chuffed to catch sight of that broad grin that he always carries everywhere with him – if your *'inside'* with Tex standing beside you, believe me you're as safe as you could possibly be under the circumstances.

Unfortunately a few years after our release Tex was shot in the stomach from a distance of 3 feet with a shotgun while sat on the toilet in a flat on the Oakridge estate in Basingstoke. Only he could get shot on the bog. Miraculously he survived after major surgery, and even on that night a police report stated that after being shot he had managed to stand up, claim a hammer from inside the house and pursue his attacker out onto the landing outside that linked the flats together, smashing a dozen windows with the hammer as he stumbled along the landing in pursuit of his assailant, holding his stomach together with his other hand as he ran, before collapsing unconscious on the floor. After major surgery he managed to survive and although I've no idea where he is now, I wish him well wherever he is.

Another good man who had been in prison with me was my old friend Steve Hale. I had known Steve for years even then. He was being held on the remand wing of the prison as he hadn't been convicted of anything at that point, in fact I believe that the charges were dropped against him and he went home after a few weeks with his head held high. As he was on another wing the only time I got a chance to sit down and chat to him was when I went to the prison church service, which was held on a Sunday morning. So it can be said that Mr. Hale is responsible for the fact that I had to take up the good book while serving my sentence.

We had such a laugh while sat at the back of the church, with the vicar yapping on about the bible. Both Steve and his girlfriend Tasha have been solid friends of mine for nearly 25 years, and so it would be unfair of me to write a book without mentioning them. Whenever I have needed some support during my life they were there for me, and now is my chance to say that it is very much appreciated.

It has to be said that prison is one of the most boring places that I've ever been unfortunate enough to visit, although the authorities did go quite a long way with their efforts to lay on activities for the evenings. On Monday evenings I used to go down to the gym and play volley ball with the other inmates, on Tuesday's it was five-a-side with Tex. Thursday's I went to the chess club and had a relaxing couple of hours trying to keep my brain functioning by playing as many games of chess as possible in the allotted time. Apart from going to these events the other evenings were spent banged up in my cell with Micky and we would sit there chatting with the radio on enjoying a quiet game of chess.

Weekends were a total nightmare as I didn't go to work on Saturday or Sunday and was therefore banged up in my cell for 23 hours each day, only being allowed out to attend church on Sundays or for an hours exercise in the afternoon. This entailed walking with the other inmates round the circular path in the prison courtyard – even out there we had rules and everyone had to walk in the same direction so as to avoid arguments.

On a Sunday afternoon the prison would lay on a film for all the inmates to watch. I have to be honest and say that I never bothered to go to this particular event, instead myself and Micky would spend the 2 hours completely stripping out the cell and giving it a good scrub. I'm sure some of the films must have been half decent but this was the only time that we could put the tables and bucket out on the landing while we cleaned, without causing offence to the others on the wing.

It was the same old routine every day and only a couple of things occasionally broke the monotony. One of those would be a *'visit'*. Just as it sounds this is when your family, friends or your probation officer would turn up to see you. Each convicted inmate was allowed one visit per month, and only two people could come at any one time. To arrange a visit, first you had to go to the duty officer on the landing during office hours and put in an application for a visiting order. This was known as *'putting in an app'*, and you had to follow the same procedure if you wanted anything at all during your time on the wing. If your behaviour merited it and you had not broken any of the rules during the previous month, then a visiting order would arrive at your cell within a couple of days, usually with the mail from friends on the outside, all of which were opened and read by the prison officers. Once you had received your 'V.O' you would then have to give full details of the person or people that were going to visit you. Once completed, the form was then handing back to the duty officer and a couple of days later it would arrive back at your cell, complete with the official prison stamp that was needed to authorize it. To complete the formalities the V.O. would then be mailed to your intended visitor and with any luck, on the due date they would arrive at the prison. They would then have to wait a while until it was their turn to be individually searched by an officer, who would often be accompanied by a prison dog. They would then be led into the visiting room to wait, while you were summoned from the relevant wing. Visits were held in an open planned room with prison officers situated in each corner and also along the sides. There was a rule of no touching so as to reduce the number of illegal items that somehow always seem to find there way into even such a controlled environment.

Although I would obviously always be really excited about seeing family or friends, when they left I was always left with an empty feeling. Walking back to the cell after a visit was always a lonely walk, as all you could think about is how lucky they were to be going home. Something that people on the outside fail to realize is that even the smallest and most insignificant comments made during a visit can mushroom into a major disaster when an inmate returns to be locked in his cell for hours on end, with nothing to do and nothing to think about except those few words that were spoken to him a few hours earlier. I saw many grown men break down in tears at the desperation they felt about not being able to help a friend or family member due to the fact that they were in prison when these people needed their help and support the most. For many within the prison system that guilt alone has proved to be too much, and as I sit here writing I can recall 4 good friends, who for one reason or another were sent to prison and tragically died within those walls – I can't help but think that its so very sad that not only did these people take their own lives, but circumstances had led them to do it within the confines of a prison which was designed to be the one place that they should have been helped to cope with their emotions. I don't think that there's any doubt that this should always be part of the rehabilitation process that was meant to take place to ease them back into society as better human beings – well to put it bluntly, that seems to have failed in a number of cases and I personally find that very sad indeed.

Apart from the monthly visits the only other thing that took place out of the ordinary was a 'spin'. A spin was when for one reason or another the prison officers decided to search your cell. This could happen at any time of the day or night and if you were lucky they would decide to do it while you were out of the cell getting one of the daily meals. If they decided to give you a spin while you were in the cell, the first thing you would know about it was when the cell door would suddenly fly open and in would charge 5 prison officers in full riot gear complete with 4 foot riot shields. These were then used to charge the inmate across the cell and up against the back wall, where he would be totally immobilized by the shield, due to the force being exerted by the officer holding the shield in front of him as he ran through the cell. Once the inmate was under control he would be removed from the cell and placed outside on the landing while the officers systematically search ever square inch, looking for anything at all that shouldn't be there. They rarely found anything, after all where are you going to hide something in such a small room? I'm sure it was done just to keep the masses in their place and to remind everyone who was in charge.

One of the things that the inmates were always trying to smuggle into the prison was drugs. What I saw most of first hand was marijuana. Now this drug had a very unusual way of arriving into a prison. The most common way to get a decent amount smuggled in was to insert it into ones back passage before attending court. I remember a guy who managed to bring 4oz with him using this method – and 4oz would have to go down in anyone's book as a major achievement! Now it's all well and good putting it in there, but at some point it is going to have to come back out again. This led to what the prison fraternity calls the '*shit parcel*'. You would be forgiven for thinking that a shit parcel would be a very rare commodity in a prison but you would actually be very wrong indeed. If you went outside the prison wing and walked round to the back of the building and looked on the grass below the cell windows, you would see literally hundreds of little bundles of newspaper littering the lawn, and each one would be the masterful creation of an inmates shit parcel. Over the years it had become a serious hobby for some people and it was fascinating to see what someone could make from a few pieces of newspaper and the remnants of their arse when they had time on their hands.

I knew when I started this book that there would be times when I would have to write about difficult times and events that had occurred over the years, and one of those things was the fact that while in prison, I had been introduced to the tradition of smoking marijuana. This was always going to be the difficult part, mainly due to the fact that some of the people around me might feel disappointed or offended if I chose to 'do my dirty washing in public'. I've thought long and hard about it all and no matter what I came up with, the end result was always the same. I couldn't find a way to alter the fact that in order to achieve my objective - which was to write an open, honest and balance view of my life, then I felt that this was going to be impossible without causing offence to someone. In all honesty I've spent 35 years worrying about everyone else in my life and I just figured it was time to stand up and be counted, and for once I should just do what I had to do. Anyone can write a biased view of anything but it takes character to open the doors to one's soul, and I believe that I have character. To get my message across I feel that in this case the end justifies the means, and so for that reason alone I need to be open and honest to enable me to place all my cards on the table. Marijuana was absolutely everywhere in Winchester prison. As cash was banned drugs and tobacco became the 'currency'.

I'm not going to attempt to make any excuses for my actions, I certainly knew right from wrong at that point in time, but in mitigation I have to say that I really was at a low point in my life.

It wasn't just the fact that I was in prison that bothered me, as to be honest that was just like being back at boarding school. I don't mean that in a negative way at all, merely to point out that both prison and boarding school have a strict routine for everyone to follow, and that I was more than used to a structured day, and so to me it felt like a home from home, only with a hell of a lot more violence. It was things that were happening on the outside that were bothering me, my girlfriend Kate was pregnant and also the mortgage lenders wouldn't wait for me to return. They had written to Kate to confirm that they were now starting the process of re-possessing the flat that we had bought. The company that I had my car finance with wouldn't wait for payment either and they turned up one day to re-posses the car, that's all she needed wasn't it – talk about kicking someone while they are down. I wasn't in a position to stop any of it because by the time I received the letter from Kate via the dreaded prison mail system and replied, they had already taken the car.

It quickly became obvious that prison was going to cause a major headache in my life, and so a month into my sentence I was advised to declare myself bankrupt to enable me to make a fresh start once I was released. All the technical stuff was handled by either Kate or some other third party on the outside. I meanwhile just had to sit there and wait to receive the bad news a couple of days after it had happened. I don't want to sound bitter but at the time it really was an unnecessary kick in the teeth, we are talking about 4 months and I believe that it would have been possible to make those repayments reasonable quickly upon my release. The fact that no-one would wait made it feel like I was destined to fail. I'd now lost so much and it just felt like everything I had worked for had been taken away from me along with my freedom. When you are sat there, pretty much alone in a prison cell, isolated from all rational thinking and you are watching your whole life's work dissolve before your eyes, it is so tempting when someone walks up to you and says 'Here mate, have a joint with me and it will all go away'. To fully understand the true effect of being isolated from reality while the vultures strip you of all your worldly possessions and stamp you into the ground, then I'm afraid that you would have to live the experience first hand, but I can tell you that it's the worst feeling in the world. It was like I was being punished twice for what I had done.

With hindsight, and I'm not trying to justify myself at all, it wasn't surprising really that in the end I succumbed and took the joint. Up until that point in my life I really was anti drugs. I was a fitness fanatic and couldn't see the point of polluting my body with such substances, and yet all my rational thinking had gone, and in my heart if I'm honest, I sat there and just wanted it all to go away. What did society want from me? - I'd said I was sorry and I meant it and yet it felt that I was still being persecuted for past sins. Prison is definitely the wrong place to be while having to deal with so many problems, therefore anything that blanked things out was ok by me. As I sit here now I'm just thankful that I wasn't offered anything stronger at the time, because over the years marijuana has caused me serious problems and had it been anything else then I doubt that I would have made it through to sit here and recount the story to you.

I stumbled through the rest of my sentence eagerly wanting to get back to my cell every evening so that we could share a joint. There is no craving with marijuana as with most other drugs and so it was just the fact that I wanted to block things out of my mind that attracted me to the drug culture. What I did was done purely out of choice, the strange thing was that as with all drugs, people only tell you the information that they think you want to hear when they give you the sales pitch. They forget to tell you that heavy marijuana use erodes your motivation, destroys your concentration, causes paranoia and heart palpitations and totally eradicates your short term memory. If I had known all that I don't think I would have bothered to have that very first joint. The moral of the story is that from my experienced position I feel that nothing good came out of my experiences with soft drugs, either in the short term or long term. Therefore my advice to anyone who will listen is; just don't start on drugs, either hard or soft, as it is a long road back to recovery and it's all uphill. So save yourself the hassle and face the problem that is bothering you head on. No matter what anyone tells you, I have yet to meet a single person who has actually improved his or her situation in life by using drugs, so save yourself the effort and try another solution to your problems.

Something else that had been playing on my mind at this time was the fact that I still had an outstanding charge to face from before I was in prison. I had been arrested earlier for Affray, which in layman's terms is a fight that involves more than 6 people. Myself and a friend had been walking home from the pub one night and were set upon by 4 young men, it didn't take us long to neutralize all four of them but when the police arrived they said that they felt we had used excessive force. Well excuse me, but to this day I believe that if you are walking aimlessly home after a night out and a group of men decide to attack you, then I believe that they deserve everything they get. We were lucky as we were both capable of defending ourselves or the consequences could have been far worse. As it turned out things were already bad enough and yet here I was, stuck in Winchester prison, and my case was due to be heard exactly 2 weeks before I was due to go home. This meant that all the time I was in prison I didn't know when I would actually be going home. I figured that as I was already in prison, then I was bound to get another sentence and would have to stay there to complete it. It's hard when you don't know your release date as you have nothing to aim at and in reality all you do is just end up drifting from one day to another, unable to dream about your release or plan for the future.

The day arrived and I was woken early and escorted to Winchester Crown Court to hear my case. I decided to plead guilty as there was little doubt that I had been involved in the fight. In short I was sentenced to a further month in prison and I was also placed under a one year supervision order with the Basingstoke Probation Service. In addition to the above I was also ordered to complete two courses at the Baring Centre in Basingstoke upon my release. One was a 'Temper control' course, and the other was for 'Anger management'. I wasn't fined or ordered to pay any costs, which was fortunate really as I didn't have anything left to pay with!

I came away relieved it was over and now at least I had a genuine release date and I could now start to look forward to going home. The time passed quickly, mainly due I think to the lads inside who kept my spirits up on a daily basis. Being in prison together and sharing all that hardship and suffering does build an extremely strong bond with all ex-cons. I'm not saying for one moment that I enjoyed my time in Winchester Prison but I definitely met some interesting people while I was there, and due to our environment I saw a completely difference side to them, one that very few people ever get to see.

Before I knew it the day arrived when I was due to be release. Just before the doors were locked on my last night, a few of the lads decided to have some fun at my expense. They burst into my cell and about 7 people took a turn to empty a bucket of water over me and all the items in the cell, they were laughing their heads off as they drenched the place. Apparently it meant that I was a good egg. At least it gave me something to do as time was standing still. You know the feeling you get on Christmas Eve when you're a child, well that's exactly how you feel the night before you are released from prison.

In the morning I was up and dressed when the duty officer came to collect me, and so off we went following the same procedure as when I had first arrived, except this time in reverse order. We left the wing and headed back to towards the reception area and the main entrance, I was waving and shouting goodbye as I trundled along. I said my final goodbye's and collected the jacket that had been taken off me upon my arrival. I was then escorted to the main gates for the last time. I stepped outside wondering who or what would be waiting for me – but there was no-one there. The feeling of emptiness and abandonment was overwhelming as I stepped out into the sunshine for the first time in months. It was August 16^h 1990, a day I'm unlikely to forget. I made my way along Romsey road which ran past the front of the prison, and as I walked along I glanced up and suddenly spotted my younger brother, sat on the wall like a little pigmy with a big grin spread right across his chops. It was good to see him, my brother and best mate rolled into one.

We turned and headed towards the railways station to get a train back to Basingstoke. Eventually we pulled into Basingstoke station and I was so glad to be home again.

CHAPTER 9

STARTING AGAIN

I arrived back into society quietly and headed to my mother's home which was now in a village just outside Basingstoke – in Silchester. Kate meanwhile had moved back to her parent's house in Sherborne St John. We were now about 6 weeks away from having our first baby, the whole situation was a nightmare and it was going to take a lot of character to rebuild from here. Although it's fair to say that I have experienced many different emotions during the course of my lifetime, some good and some bad, I would have to say that none can compare with the feeling I got upon my release from prison. There are no words to describe the adrenalin rush that you get when those big steel gates open wide enough for you to take those final steps to freedom.

The first thing that we needed to do now was get ourselves a home, the problem was that we had both been declared bankrupt during my time in prison and so therefore we couldn't get a mortgage, the situation was far from ideal. It's interesting to note that upon my return, every single person that I spoke to who knew Kate and I had said exactly the same thing to me - all were in agreement that I would be better off without her. Although she was heavily pregnant at the time, the feeling was that my life was in a mess and I now had the ideal opportunity to start afresh. Everyone felt that the whole process would simply be a hell of a lot easier without Kate in the equation. Although I fully understood their feelings, I just couldn't bring myself to abandon my unborn child. I therefore decided to give things one last try, but then again I never was one for taking the easy option. Now over 15 years later I can honestly say that I don't regret that decision at all.

The following months were a complete nightmare; Kate was heavily pregnant and she also hated living at her mother's house. I think it's fair to say that they have endured a fiery relationship over the years and rarely saw eye to eye about anything. As the weeks passed we knew that we had to get things sorted out, and quickly. The local authority had told us to come back to them when the baby was born, as we could then enter the housing system and start to move towards being housed.

As winter approached I received a letter from the Barring Centre in Basingstoke regarding the two courses that I had to attend thanks to the earlier affray. I was due to start the Anger management course in mid November and then that would be followed by the Temper control, a week later. There was a hell of a lot of pressure on us at this time, don't forget we were just another young couple starting out in life and here we were with no house, no car, nothing, what a state to get yourself into and I'd have to agree that its no way to bring a child into the world. From now on we would have to do better. The one consolation was that the new baby would be too young to remember anything that happened at this point in our lives. We therefore felt that this gave us about 2 years to get re-housed and to get our lives back on track.

Then one night in early October while I was out for a beer with some mates I was arrested for *'Using abusive or threatening words or behaviour likely to cause alarm or distress'* - to 3 police officers, and also for *'Possession of an offensive weapon in a public place'*. And so it was back to the magistrate's court and I was fined another 90 pounds for my troubles to go with the lectures I got from just about everyone in my immediate family.

The last couple of weeks before the birth passed without incident and on 31st October 1990 my daughter was born at Basingstoke Hospital. At last we had some good news to share; she was gorgeous in every way. You can't put into words what a father feels, having just witnessed the birth of his child – I was blown away by the pure beauty of my new baby girl. Kate had only been given gas and air while in labour and so the next day she was up and about strutting her stuff, like a new mother does. That evening she came out of hospital and returned home to her mother's house.

Within days of them returning home from hospital there were problems in the house. Apparently her mother had decided that Kate knew nothing about babies and decided that she knew better in every department. This caused the pair of them to clash as Kate felt that she wasn't even getting the opportunity to feed or change her own daughter. Knowing how vicious Kate's mother could be I quickly realized that we needed to get both Kate and my daughter moved out of the house as soon as possible. Unfortunately while Kate and I were in the process of working out what to do with regard to housing, war broke out. I've no idea how it started but Kate ended up in a fight with her mother in the entrance hall to their bungalow. Unfortunately my newborn daughter was asleep in the hallway, neatly tucked up in her pram. This important detail didn't stop them from throwing punches at each other. To cut a long story short, between them they wreaked the hallway and they only stopped when they had managed to break the glass panel on the front door, which in turn sent a shower of razor sharp shards of glass all over my beautiful baby girl. To say that I feel that their actions that day were reckless would have to go down as an understatement. The seriousness of the events obviously raised more questions within my family, as none of us could quite work out how things had got so out of hand. There is no question that a grand mother should never behave in such a manner. In the real world we would all probably forgive a woman who had recently given birth, if she was to be slightly touchy over the following weeks. A blind eye would be turned to any strange behaviour because we all understand that a women's body goes through quite a traumatic experience during both labour and giving birth – the hard part was trying to understand what a fifty year old grand mother was doing fighting with her daughter and sending glass all over the place. That was the part that we were all having difficulty with because whichever way you look at it, there can be no reasonable excuse for what went on in that house that day – they should be ashamed of themselves, but alas my instinct tells me that neither of them would be in the slightest bit concerned about their actions that day.

The next day Kate and I returned to the local housing authority to request that we now be housed, due to the fact that neither Kate nor my daughter would be safe should they return to their home address. After a couple of hours of filling in official paperwork, we were given a train ticket to Reading and also an address of a hotel where we would now be housed as 'bed and breakfast' guests, until such time as Basingstoke Council could find a permanent home for us. It turned out that we were only in Reading for 3 weeks but as is sods law it happened to be the three weeks that I was supposed to be at the Baring Centre in Basingstoke to attend my courses, bloody typical I thought!

While we were staying at the Early Court Hotel in reading, we received a letter from the housing department at Basingstoke Council telling us that a 3 bedroom house had become available. A week later Kate and I moved into our new home in Chineham, along with our new daughter. We were told that the house was due to be knocked down to make way for a roundabout in the near future, and it was therefore only temporary accommodation. We were over the moon as we were now in the system, even though as soon as a house became available for us, we would have to move again.

We quickly settled in and started to form our new home. By this time I had returned to my old job building swimming pools, but to be honest it just wasn't the same. I quickly learnt how shallow people can be, sure they made me very welcome but as most people that have been in prison for violent offences will tell you, you soon get fed up with everyone agreeing with everything you say all day, and so after a couple of months I decided that I fancied a new challenge and began to look for another job. It wasn't the money, as building swimming pools had paid me a fortune over the years; I just felt that in order to move forward I would have to start looking for employment elsewhere.

I know you cant just forget about the past, and I'm the first to say that as individuals we must take responsibility for our actions, but as very few people had even bothered to ask me what had actually happened that night, and even if they did then they didn't really listen to what I was saying, instead they always just seemed to jump to their own conclusions and think that as you had been inside then you were probably bad news. To be fair they had a point, I guess it's just that I've never looked upon myself like that. At the time you don't realize what a devastating effect prison is going to have upon your life and not only that, it also continues to cause you pain and suffering well into your future – so be warned.

Apart from getting a little fed up with building swimming pools, things generally were starting to improve. One of the best parts was coming home from work to my little bundle of love, she was only 5Lb 7oz at birth - so small and beautiful, and with the darkest brown eyes you've ever seen. I can't think of anything better in our world than new life. This obviously bought with it a great deal of responsibility to my life and I think that's just what I needed at that time.

We plodded on to the end of the year just thankful that there had not been any problems and as we saw in the New Year and welcomed 1991, Kate and I promised each other that we would strive to improve the quality of our lives during the next twelve months.

We were doing quite well for the first half of the year and then suddenly on 24th May 1991 our lives would again be thrown into chaos – only this time through no fault of our own. At 11.32pm on that fateful Friday night, after being out with a group of friends to the swan pub in Sherborne St John, I was hit by a blue Vauxhall Astra motor car while crossing the road on Popley way in Basingstoke. I already knew of 4 people under the age of 20 who had died on this road, by coincidence it is the main road that runs past the front of my old school 'John Hunt of Everest'. I was well aware of the dangers that came with crossing Popley way as I'd done it daily for 2 years only a few years earlier, and yet it still happened to me – I think that speaks for itself and gives you an idea of just how dangerous that road used to be.

I had been on a bit of a session with some mates and as the beer flowed we decided to leave my car at the pub and get a taxi home. I left the pub in a taxi with 2 friends, firstly my old friend the late Adrian Payne, whom I had known since he was a boy as it was his father that I was working with on the swimming pools.

Also with us that night was another long time friend Sam Axton. It was to Sam's house that we were heading that night and the accident occurred near enough to her house for her next door neighbour to be one of the first people to the scene, apparently they had heard the impact from their lounge and had come running over to try and help.

The three of us had been dropped off in a bus stop, on a sweeping bend; visibility was about 150 yds in either direction and even though it was dark, visibility was still pretty good due to the street lighting that lined both sides of the road. We got out of the taxi and I paid the fare through the driver's window, we said thanks and good night and proceeded to cross 2 lanes of traffic followed by another bus stop on the other side of the road. Separating the two lanes of traffic was an 'island' which consisted of a couple of high visibility bollards.

We were crossing the road, walking in a straight line with me in the middle, Adrian on my left and Sam on my right – the first half of the journey was fine as we made in to the traffic island without any problems. The next thing I can remember seeing is the headlights of a car about 10 yards from me, coming from my left side, everything then seemed to be happening in slow motion. I distinctly recall putting my left hand out and feeling the cold steel of the car's bonnet shortly before I felt the impact of the windscreen to the left side of my face. I went straight through the windscreen on the passenger side and headed face first into the passenger of the vehicle, and as the driver applied the brakes I was sent sprawling back out through the windscreen and onto the bonnet. Shortly after I felt the impact of the road down the left side of my head/shoulder area as I subconsciously tried to form a ball to roll out of the danger, not realizing that it was already far to late. Then came the eerie silence that people always seem to associate with all major traumas.

I remember lying in the road and starting to feel really wet on my head and also down the left hand side of my face. As best I could, I stumbled to my feet and when erect, I looked down and my beige trousers were turning red before my eyes. A dark haired woman then approached me and suggested that I lie down and wait for the ambulance to arrive. I apparently mumbled back something about having to get home as I was late. I then heard a shout in the background, followed by a scream, as the dark haired women guided me towards the floor and into the recovery position.

Within what felt like a few minutes the face of a middle aged man appeared over my shoulder and asked me my name; lying there in the road after an accident believe me its one of the best feelings in the world when that unknown face appears and you feel the surge of relief thunder through your body as you now know that your going to be all right. It was the first time that I had ever been close up to an ambulance and its crew and I think sometimes we forget how lucky we are in England to have such compassionate people risking their lives daily to help us in our hour of need.

They immediately pumped something into my thigh and I guess I drifted off, as the next thing I remember is lying on a trolley in a side room at Basingstoke hospital, with someone leaning over me tugging at my face. As it turned out that they were trying to remove the gravel and grit from the left side of my face, so that they could asses the extent of my injuries; the strange thing was I couldn't feel any pain. It's difficult to explain exactly what it felt like to be strapped to a trolley and have someone leaning over you with a scrubbing brush, scrubbing away at an open flesh wound on your face, without feeling any pain – it was totally surreal. Then I was whisked down to x-ray, trolley and all. They put me on a conveyor belt and dispatched me into an enormous x-ray machine, apparently this thing photographed the whole body and would show up every single injury on my torso – or should I say that I believe that was the theory behind it all.

The hulking lump of steel revealed that I had the following injuries; 17 stitches needed in various lacerations to the left side of my face, most of the skin had gone from the left side of my chin, more stitches needed in 3 deep lacerations stretching from my forehead to the back of my neck, which made me look like a badger for the next 5 weeks. I also had a deep laceration on the bridge of my nose that went to the bone, stitches and bruising on my right thigh, half a dozen stitches scattered over the back of each of my hands, due to the fact that they had scrapped along the road when I had landed, damage to the ligaments in my right knee, after it had struck the car's front headlight and bonnet upon impact and grazes to both feet. The worst part of all was the feeling that I had indeed been hit by a car, I ached all over and every inch of me felt like it was bruised. It's difficult to explain as I've never had that feeling before or since but believe me when I say I felt like I'd done 12 rounds with Mike Tyson – it hurt!

The medical report from the accident used for my insurance claim stated that I was 'conscious and cooperative' upon arrival at the hospital; conscious and cooperative eh, medical terms amaze me – in layman's terms I would have described myself as almost dead!

Having had the benefit of the best that the National Health Service had to offer, I eventually found my way up onto a ward on 'D floor', where I tried to settle down for the night to get some sleep. The pain was unbearable and I was awake all night, every time I moved any part of my body I felt a surge of severe pain. It was one of the longest nights of my life and in the morning, after a brief inspection by the duty doctor I was discharged from hospital, despite the fact that I was in a terrible state. It just seemed so absurd that after approximately 15 hours after a major road accident I was being sent home. By now my whole body was turning blue as the bruises had started to appear due to the initial impact and I could barely stand, let alone walk – still the order was given and I was discharged.Think what you will about the National Health Service and believe me I was pleased to see the ambulance crew when they arrived, but now my gut feeling was that the accident and emergency department seemed to be making a mess of it. My feelings were proved to be correct when 2 days later I returned to the hospital for a follow up appointment with the plastic surgeon, and after another x-ray it was discovered that I had a broken left arm, and just for good measure I had dislocated my left shoulder – the same shoulder that I had broken, no wonder the bloody thing hurt so much in the night! They had missed it and sent me home for 2 days; at least now I understood why I was in so much pain every time I moved a single muscle. After much scratching of heads and some very panicky telephone calls, I was re-admitted to the hospital for an emergency operation the following morning to repair my shattered left arm. They cut open my shoulder and to relocate my dislocation they inserted two 12" bars through my arm and drilled them into the bone to hold everything together for the next 6 weeks. To finish off they stuck a cork on the end of each bar just in case I walked into a door, to try and minimize the pain that such an event would bring. To add to my list of scars I now had a 16cm scare running vertically down my left shoulder from the surgeon's knife.

This time I was to stay in the hospital for three and a half days so that the injury could settle down before I returned home. During this period I had to carry a glass jar in my right hand every where I went, a clear thin pipe ran from the jar to the top of my left arm and disappeared inside me at the point where the surgeon had operated. Apparently it was used to drain away any fluid that had been left in my shoulder joint from the operation.

Coming home was a nightmare for all of us, firstly all the colouring of the bruises were now showing themselves so I looked a right old state, and on top of that I could hardly walk as the initial impact to my body had really left it's mark on me. We managed to get me upstairs and into bed and after another dose of painkillers I drifted off to sleep. I was so relieved to be home as the last week or so had been so emotional, it's difficult to explain what goes through your mind after such a near death experience. I was warned by the hospital staff to expect 'flashbacks' over the next couple of years but in all honesty I've never had one to this day – and the accident was 14 years ago now! It was the other things that no-one warns you about that affected me, I started to question everyday things like the direction that my life was going, what I had managed to achieve in my life and what I now wanted to do with my life – in short I started to question just about everything around me. I guess that something like that would make most of us have a good look at ourselves and I was no different.

I wasn't to realize it at the time but sat here looking back on my life, it's strange that it was around that time that all the built up aggression that seemed to be inside me, just seemed to vanish. Maybe it's just a coincidence but the fact remains that maybe, just maybe, the bang on the head that I received that night was enough to knock some sense into me. I'm not saying that I had a total personality change but I definitely became a much more caring and emotional person after that night.

Over the coming months with the help of the local physiotherapy department I made a full recovery, although I did get problems with my right knee for a couple of years. Generally though it would be fair to say that I made a full recovery, I was lucky and I knew it.

It had been quite a rough ride though, firstly as I've already mentioned the hospital failed to notice my broken and dislocated arm. Also a few months after the accident while at my local doctors due to an ear infection, the doctor found stitches in my right ear that none of us realized had even been put in. He then asked the duty nurse to check me over, and on inspection she found another seven none dissolvable stitches on my head. I know it sounds ridiculous to think that a grown man didn't know he had stitches in his body, but you have to remember that I was cut and bruised all over and unless you see them actually putting the stitches in then it's very difficult to know where they all are. If you walk into a hospital having cut yourself while making dinner then it probably wouldn't happen to you, but I had deep grazes and lacerations all over my body and the stitches were often put in individually just to hold things together while my body got on with the job of repairing itself. I had been to a few follow up appointments at the hospital in the months following the accident and each time the doctor would pull out a diagram of the human body from my file, on it were marked all the injuries that I had received that night, along with details of all the stitches that were put into me at the time – I've looked and none of them show stitches in my ears or the top of my head.

Over the following months I spoke to various people and discovered that the scream that I had heard just after the accident was in fact from the driver who had been punched in the mouth by Adrian, after he stepped from his vehicle and sarcastically said *'is your mate ok'* – to which Adrian had obviously taken offense.

By the end of the year I had made a decent recovery and felt that it was the ideal time to change direction, the swimming pools had been boring the hell out of me for quite a while and the building trade in general was heading into a deep recession, as was the whole country in fact. Instead I headed down to a recruitment agency in Basingstoke and enrolled for work. Within a few days I started working at a local factory that produced hot and cold drinks for its own vending machines, machines which the company also just happened to build at another of its factories 100 yards further up the road.

I joined 'blue' shift and worked twelve hour shifts which included both days and nights. The factory Rota was 3 days on then 3 days off, followed by 2 nights on and then 2 nights off – to complete the cycle it then reversed and you would do 3 nights on with 3 nights off, followed by 2 days on and 2 days off. It sounds complicated but in fact it works very well. It was perfect for me as I was still going to physiotherapy quite often and I also had both hospital and solicitors appointments to keep, as I was now in the process of making an insurance claim against the driver who had run me over.

Then one day in mid 1992, out of the blue, we received a letter from Basingstoke council saying that a 2 bedroom house had become available on the South Ham estate in Basingstoke and that it was now our turn on the housing list. We drove round in the car to have a look and decided that everything looked ok. Within 10 days we had moved into a 2 bedroom house in Bardwell Close.

My new job was straight forward enough; the difficult part was getting my body moving again. After a shift at work I would come home aching from head to foot as my body was just so out of condition after the long break I'd endured during my recovery. I have to say that all the staff at work were excellent to me during this period and I made some good friends during my time there. I don't see many of them these days due to other commitments but its fair to say that I still look back upon many of them with affection.

Also In 1992 my insurance claim for the accident was coming to an end. You soon learn in life that if any money is going to come your way then following closely behind will be the pack of vultures that suddenly appear with a claim to your new found riches. The insurance company turned out to be only the first person to grab a slice. I had been in receipt of incapacity benefit for about 9 months and so even before the final cheque had arrived, the department for work and pensions relieved me of four thousand pounds. Then the legal eagles took their turn eating from the pie and when everyone had finished helping themselves to my new found fortune, from a settlement of over twenty thousand pounds I was left with exactly four thousand six hundred and eighty eight pounds and seventy nine pence. Yes it was worth having, especially under the circumstances but it didn't feel much at the time for nearly loosing my life. Nevertheless the money helped Kate and I to provide some of the things that we desperately needed for the house and also for our daughter.

CHAPTER 10

GETTING HITCHED

As things seemed to be improving all round, Kate and I decided to tie the knot, and on 25th March 1993 we got married at Basingstoke registry office. It was all done at very short notice, 3 weeks notice in fact. We had been living together for a few years and now we had the baby with us, and so it seemed the next logical step. We had talked about it over the previous couple of years and when we looked into it, we realized that as I was working full time, I would get a tax rebate back to the previous April once we got married. Well we realized this minor detail at the end of February that year – hence the fact that 3 weeks later we were married. It just happened to be a couple of weeks before the end of the current tax year which worked out nicely and 5 weeks later, as promised, I duly received a tax rebate of approximately three hundred pounds.

Things were going as well as could be expected. I hadn't been arrested for quite a while and I was also getting back to being my old self and really enjoying life. Work was going great and the days passed quickly, although financially things were really tough as Kate had given up working full time when our baby had been born.

During the summer of 1993, we got the news that Kate was pregnant again. We climbed up into the loft and sorted through all the baby stuff and started the process of getting ready for a new arrival. All the necessary arrangements were made and on 15th January 1994 along came our new baby boy. I was overjoyed as we now had a boy and a girl, what more could anyone wish for. I had been trying for years to bring some sort of order to my life and as I sat there watching my daughter running round the lounge while I made my son's milk bottles up for the next day, I couldn't have asked for much else. It seemed that at long last I had found some of those elusive feelings that we all searching for - inner peace and tranquility. It was like I had just cracked the 'code of life', for years I had been a bit confused as to why exactly I was put on this earth. So far nothing had gone to plan and nothing had turned out the way I had expected. Maybe I was just expecting too much of others because as you get older you definitely start to realize that it's up to each one of us to carry our own water from the well. If you sit around and wait for things to happen, thinking that the world owes you something then I'm afraid that you won't get very far. If you really want to move forward with your life then it's going to be very much up to you, as an individual, to gets things done.

I felt that I had worked hard for quite a while at this point, trying every day to be a decent human being and as far as I was concerned I was now reaping the rewards of all my efforts. Fatherhood had bought me new emotions and feelings and I was enjoying every minute of it. I can't explain why but from the very first day that my children were born, I instantly felt that I now had a purpose in life, and my natural instinct to love and protect them was overwhelming. I had seen quite a bit of aggression in various forms over the years but I can honestly say that the feeling of love that a father has for his children is 100 times more powerful that any punch a man could throw.

Unfortunately Kate's behaviour started to change dramatically for the worse within a couple of months of my son being born. It's difficult to put into words because it was the little things that she did that became so difficult to understand. In layman's terms most would say that it was as though she resented the situation that she now found herself in, but from within the marriage my own perception was completely different, as I knew that she now had everything that she had ever wanted.

It was around this time that I was driving down a country lane one day when I came across a group of half a dozen children who were teasing and throwing stones at what appeared to be a puppy. I pulled over and after a brief discussion with the owners I came away with the dog, having parted with fifty pounds for the privilege. It turned out to be a male German Shepard named 'Lucas', which I changed to 'Luke' to give him a fresh start. He was in a right old state, his coat was matted together and his ribs were showing due to an obvious lack of food. It was obvious that he'd had a hard life but after a bath and a good brush he looked like a different dog.

Over the coming weeks I formed an extremely strong bond with him; it was like he wanted to thank me every single day for rescuing him from his living hell with all those children. When we were at home he would curl up next to my children, never letting either of them out of his sight. It was wonderful to watch as now even the dog was happy and settling in well. I was delighted that the dog had such a strong bond with the children, as it meant that he wouldn't let anything happen to them. I could then concentrate on going to work without having to worry about what Kate was doing at home with the children. It's difficult to explain what exactly was wrong at the time, and as we are all so aware, hindsight is a wonderful thing, but like I have said it was the little things that caught my attention. Like the derogatory way that Kate would speak to our daughter – she was only about 4 years old at this point and yet Kate would order her around as though she was in the army, taking great satisfaction from the fact that she was 'in charge'.

Now forgive me if I'm wrong but children aren't there to be bossed about and belittled, but rather to be encouraged to grow and develop. She was downright vindictive and aggressive toward the children and it wasn't long before the dog picked up on this. I often came home from work to the sound of Kate complaining that while I was away the dog would growl at her if she went too near the kids. I did however build a barrier so that Kate could shut the dog in the kitchen if he became a problem during the day, and we agreed to keep an eye on things as it would be impossible to keep the dog if he wasn't going to let Kate move freely around the house while I was at work.

It didn't take long for the rows to really start and the strange thing was that we would always argue about the same thing, and that was how Kate spoke to the children. She would say that I was too soft and that they would hate me when they were older, and I would say that she needed to have more control and respect for our offspring. Before you jump on the bandwagon and harp on about stress and childbirth I have to say that it was nothing to do with those things, Kate was fine in herself and there was no doubt that she loved our kids just like any other parent would, its just that she went about in a different way and would not listen to any advice – it was definitely her way or no way. She took such great pleasure from having someone around that she could order about, the problem was that this was a 4 year old defenseless child and it was bothering me a lot. Deep down I knew that she cared and loved them both but we just couldn't agree on how to handle them on a day to day basis. I have always been very anti bullying and yet here I was in the comfort of my own home and daily I was being forced to witness what I can only describe as bullying upon my children by my wife.

I wasn't alone in my thoughts and I can recall many family occasions when eyebrows were raised by various people over the way Kate would assault the children without warning. You see with Kate the thing you have to realize is that there is never a verbal warning. Most parents would call or shout at their children for doing something wrong but not her, the first thing they would know is that she would lash out at them from behind.

One event that has stayed in my mind is the day that Kate attacked our son without warning, during a Christmas gathering at my mother's house. I had gone into the garden with my brother for some reason and my son, who was only about 2 years old, was sitting on the settee in the lounge. When he realized that I was outside he stood up and turned round to look at me through the glass window. The next thing I know all hell broke loose in the house and my mother, who is normally a very reserved person, began yelling at me to come inside and have a word with my wife.

Apparently as my son was quietly peering through the window, Kate had entered the room and without warning had ran over to him and slapped him so hard across the upper thighs that he was thrown from one end of the settee to the other - then she told him off for looking out of the window. Why anyone would feel aggrieved by a child looking lovingly at his father through a window god only knows. I know it may not sound much too many of you but no one in that house was used to seeing anything quite like that and to be honest I'm surprised that she wasn't lynched there and then. Everyone present at the time had said that they were very concerned about the aggressive nature of the attack, and just as important was the fact that no warning had been given, the poor boy didn't stand a chance. Its probably worth noting that no-one in my immediate family would mind a 2 year old child standing on their sofa looking out of the window just as long as someone was next to him to make sure that he didn't fall off – that attack was out of pure spite and nothing else, the only difference was that this time she had made the mistake of doing it in front of a lot of people, and it would never be forgotten.

Kate's response to others daring to question her ability as a parent was swift and merciless. The following day, while I was at work she arranged for the destruction of our family dog at the local vets. Both the children and I were distraught when we realized what she had done and yet far from being sorry, Kate just strutted about the house with her chest puffed out, giving off an air of victory – once again as she couldn't get her own way, she had victimized the most precious yet defenseless thing that she could think off, and she had done it in such a cold and calculated way that it caused the ultimate hurt to those who in her view were responsible for daring to criticize her. She was now starting to show serious signs of very controlling behaviour and the only consolation for me was that now others could see for themselves exactly what I had to put up with during my marriage. Maybe people would now start to realize what a disturbed individual I was living with.

It was now early in 1996 and as we had 2 children of different sexes, we were allocated a brand new 3 bedroom house on a new estate that was being built on the old hospital grounds in Basingstoke – the new Rooksdown estate. As you can imagine, when we first moved in, the garden was just a pile of mud and so during the following year I set about building some retaining walls and a patio for the children to play on. I had also always wanted to keep some birds so I build an aviary at the end of the garden and slowly gathered together a collection of Australian parakeets, along with various small finches from around the world.

The rows continued as Kate started to believe, for some strange reason, that she was now better than some of her friends. Slowly they stopped coming round to see her due to her new found arrogance and yet in her small head she convinced herself that it was my fault that her friends didn't visit anymore. She also decided that I needed a better job to go with her new found status and although I found it difficult to understand how someone could be so shallow, after a few months of constant bickering I agreed to apply for a new job in the computer industry. I gave my notice at the drinks factory where I worked, and after an emotional goodbye I left to pursue a career in an office for the first time.

For the first time in years, Kate was so proud of me as I left for work each day in my shirt and tie, and yet on the inside I really wasn't happy. I'd always been quite a deep and thoughtful person and yet somehow I had managed to marry a woman who could make a paddling pool look deep. Nevertheless I persevered and to be honest I enjoyed many aspect of office work, I made some good friends and went to some wild and wonderful work do's at various hotels across the south of England but it just wasn't me, I hated the false environment of an office, where everyone wore a false smile and did 'lunch' with business contacts.

I tried to remain focused although it was very difficult as my wife was becoming more and more unpredictable, on many occasions I begged her to get some help or counselling but it just fell on deaf ears. She believed that I was wrong, and in fact she often stated that she felt I should seek counselling for myself.

Then in the summer of 1997 after a very short illness my father died, aged 57. This coupled with all the aggravation that I was getting at home, started to push me towards a breakdown. It was a terrible time as I was unhappy at work and yet when I returned home for some solitude, I would be faced with constant abuse from my wife. I don't believe that any individual, faced with the same situation, would have been able to cope. Every time I turned round there was a problem and I believe that the death of my father was the final straw that just made me stop and question what was happening in my life, where I was heading, what I had achieved and also what I wanted to achieve.

After a couple of months of total misery it was suggested that I should go and see a doctor, as friends were telling me that I just wasn't myself – if only they knew what I had been having to put up with on a daily basis maybe they would have understood a little better as to why I was so very miserable all the time. I was duly signed off work with 'depression' and I started a course of anti-depressants to try and put me back on a level playing field. Now the problems really started. If I thought that the last year had been a nightmare then although I didn't know it at the time, I was now heading for something much worse, and the strange thing was that at the time I just didn't see it coming.

I eventually spent 11 months off work with depression and during that time Kate really started to show just how selfish she had become. I was off work on full pay + bonuses so financially we were doing ok, but as an individual I was really struggling to function in a normal manner as I had lost my drive and determination. I couldn't sleep and so therefore had no energy. I was tired all the time, as though this wasn't enough on its own I also ached from head to toe – I'm not sure what causes the muscles on the human body to tighten up but I can tell you it's a living hell, it really is. Each morning I would climb out of bed after another sleepless night and make my way to the bathroom for a nice hot bath, by the time I got out of the bath I was usually ready to face the day, although it has to be said that sometimes I didn't even have the energy to get out of bed, and on these occasions I would simply stay there all day.

At this time Kate decided that she might as well return to work as I was at home all day, it's a shame that she was so wrapped up in her self that she couldn't see the pain and suffering that I was going through. Her response was to get herself a job at a local electronics firm. The fun really started when Kate first got paid, she sat down and started making a shopping list and when I peered over her shoulder I realized that it was all items for her, items like clothes and makeup. After a brief discussion I realized that she had no intention of paying any of her wages into the family home, instead she was going shopping for herself – she flatly refused to pay any household bills or to contribute in any way at all towards the cost of running our home. Obviously the situation couldn't continue for very long as we had two young children to consider. It was clear that the situation was now beyond repair and that something was going to have to give, somewhere along the line.

We managed to survive Christmas that year although it was traumatic to say the least and at the beginning of March 1998 Kate sprang another of her specials on me. It was difficult to know what she was thinking at the time as she was being so irrational with both her actions and her thoughts. One evening when I returned home and walked through the front door, she immediately tried to provoke me into an argument. By this time I was more than aware that this was likely to happen, as it was happening 3 or 4 times a week anyway, and so I didn't bite but instead made my way upstairs towards the bathroom and ran a nice hot bath to enable me to keep out of the way for half an hour until she calmed down.

She was still screaming abuse at me through the locked bathroom door when I heard a knock at the front door and I just thought thank god for that, maybe now she would calm down a bit and I could get some peace. I could hear talking in the hallway but couldn't make out what was being said. Minutes later there was a knock on the bathroom door and a voice identified itself as a policeman. I got dressed and made my way downstairs, still wondering what they wanted as I hadn't been up to anything that I could think of, it really was a mystery. When I got downstairs the first thing I noticed is that the children weren't there and I asked where they were. Kate replied that they were at her mother's house. The police then went on to explain that they had responded to a call from a woman at this address with regard to a 'Domestic in progress'. I explained that as they had just seen I was in the bath and so I could not possibly have been involved with an argument with my wife. They then knocked on the neighbour's front door and after a brief discussion they returned and suggested to Kate that next time she wanted to report a domestic incident, it would be a good idea if she waited for the argument to actually start first before calling the police as they were very busy. At this point it became obvious that Kate had decided to get me arrested for threatening her, unfortunately her plan had backfired when I failed to take the bait. She had taken the children over to her mother's house earlier in the day and then gone home to wait for my return. The plan was to start a row and get me arrested so that she could tell everyone what a terrible person I was. I realized at this point that my marriage was over, as not only could I no longer live with my wife but now I couldn't even communicate with her either. What worried me most was the fact that her actions showed a 'thought process', or to be exact 'a very devious thought process'. Its one thing to have a difference of opinion but Kate was being cold, calculated and malicious in her actions and I knew we were in a very dangerous situation as I believe that someone who has a thought process as warped as that needs to be watched at all times.

I called my mother and she drove down to pick me up as I was in a terrible state, everything I had ever wanted was now going to be destroyed. It's difficult to explain just what it feels like to realize that after 13 years of living with someone that they aren't the person that you thought they were. She had changed so much from the nice quiet sociable girl that I had first met on the bus that day into a nasty, vindictive, deceiving individual and there was nothing that I could do to help her as she totally believed that her actions were acceptable. Having spent time over the years in the company of her mother, I could understand why she had come to that conclusion. All Kate was doing were things that she saw everyday during her own childhood and so it's hardly surprising that she thought her actions were normal.

As I climbed into my mother's car and we pulled away it suddenly dawned on me that the children would be devastated. I had always been so very close to both of them and inside I felt such a failure for abandoning them, but there was just no other choice, as far as I could see the situation at home was starting to become dangerous. I honestly believe that at the time Kate was capable of doing absolutely anything to me and as I was still off work, it was decided that the best place for me to be was back at my mother's house in Silchester.

The following months were difficult, but one thing really stood out and that was that no matter which one of my friends I asked for advice, the answer was always the same, and that was: keep walking and don't go back to live with Kate under any conditions. It seemed logical to me that they couldn't possibly all be wrong at the same time and so I decided that my marriage was definitely over and I agreed with Kate that we should file for divorce as soon as possible.

In the meantime we gathered together all the outstanding household bills, which surprisingly added up to just over eight thousand pounds. These included a car loan of five thousand and the rest was made up of various smaller amounts. I decided that it would be in all of our interests that I take these with me and clear them, enabling Kate to concentrate on caring for the children with no immediate financial pressure. I also left her with one and a half thousand pounds in cash so that she could buy herself a small car to drive herself to and from the school each day with the children. All I had left from almost 13 years with that woman was a feeling of total failure and a dept of eight grand; it didn't seem to be all that I had hoped it would be when I first walked down the isle. As though that wasn't enough I also felt that my heart had been ripped out as I missed the children every hour of every day – how was I ever going to explain to them exactly why I had to desert them in their hour of need, I prayed everyday that they would understand.

At first I couldn't concentrate on anything, but slowly as the months passed, I started to feel slightly better in myself. Finally after 11 months of a living nightmare, I was well enough to think about returning to work. Months earlier I had decided that now I was single, I was going to find a job that I enjoyed and not a job that someone else wanted me to do for their own self conscious image.

I spoke to many friends and one of them recommended a local building firm that specialized in the restoration and renovation of period and country homes. My younger brother already worked there, as did numerous other friends and so it seemed the logical thing to do as I took the first steps back into reality. Although I was still in a mess emotionally, I felt that using my brain would at least take my mind of some of the other trials and tribulations that were going on in my life.

The divorce was going along as amicably as could be expected and I had unlimited access to the children. I saw them at least every Saturday, when I would go down to their house and drop of my maintenance money. They would also stay at my mother's house every other weekend which was always a nice bonus, all in all things seemed to be working out fine and I was beginning to wonder why I had stayed in the relationship for so long. In my heart I knew that I was always going to struggle without my kids, as they were the only thing that mattered to me. They had given me such a feeling of purpose and responsibility. I began to except that from now on it was up to me to make a go of things as after all now I was alone and there wasn't anyone else left to blame if things went wrong. It was time to stand up and be counted, time to carry my own water from the well. The first thing that I did was go down to the local council offices and got myself registered for housing, so that in a couple of years I would hopefully be allocated a flat.

I started my new job in the building industry and just hoped for a brighter future, at least now I didn't have the weight of a neurotic woman to carry around with me.

CHAPTER 11

THE CALM BEFORE THE STORM

I now had a new job and I was living back in Silchester with my mother - each new day felt like a burden had been lifted from my shoulders. I was still getting along relatively well with Kate and I was seeing the children as often as possible. She meanwhile, had met someone new and all seemed well from the outside. I honestly couldn't have asked for much more – everyone seemed happy considering the situation that we were now in.

Then early in 1998 my younger brother announced that he was going to get married, and he asked me to be his best man. He then went on to inform me that the wedding was going to take place in East Africa, in a seaside resort called Watamu near Malindi in Mombassa. He added that before the actual wedding, we were going to safari from Nairobi through to Sambaru and then up to lake Nukuru and onto the Mara to see the Massai tribesmen, and then finally on to Malindi for a week to get some rest before the wedding that would be on 5th October 1998. I've written about my journey back to East Africa in the first chapter of this book so there's little point in going over old ground again, suffice to say that the wedding was absolutely stunning and although to be honest my experiences of married life have now made me believe that I would be unlikely to ever marry again, it is safe to say that should I ever get the urge to walk down the isle, then I would love it to be on the beach in Africa as it was the best wedding that I've ever been to – absolutely perfect and richly deserved for my brother and his wife.

The whole occasion had also given me the ideal chance to rest my body and to have a good think about what I wanted to do with the rest of my life. It had given me the time to asses my situation and I could now begin to plan for the future. I returned from that journey back to the place of my creation filled with a feeling of inner peace. On my travels I had mixed with several different cultures and realized that life didn't have to be spent in the wet and cold of the English winter. I now realized that if I worked hard and saved some cash, I was free to go anywhere in the world whenever I felt like it. I had definitely caught the 'holiday bug' and I couldn't wait to get back to work to earn some money so that I could plan my next adventure. At last I was starting to feel good about myself.

A couple of days after I came home, I made my way down to visit the children with some small presents that I had bought in Africa. When I got there it was as though Kate was enraged with jealousy about my holiday. I came away having given the children their presents and in the back of my mind I knew it wouldn't be long before she would come up with some sort of response. As expected a couple of days later she called me and demanded that I should increase her maintenance money that I was paying her every week towards the upkeep of the children, as she was finding it difficult to manage on her income. I politely told her that I would increase the payments by five pounds per week in the New Year as I did every year. She wasn't happy but at least we had reached a compromise, which felt like an achievement in itself.

I could tell that the situation was still bothering her, and then one morning during one of my routine visits she invited me in, sat me down and made me a cup of tea. She went on to announce proudly that she would be re-marrying in the summer of 1999 somewhere in the Bahamas and asked me if I would look after the children while she was away for the wedding + honeymoon. I was delighted, as not only would I get to spend 10 days with my children but also I was over the moon that Kate had found someone else to occupy her thoughts, which in turn meant that hopefully she would probably stop making life so difficult for me. The wedding came and went and I have to say that from an ex-husbands point of view the situation couldn't have been much better. Kate and Richard seemed really happy and so did both of the children. I was glad because when you get divorced I think that whatever people say, in their heart they just want themselves and their partners to be happy, that way there are no worries about the children and you can begin to move on with your life – apart from a few minor disagreements we all got along fine. Although I still felt a deep burden of guilt and failure on a daily basis regarding my two children. It had now been well over a year since I had split from my ex-wife but those inner feelings were so deep inside me that they were still as strong as ever.

Work was going well and I started to build up some money. Then one day while I was at work, I starting talking to an old friend of mine called Tony Russell. We started chatting about all the different countries in the world that he had visited, after a couple of hours of discussion we came to the conclusion that we should stop talking about it and go and buy ourselves a plane ticket to somewhere nice and hot and spend the coming winter sat in the sun on a beach, after all we were both single so there wasn't much stopping us. Tony wasn't your average package holidaymaker, he had travelled to some serious places in the world alone with his backpack in search of endless wisdom that he bought back with him and began to install in all those around him as he worked by day as a plasterer in Basingstoke.

Over the coming months we worked as hard as possible and we gathered our money together ready to set off on a journey of discovery, not only in geographical terms but also on a personal level as I was really looking forward to spending some quality time with Tony as he is without doubt one of the wisest people that I've ever had the pleasure to meet. On Christmas Eve 1999 we set off on a 6 week adventure to see in the millennium on the other side of the world – we headed to Bangkok International Airport in Thailand to absorb some serious Asian culture, with Tony 'full blown' Russell cast in the role of expedition leader.

It has to be said that I took it as an honour to travel with Tony as he had been around when it came to backpacking. Any traveller will tell you that it is one of the best feelings in the world when that old cloth bag hits the centre of your back and you realize that you are on your way to another adventure. They will also tell you that the first rule of backpacking is: be very selective of who you travel with as you are stuck with them 24/7. They are going to need to be fully awake and alert at all times, especially when travelling through south East Asia. I therefore took great pleasure from the fact that Tony had invited me along because it meant that he felt I could look after myself both socially and physically – opportunities like this only come once in your life time and it would have been foolish of me to turn down the chance to learn form Tony's previous experiences.

We landed at Bangkok International Airport in the early

afternoon on Christmas day and after collecting our luggage we climbed into a taxi and headed for the notorious Koh San Road in central Bangkok. This was a road that the Thai authorities had specifically allocated to catering for the constant stream of backpackers that were sweeping into the country at the time. The idea was a simple one – keep all the different nationalities in the same street and then you could keep an eye on them all without too much difficulty. The only downside was that as just about every first time tourist ended up there, this caused the prices to be pushed higher and higher and although it is still very cheep to stay at a hotel on the Koh San Road, you would have to call it expensive compared to the rest of Thailand. Having said that, at least if you do head there you will find everything that you need to survive in Asia all in one place and it is without doubt an ideal place to re-stock items or to arrange to meet people. By the time we arrived at the Koh San Road it was about 4 O'clock in the afternoon and after a quick shower Tony announced that when you went backpacking it was traditional to hit the local town as soon as possible after your arrival – this was known as arriving 'on the run', and was a must for any serious traveller - who was I too argue, I just summoned some reserve energy from the depths of my soul and followed my leader.

After a good look round central Bangkok and having enjoyed a lovely meal, we returned to the guesthouse and I was ready to collapse. We had done some hard travelling in the last 18 hours and I was like a zombie at this point. As I lay on the bed exhausted Tony popped out to the shop. I was drifting off when he returned, but he just waved a pair of tickets at me and said that we were getting on a coach in 40 minutes and heading south to the islands that littered the southern tip of Thailand. What he didn't tell me was that the up and coming coach journey would take approximately 13 hours to complete. The wise old fox knew that if we went to sleep we may never get there at all.

Our destination was the seaside town of Krabi; from here it was possible to hop on a boat to a large selection of the southern tropical islands. I was informed that we were heading to an island called Koh Lanta, and that this was an island that Tony had visited some 4 years earlier.

Despite our tiredness we couldn't stop ourselves from chatting through most of the coach journey. Tony explained that on the island there was a beautiful deserted beach, he also added that they had no electric on the island, and so in the evening everyone would gather round a camp fire to chat, it sounded like paradise and exactly what I needed. It's such a shame that so many people visit Thailand and get stuck in the bars that line the streets of Bangkok and yet the southern islands of Thailand are amongst the most beautiful in the world and definitely worth a visit. I was thankful that I was travelling with a man of culture who could appreciate the wonders and beauty of this distant shore.

13 hours later we arrived in Krabi and booked ourselves into a guesthouse for the night. Although we were now both almost dead on our feet, I thought that it would be a good time to get my own back on Tony for making me hit Bangkok on the run, now I decided that we were going to hit Krabi on the run as well just for good measure, and so without any further ado we headed straight out into the night and headed for the centre of Krabi to check things out.

In the town we found a small market and as we walked around we came upon a tattooist, now before you ask I've no idea why I did it but I found myself flicking through a book of designs and announcing to Tony that I was going to get a new tattoo to remind me of our journey. I quickly decided that I wanted to have a scorpion done in traditional black ink, and I soon found an A4 sized scorpion that looked ideal. Thank god I had the wise one with me, as Tony quickly stepped in to give me some more of his sound advice. Now the thing to remember about Tony is that past experience has taught me than when he speaks he is usually worth listening to. He suggested that the scorpion was far too big for my body and that it would look much better if we shrank it down a bit and put it on my chest. At the time I was capable of anything and although Tony was in a similar state, he still found the time and energy to make sure that his mate didn't return home looking like he had fallen into a large pot of black ink, that says everything about the man. To cut a long story short I am now the proud owner of a small 2 inch black scorpion on the left side of my chest and until my dying day it will remind me of the good times I spent in south East Asia with Tony Russell.

As we left the tattooist I knew in my heart that I had not achieved anything and that Tony had in fact won the day again - as I felt the strap of my backpack tear into the open wound on my chest. I winched with pain but didn't want to complain. As I turned to look at big Tony, he turned towards me with a big grin spread across his face; he didn't have to say a word.

We duly arrived on the island of Koh Lanta and managed to locate an old friend of Tony's who was known as 'Ling' (which I later found out means 'Monkey' in Thai). Ling was going to look after us during our stay on the island, although at the time we had no exact plans on how long we would stay there as we were literally free to move about the country as we wished.

Within minutes we were herded up with a dozen other backpackers and guided towards a pickup truck that was parked nearby. We chucked our bags in the back, climbed aboard and just held on for dear life as we hurtled along the dirt track that seemed to be disappearing into the jungle. After about half an hour the truck came to an abrupt stop, I climbed off the back of the pickup and was faced with the most awesome view out across the ocean. As I walked a few steps forward I began to see that directly below me was the deserted beach that Tony had been so descriptive about – there was little doubt that Tony had been right and that I was indeed now looking at paradise. We were now standing on a hilltop overlooking the beach. Within the forest that lined the hillside the locals had crafted a dozen or so very basic little bungalows to house their foreign guests. They had also built an open air restaurant and a traditional watering hole where we could drown our sorrows. The bar which was constructed entirely of oak was supported on wooden stilts and it gave you the feeling that you were suspended in mid air out over the bay.

We booked ourselves into a bungalow and unpacked our stuff, and then just collapsed in a heap on the beds. It had taken 2 long days of travelling to get here and we were both now totally shattered, but I have to say that the view alone had already made the journey seem worthwhile. We slept like little school boys for about 20 hours and when we eventually woke up, waiting to greet us was the glorious sight of a clear sky and beautiful sunshine.

As we dressed and wandered down towards the beach for my first close up view, I realized that big Tony was going to wear his familiar grin for the duration of the next week, as due to the new tattoo that I now had etched into my chest, I was going to have to sit on the beach and watch him snorkeling away without a care in the world. Every time he reappeared from the beautiful Adaman Sea he would always greet me with the immortal words of *"how's the tattoo'* – the moral of the story is that if you wish to get a new tattoo while you are on holiday then that's fine, just do it during the last few days of the trip and not like I did on the first day, thus saving yourself the embarrassment of being the only person on the beach who was acting like he had a serious allergy to sea water.

We stayed with Ling for three and a half weeks and in that time I found emotions deep within me that I never knew existed. I reached a state of total relaxation of both mind and body during that period and I needed it so much. Tony was indeed right when he had told me that on Koh Lanta I would discover my true self and return to England a changed man. It was hard not to change as everywhere you looked you saw things that made you realize that life was not all about the rat race back home, but that there were indeed great pleasures to be had, and secrets to be learnt, by visiting different cultures around the world.

As we approached the end of our first month on Koh Lanta Tony informed me that we would have to cross the boarder into Malaysia in order to renew our visas, as they were only valid for one calendar month. We gathered our stuff together and made our way back to Krabi and onto Malaysia, which was about 10 hours away in the minibus. We decided that we would only stop there for one night and then make our way back to the beach to carry on our soul-searching. All the way there Tony was giving me some positive spin about how good it was in Malaysia and telling me all about the country's culture. Amongst other things he said that I should try to find the time to enjoy a traditional curry from one of the street vendors and his eyes lit up as he told me that it was served and eaten on a large deep green banana leaf. It all sounded too good to be true even coming from Tony, and sure enough my experience of Malaysia didn't quite turn out as expected.

We found ourselves a guesthouse and booked into 2 single rooms, directly opposite each other on the 3rd floor of an 8 storey building. All went well until about 5am, when our sleep became disturbed by the sound of a group of men arguing. I got myself dressed and packed everything away just in case we needed to make a quick exit from the premises. I then took up a position behind the door just in case anyone tried to get into my room to escape the mini riot that was now going on only a few feet from me, on the other side of the door. It's surprising how much noise a group of drunken men can make at 5am when everything else is so quiet and still.

Suddenly the calm night air was pierced with the sound of throat curdling screams that lasted for about 30 seconds and then as quick as it all began, it all went eerily quiet. I chucked my backpack up onto my back and gently opened the door at which point Tony peered out from the darkness of his room, with just a nod of the head we both crept out onto the landing to be faced with an extremely large Nigerian laying face down in the hallway, he wasn't moving at all but just laying there groaning. It was obvious that he had suffered an extremely brutal assault and clearly visible were a number of knife wounds over his back and down his legs. Without a word we both stepped over him and made our way out of the guest house and off into the darkness.

Sat in your nice warm house reading this then I guess our actions might seem a little harsh but believe me you need to wake up to reality in that kind of situation as you are likely to witness all sorts of strange events if you spend a decent amount of time in guest houses around the world. If you are not directly involved then you really don't want to be in the vicinity when the Thai police turn up to stop a fight, complete with CS gas and truncheons. As the saying goes "When in Rome, do as the Romans do....." The harsh reality is that if you go to another country and start a fight then you had better be able to take care of yourself as you will quickly realize that you are all alone when it goes wrong. No sane minded person is going to help you due to the communication problems with the police, it's therefore up to you to carry your own water from the well.

I expect that the Nigerian ended up staying in the local hospital for a couple of days which was probably not a pleasurable experience in itself, but I bet he learnt the valuable lesson that when you are travelling abroad you must never start a fight with the locals as it might actually end up costing you your life. It's fair to say that there are no Queensbury rules in South East Asia at 5am in the morning.

Having decided that I had seen enough of Malaysia to last me a lifetime we headed into town and bought a ticket for our return journey back across the boarder to the safety of Thailand and headed back to the beach on Koh Lanta - but not before stopping to enjoy a banana leaf curry from a street vendor as promised!

It was a great feeling to return to the tranquility of the secluded beach on Lanta Island with all the friendly local faces. We settled down for the remaining couple of weeks of our holiday for some serious sunbathing.

Our days were spent soaking up the sun or gently sailing round the island with a couple of Dutch men that we had met. They had sold their restaurant in Holland and now lived on Lanta. Robert and Ronnie were very genuine and welcomed us with open arms. They had transported their mini catamaran out there with them and it was pure paradise to gently float round the island without a care in the world.

Another couple that were regular visitors to Lanta were my good friends Sasha and Inga - Sasha was German and I believe that Inga was Swiss. I have to say that they were two of the nicest people that I have ever had the pleasure to meet. We had many deep and interesting conversations during the evenings while we sat watching the sun go down.

During the holiday myself and Tony discussed the possibility of working together upon our return to England. Tony had already been doing his own thing for about a year, and as things were busy he thought it would be a good idea if we joined forces as we got along so well. Obviously there is much more to business than being friends. In my opinion trust is important in most walks of life and especially in business. It's fair to say that I trust Tony completely, and so the decision was made that upon our return I would leave the building firm that had been so good to me and I would take the plunge and have a go at standing on my own two feet.

During my stay in Asia I had used the time to reassess my life and had realized that there were some interesting things that one could do other than just being like all the other sheep back home with their mortgages and car finance. I would say to anyone that before you settle down and have children you really must go and see the world, as not only will you get a nice sun tan but you will also learn so much about different nationalities and cultures that will help you understand your fellow human beings much better for the rest of your life. You will also learn so much about yourself, which is always a good thing. I had returned to England after spending the best part of seven weeks in the sunshine, on what had become of voyage of discovery for me.

Within days of being home I received a letter from the housing department at Basingstoke council to inform me that I had been allocated a 2-bedroom flat in Tadley, which was on the outskirts of Basingstoke – it was now the end of February 2000. I was overjoyed and although I had only been on the waiting list for 2 years it felt like an eternity. At least now I had a home of my own again and could come and go as I pleased. The news really couldn't have come at a better time for me, and although I was still quite fragile within myself I still hoped that the new flat would be the tonic I needed to lift my broken spirit. The break in Thailand had done me the world of good and now it was time to see exactly what kind of repair job we had achieved while sitting in the sun – in my heart I knew I was ready for the next challenge.

I left the building company that I had been working for and went of to work with Tony as planned, it was hard work but the rewards were great, as there was a general shortage of plasterers. The situation was even worse for plasterers that could specialize in external work and or traditional lime work, and so we set about cornering ourselves a small slice of this niche market. Our system worked well as within a few months we had work booked up for the next year and a half.

Around this time I found myself a new girlfriend after being single for the best part of 2 years, and that coupled with the fact that I had been on another expensive holiday was enough to send my ex-wife wild with rage at the beginning of 2001. Again she demanded that I give her more maintenance money every week. It was as though she genuinely wanted my whole life to be destroyed and was determined to do all she could to make life difficult for me. When I told her that I would only give her an increase of five pounds per week as I always did every year, she started to sulk about it and over the coming few weeks she started cancelling some of my Saturday visits to see the children at short notice, saying that one or the other of the children had toothache or tummy ache.

As time went on and I still refused to bow to her pressure, she cut my access down from every Saturday to every other Saturday, saying that as I wasn't paying her enough money in her opinion, then from now on I could only see the children every other week. I was absolutely devastated but didn't want to give her the satisfaction of showing it. There is nothing more irritating in life that someone who uses their children as a weapon against their ex-partner. Things like that are an everyday occurrence for divorced fathers across the country but that doesn't make it any easier to handle when it happens to you, it's always a difficult thing for any father to take. Just for good measure, to make sure she got her message across loud and clear she also banned the children from waving at me whenever they passed me in the street. This was an extremely malicious act as the children often passed me in their car as my new girlfriend lived on the same street, and they would drive past heading to and from the local school. It's difficult to explain what it feels like to have to watch your children drive past you staring blankly through a car window twice a day, unable to raise their hand to do what could be described as the most natural act for any child; that is to wave at either parent whenever they saw them. I can't begin to explain to you what satisfaction someone might get from enforcing such action upon a child – in my view it can only be explained as extremely controlling behaviour and when its carried out to such an extreme upon an innocent child then there is no place for it in any home.

I stumbled on through the year trying to keep the peace with Kate, although sometimes it was difficult as she just always seemed to be trying to provoke an argument every time I went round. Within myself I was feeling much stronger since having my 7 week break in the sun and during that time I had managed to put her actions to the back of my mind. When I first got divorced I was so very fragile for months, as I carried the burden of feeling such a failure around with me bearing heavily upon my shoulders, but now I was well rested and mentally much stronger – I was now ready to deal with whatever she was going to throw at me.

It was around this time that a series of events began to unfold that would have a drastic effect upon my life in the future. A man had been beaten up outside a night club on the outskirts of Basingstoke, while queueing for a late night burger with his wife. Apparently 4 or 5 men had pulled up in a car and beaten him senseless with knuckle dusters and baseball bats. 2 men were subsequently arrested and then released without charge. The police investigation went on for the rest of the year as they tried to find out exactly what had happened.

Work wise things were going really well and soon it was time to plan my next adventure abroad for the coming winter. Tony had already decided to stay and look after the work side of things, and to be honest I felt guilty when it was time to explain to him that I wanted to take another six week holiday during the coming winter, he fully understood the situation, after all the travelling bug was also rooted deep within him.

As I've said one of the most important things about travelling is who, if anyone, do you take with you. If you look around it probably won't take you long to realize that most of your friends or associates would be a downright liability in a crisis – to backpack you need to be able to leave all your western comforts at home and be fully prepared to rough it on occasions. At this point I decided that I would indeed travel to Thailand again, only this time I was going to do it alone. Tony also felt that it was time for the pupil to leave the master. He explained that to truly say that I was a veteran backpacker I would have to do a solo trip, and now seemed as good a time as any.

Over the following months another old friend called Malcolm Davies decided that he too would like to see a little of Thailand. We discussed it and decided that he would fly out for 3 weeks while I was out there, and I arranged to meet him in Bangkok to show him how it was done. Malcolm is an old throwback to the doorman of yesteryear. All of his adult life he had been involved in learning or teaching various forms of combat, and at this point he had been a doorman at various nightclubs in the south of England for over 25 years. His passion was Jujitsu, and I do mean it when I say that he was dedicated. He worked as a lorry driver by day and then 3 evenings a week he would teach Jujitsu and 3 evenings a week he would go to his own club to learn Jujitsu, with a couple of ex special forces mates of his called Peter and Eddie. Talk about the 3 musketeers – believe me you wouldn't want to upset those three down a dark alley, as each of them possessed enough knowledge to immobilize numerous people at any one time. The three of them would often spend hours together doing what we call 'reality training' – in layman's terms they would regularly beat the hell out of each other in order to perfect their individual techniques. It would be fair to say that their classes were not for the faint hearted. What I'm trying to say is that Malcolm was certainly capable of looking after himself, and that he was also a very good communicator, as he dealt with people routinely during the day. He also happens to be a very good friend of mine, who I had no doubt, would enjoy his time in Asia.

Meanwhile the police investigation into the fracas at the burger van had been going on for over a year, and then out of the blue 2 men, Ivor and Brian Aubrey were arrested and charged with causing grievous bodily harm to a Mr. Richard Hart at a burger bar in Basingstoke. They were both later found guilty at Winchester Crown Court, where Brian received a six year sentence and Ivor received four and a half years

Towards the end of the year, around November if my memory serves me well, I received a letter from their solicitor based in London asking me if I would be prepared to give a statement with regard to the incident. The letter claimed that there had been a miscarriage of justice and that both brothers would be launching an appeal against their conviction. Although I didn't want to get involved I was assured that there were other witnesses who claimed that both parties may be innocent of this particular offence.

It would be over 2 years later that I would feel the full force of the repercussions of my actions that day. I should have known that everything comes at a cost but for whatever reason I was totally oblivious to any negative response that might be triggered by my actions at the time. In short I gave a sworn statement to the police regarding the events that had occurred during the fight at the burger bar in Basingstoke.

My involvement with the Police was brief and to the point, shortly after I had forgotten all about it as I made the final plans for my next trip to South East Asia with big Malc. I was a little apprehensive about the trip as not only was it going to be my first solo trip but I also had to think about meeting up with Malcolm and also where he would want to go and what he might want to do when he got there.

On a personal level I just wanted to board an airplane as quickly as possible so that I could leave the country and get back to the solitude of Koh Lanta where I could relax and enjoy myself. At this point I knew that Saha and Inga would be waiting to greet me on the island and also that Robert and Ronnie would be there, as they were having a new house built near the beach. I always had good times and fond memories of my time spent in their company and it would also make a nice change to all the aggravation that I was getting back home.

The last few days dragged as they always do but eventually it was time to head back to Heathrow airport and board the plane ready to head off to the sunshine.

We arrived in Bangkok on 22nd December 2001 and although Malcolm didn't realize it, we were going to hit the town centre 'on the run', only this time it was me cast in the role of expedition leader and Big Malc was now the student. Having been out and seen the sights and delights of Bangkok it was then straight onto the coach for the dreaded 13 hour journey overland down to Krabi, where we could catch the boat to Lanta Island.

As expected we arrived on the island absolutely shattered and looking forward to a good long rest. As we climbed from the pickup truck I smiled as I remembered doing the same thing with big Tony a year earlier, only this time I was a little wiser – no new tattoo!

The bay was just how I remembered it and the feeling of complete peace only took a few hours to get a grip of my body as I lay in my hammock with a book in my hand and gently drifted off to sleep.

On our travels Malcolm met a young Thai girl called Joy. I can still remember on our last night together in Thailand, when he turned to me and said that one day he would marry her. Malcolm didn't say things that he didn't mean – when he said that he would marry her, I had absolutely know doubt in my mind that he was serious.

One of my fondest memories of that trip with Malcolm is that one day, while we were out on the motorbikes that we had hired, I had been carrying Malcolm's camera in a basket on the front of my bike when a water bottle exploded in the bag and soaked his prized camera. The story starts on Lanta island when one night Malcolm had left his camera on the side while he had a shower, I couldn't resist the temptation to stuff the camera down the front of my shorts and take a picture. I then put the camera back before

Malcolm realized what I had done. It was done very spontaneously and at the time my only thought was that it would give Malcolm a giggle when he got back to England and returned to work while I continued my adventure in the sun.

Well I had forgotten all about the day I took that picture, but a month later poor old Malcolm had excitedly taken his films down to Boots in Basingstoke to get them developed. Upon collection he had explained to the female assistant that while on holiday his camera had got wet and he asked her to check that the pictures were ok and not water damaged, before he paid for his order. I really would have paid good money to have been a witness to their faces as they flicked through his holiday snaps to be confronted by a full frontal picture of my manhood staring them in the face, and Malcolm looking so embarrassed trying to explain that he had no idea how such a picture came to find itself on his camera. The look of total horror on his face as he stood there at the counter would have been a joy to witness, unfortunately it wasn't to be but I did almost break a rib laughing as he went on to explain it all to be upon my return to England. Memories like that will stay with me until my dying day, and even now I chuckle to myself whenever I go to get films developed – and just for the record I never go to Boots in Basingstoke!

There is another story that involves big Malc that has stayed with me and will probably never leave my soul. One night while sleeping in my beach bungalow on Lanta Island, I was awoken by a strange commotion that was occurring in the corner of the room. I leapt from my bed and ran to the light switch, turned with my fists up ready to pile in and help Malc with the intruder, only to be confronted by the sight of the big man savagely attacking my plastic airbed. Malcolm was getting right into the attack and was throwing lovely combinations of punches in the direction of his air filled assailant, when he realized his mistake. When the red mist cleared and he eventually calmed down, we realized that I had placed my airbed behind the door and during the night it had fallen against Malcolm's feet, at which point he had jumped from his bed and launched his merciless assault. We giggled about it long into the night and I eventually drifted off to sleep, safe in the knowledge that nothing on earth was likely to actually make it across the room to reach my bed, as first they would have to get past the big man, and that was no easy matter I can assure you.

The rest of the holiday passed without incident and eventually the time came for me to head back home. Upon my return from the trip with big Malc I headed down to see the children to deliver some small presents that I had bought for them on my travels. It was now the end of February 2002 and again my ex-wife goes up the wall about me having such a long exotic holiday abroad and demands that I give her more money.

I should point out that over the last couple of years I had been raising her weekly maintenance automatically and that this is not a case of some hard done by women who had been deserted and left alone with her children. It is a fact that I had taken over eight thousand pounds of dept out of her life at the end of our marriage and had also paid her maintenance money regularly every week without fail – no she wanted more, she wanted everything. She also still felt the need to be vindictive and to hound me at every opportunity, and that was starting to raise more serious concerns about her mental state with various friends and relatives.

Again I told her that she would get a rise of only five pounds per week as usual, and not a penny more. I thought she had accepted my proposal, but then a couple of days later she called me and demanded that I sign adoption papers so that her new husband could adopt both of our children. I have to say that I found this rather strange considering that she had known me for over 15 years at this point, and she was well aware of the fact that I would rather be shot than willingly sign any adoption papers with regard to my beloved children. The saga dragged on for a couple of months and when I wouldn't give in she demanded that I at least sign papers so that she could then change the children's names by deed poll.

I had learnt over the years that nothing was ever what it seemed with my ex-wife and it didn't take long for the truth to come out. A couple of days later she turned round and told me that she had been offered the opportunity by her employers to emigrate to Canada, and that she intended to take the children with her to make a fresh start. This obviously raised some serious questions amongst my close circle of friends, many of whom were extremely concerned about how the children would be treated if they were to be removed from my protective influence. I remember sitting down to discuss it with my mother, who went on to say that she felt that Kate was trying to hide something from us.

Fortunately Kate hadn't realized that before she could take either of the children abroad for more than 31 days, she would need the written signature of any other parent who held parental responsibility for the children in English law, and thankfully she had absolutely no chance of getting that from me. She tried everything over the coming months to get me to change my mind and sign away my children, so much so that I was now seriously starting to wonder what exactly it was that she was trying to hide from me, as she was so determined to move abroad at any cost.

Over the coming months she hounded me constantly about getting the children's name's changed one way or the other, she also continued to threaten me with the fact that she would be emigrating, although it appeared that those plans were now on hold until the following January at the earliest, that's presuming of course that the offer by her employer was a legitimate one. I have to say that the way things were panning out, at the time I was having serious trouble sorting out all the fact from fiction when it came to my ex-wife, as she was literally going from one extreme to another and appeared to be talking total nonsense most of the time.

It was now mid 2002 and one day while I was walking from my girlfriend's house, down the hill to see the children, one of Kate's neighbour's stopped me in the street and raised concerns about the way Kate handled our children. Apparently she had been standing in her kitchen one day while doing the washing up, when Kate had walked past her kitchen window accompanied by my daughter. She explained that she hadn't heard the conversation but had seen Kate lash out and hit my daughter around the face, and then proceed to drag her up the hill. What concerned her was that she hadn't noticed my daughter doing anything out of the ordinary as they approached the front of her house; in fact she said that both children were always impeccably behaved whenever she saw them. She could therefore offer no explanation as to why Kate had lashed out, and this was causing her serious concern. As I got on well with the woman I thanked her for letting me know and explained that I would be seeing both children in a couple of days and that I would make some discreet enquiries as to what had been going on.

Although I didn't say it at the time, I was now beginning to think that something was very wrong. I had also recently had a conversation with my mother, where it had been mentioned that the children 'didn't look right'. It was felt that they were starting to look a little quiet, or maybe even withdrawn, they just didn't seem as happy as they used to be. The problem was that no matter how hard we looked, there was never anything obvious that was wrong. Sure I had a lot of my Saturday visits cancelled at short notice but that in itself was hardly an offence. I decided at this point to keep a closer eye on things to see if I could pick up any negative vibes from the children. Even with the trust they both had in me it was extremely difficult for them to mention even the smallest things that had occurred, as Kate had such tight and threatening control over them both 24 hours a day.

Work was going really well and Tony and I had picked up some serious contracts in the Newbury area. We had targeted Newbury as it was ideal for a number of reasons. Amongst them was the fact that it was local, it was also just far enough away as not to interfere with the old building company that I worked for, and last but not least there was a market for traditional lime-work in Newbury and that is where we could make the most money. By this time we had also managed to seal a couple of major contracts that we had been working on for just over a year, and it gave us great satisfaction as this meant that we could mix it with the big boys, and survive.

A pattern was now starting to form, with my days full of achievement and success but my evenings and weekends were being spent pulling my hair out and trying to figure out what crazy idea Kate would come up with next.

As the months passed I had little doubt that I would have to get away again in the winter for the sake of my sanity, it was catch 22 as I needed the break to re-charge my batteries and to get away from all the stress this end, and yet every time I left the country Kate would hit the roof with a vengeance upon my return. It didn't take much to figure out that we couldn't carry on like this for very long; even her new marriage wasn't having the effect that I had hoped for. I just figured that as I was in a no win situation, then I might as well carry on regardless and do what was best for me as an individual. For the first time in my life I was now going to put myself first. In my opinion the only reason that I was suffering so much with regard to my previous marriage was the fact that I cared, and worried too much about everyone else – from now on I was going to do exactly what I liked. I came to the conclusion that if she had a problem with it, then that's exactly what it was – her problem.

I spoke to Tony and asked if he fancied accompanying me on another journey to a distant shore but he said that as he had a couple of minor things to sort out on the farm, he needed to stay in England. I called big Malc and he said that he was up for some more travelling and so we arranged to go back to Koh Lanta for a month. Only this time we both agreed that the novelty of the 13 hour coach trip had warn off and we felt that it would be better to catch an internal flight from Bangkok to Krabi if possible, to save us an awful lot of time and aggravation.

When I later made enquiries about internal flights, I was amazed to find out that the cost was only just over twenty pounds – to think that I had endured such hardship sat on that bloody coach for 13 hours, and all for a measly twenty pounds.

The day soon arrived and Malcolm and I found ourselves sitting in the departure lounge at Heathrow airport once again, all the excitement of previous trips flooded through my body and it was just such a relief to get away from everything that was going on here.

We arrived at Bangkok International airport as planned and made our way along to the internal flights terminal and booked ourselves in, an hour later we were in Krabi. What a difference it made to our welfare, not having to do that coach journey. We arrived so full of beans that we decided to head straight on to

Phucket to try and meet up with a friend of Malcolm's who was there holidaying with his wife and a couple of other friends. We found them and stayed there for 2 nights, then made our way back to Krabi and caught the boat to Koh Lanta.

After the 2 hour boat trip we arrived at the port of Ban Saladan on Lanta Island and were greeted by a very enthusiastic Mr. Ling. Onto the back of the pickup truck we got and off we went to find ourselves a bungalow, so that we could really start the process of chilling out under the sun.

When we arrived the bay looked as beautiful as ever and as I glanced across to the bar I caught sight of Robert and Ronnie who were soaking up the afternoon sun. After a brief chat we headed off to find our bungalow and unpack. I errected my hammock and as usual I climbed in, curled up into a ball and drifted off to sleep. When I awoke it felt like I was home once again, as the burning sun stung my face. I just sat there for a second and thought of Tony – after all it was he who had made all this possible a couple of years earlier.

During this trip Malcolm had wanted to try and locate Joy, whom he had met last year, and so we set off on the boat again, back to Krabi to try to find her. We found her and she came to stay with us on the island for the second couple of weeks that we were there. From now on Joy and Malcolm were inseparable, and so when we went out for day trips and various other adventures, there were now three of us. I sat and watched as their love blossomed. To be honest it was very rewarding to think that in a small way I was partly responsible for their happiness. Malcolm was totally reborn in her company and it was obvious to anyone who cared to look, that the two of them were falling in love. In my mind there was only one thing we could do – we would have to take a trip down to the local tattooist and choose a special design to celebrate the good news. The next day Malcolm was the proud owner of a new tattoo depicting a black panther climbing out from the centre of a beautiful red rose and underneath it, in bold letters was inscribed the word 'Joy'. He had the biggest smile in the world when we got back to the bungalow and he proudly showed Saha and Inga his new piece of artwork. It was a very touching moment when he turned to me later that night and thanked me for helping him find true love. I could see in his face that he meant every word of it.

Once again the days drifted away and before we knew it, it was time to catch our flight from Krabi back to Bangkok to complete the journey home, another adventure was nearly over. I've so many memories of my time in Thailand with both Malcolm and Tony, but the one that stands out the most is the day that Malcolm and I were due to leave Bangkok to fly home in February 2003. We had dropped Joy off in Krabi the day before and continued our journey north to Bangkok. Malcolm had been extremely quiet all day and I could tell that something was bothering him. As we made the final checks to our luggage ready for the journey home he suddenly threw his backpack on the bed and when I turned round he had tears in his eyes, he didn't need to say a word as I had guessed what he was going to say, after all it was written all over his face. He just looked straight at me and announced that he couldn't leave Thailand without her, and he meant it. We now had a dilemma as we were due to catch a plane home in about 3 hours. There was no need for discussion as I had witnessed first hand exactly how they felt about each other, and true love can't be hidden or disguised. I knew that I would have to catch my plane whatever happened, and after he had assured me that he would be ok, he went on to explain that he was going to marry her and bring her home with him. After a brief discussion with the big man about what the British Embassy could do for him, I climbed into the taxi alone and headed for the airport.

During the journey my head was spinning, I had so many questions flying through my mind: Would he be ok, would he find her and if he did, how the hell would he get himself married in the middle of South East Asia. Well it was too late for me to worry now as I arrived at the airport and took my first steps inside. I had no doubt that I was doing the right thing but in the back of my mind all I could think about was that if he did find her and end up married, then I would have given anything to have been stood proudly next to my mate while he did so.

I arrived back into the UK on a cold and frosty morning and I was collected from the airport by Malcolm's mother Bett and her boyfriend George. One of the hardest things that I have ever had to do was when I had to explain to them why Malcolm was not with me. He was looking for something new and he found it, and he did so with my blessing, after all that was the least I could do for him – he's 44 so he doesn't need anyone to judge him, what he needed was support and friendship and I'd like to think that in his hour of need, I gave him exactly that.

Once home I quickly found that nothing had changed and it was straight back to the familiar routine of work work work, in fact the only thing that broke the monotony was when a month later I received a call from Malcolm who he was still in Asia. He went on to tell me that he had indeed managed to find Joy in Krabi and that they were just about to get married. When I put the phone down at the end of that conversation I was totally torn in two emotionally – half of me was overjoyed that my mate's dream was going to become reality but the other half of me was devastated by the fact that I wouldn't be stood next to him while he fulfilled it. To those individuals that said it would never last all I can say is that only time will tell us the answer to that one, but what I can say is that 17 months after they were married, on the 7th July 2004 Joy gave birth to a bouncing baby boy who they named Andrew, and today they seem happier than ever.

The lesson to be learnt is that you should never judge other peoples lives purely on the basis that their actions should fit in with how you think things should be done, after all does it really matter how each individual finds his or her internal happiness – surely what is much more important is to celebrate the fact that they actually found it, and nothing else.

All the other aspects of my day to day existence just picked up where they had left off before my winter break. Within a week it felt like I had never been away. As the saying goes….same shit, different day! I had returned with a very positive attitude towards everything that was going on in my life and had decided to try hard over the following year not to worry so much about small individual things, I felt that if I could do that then I would probably reduce my stress levels by at least 50%.

I started to decorate the flat how I'd always wanted it and I really started to enjoy the minor details, like going to town to choose all those little things that make a house a home. You'd have been proud of me with all my colour coordinated rooms, matching carpet and curtains. Before long I had the perfect bachelor pad.

Meanwhile even my family life was better than it had been for a couple of years, maybe now my ex-wife was starting to realize that I would take a winter break whether she complained about it or not. Maybe my own attitude had softened a little, I'm not sure, but for whatever reason things felt a little calmer than they had been for some time.

Work wise things had really taken off for Tony and me. I believe that in life there is no such thing as a free lunch and so I guess our success was down to hard work and determination.

We had picked up some good jobs and with it a sense of great achievement. Tony is good company and it was a total pleasure to go to work with him every day. We would spend the hours while we worked discussing extraordinary things like 'Plato's republic', a subject that just happens to be a particular favourite with Tony.

In July 2003, Tony and I started work on a country home in Hartley Whitney, which is a small village on the outskirts of Basingstoke. Our plan was to complete the works in approximately 4 weeks, dependant on the weather. What more could I ask for, the sun was shining, I had one of my best mates beside me for company and the business was going great. It had taken me half a lifetime to reach out and find success like this and I now had no intention of letting it slip through my hands.

Unfortunately that decision was taken out of my hands as 3 weeks into the job a chain of events started that very nearly destroyed me. What followed was a sequence of events that are almost impossible to put into words, let alone comprehend, unless you have been unfortunate enough to find yourself in my position. I felt that over the years I had seen most things and I believed that I was an individual who was definitely difficult to shock – but I will be honest and say that the events that occurred on Friday 11th July 2003 shocked me to a standstill. I'm now going to do my very best to explain that chain of events to you.

CHAPTER 12

BROKEN DREAMS

On Friday 11th July 2003, I had been working all day with Tony doing some Tyrolean to the outside of a country home. The sun was shining and everything was sweet. It wasn't until I returned home that evening that I realized that I would never forget the time or the date. Little did I know that already a series of events had occurred during the day that would leave a permanent scar on me for the rest of my life.

My involvement occurred purely by chance, after I had returned home from work, made myself a cup of tea and then sat down at my computer to check my e-mails. To this day I'm not totally sure what made me check the mail so early, especially as it was a Friday night and I would normally have quickly jumped in the bath and got myself changed before doing anything. Something made me do it and as I'm a big believer in fate, I shall put it down to that - the time was 5.50pm.

I worked my way through the mail and then went on to check my 'junk' box, for some strange reason I found myself checking each mail individually, and as I worked my way down the list one mail in particular caught my eye. It would be fair to say that the chances of me even finding this particular e-mail were slim to say the least, let alone me going on to actually open it and read it. What was enclosed made my heart miss a beat and I actually felt physically sick. I read on but couldn't make any sense of what I was reading, by this point I think I was in a state of complete and utter shock.

The e-mail was from Basingstoke Social Services and in particular their Child Protection unit. It went on to say that I should ring the enclosed number with regard to my daughter – the enclosed number was for the local Basingstoke hospital. As I sat there I couldn't absorb it all, after all why had I received an e-mail from an unknown source about my daughter, if there had been a problem, why hadn't anyone telephoned me? Nothing made sense at all and my head just kept on spinning.

I walked through to the lounge and picked up the phone to dial the number. After a couple of rings the call was answered by a rather confused woman. I say confused as she was obviously unaware of the nature of my call. She had been told that I may ring at some point and when I did, her instructions were to tell me to come down to Basingstoke Hospital and head to the child protection unit, she added that I should hurry up and get down there as they would be closing for the weekend in 40 minutes. She went on to explain that any children left there would be taken to foster parents for the weekend. I wasn't having any of that and although at this point I hadn't actually been told that my children were there, I strongly warned her that if my children were there, then they would be going absolutely nowhere without my say so and god help anyone who thought otherwise – I was on my way and someone had better take the time to wait until I got there. I still had no idea what had gone on or why I was even heading down there in the first place, nothing made sense and the situation wasn't helped at all by that first phone call.

I arrived at the hospital still in a state of total bewilderment; waiting for me was a member of the child protection team. After a brief introduction I was led along the corridor where I caught a glimpse of both my children. Despite the protests of my escort I walked over to them and asked if they were ok. Both were very relieved to see me and both looked absolutely terrified of something. At this point I was ushered into a side room where I came face to face with 4 other people. They introduced themselves and it turned out that 2 of them were hospital staff and 2 of them were police officers – all of them were attached to the child protection team.

Its hard to explain the feelings that were running through my body as they went on to explain to me that there was now a child protection order in force against my children. They went on to explain that my daughter had been hit by her step-father, and then she was sent to school as usual. When the school saw the state that she was in they took her to hospital, where the problem was noticed by the child protection unit. When I asked them when all this had happened I was astounded to be told that it had happened at 9.15am that morning, when my daughter had arrived at school with marks on her face. 'Nine o'clock this morning' I shouted at them, why the hell hadn't anyone called me earlier. I'd been laughing and joking all day in the sunshine with Tony while all this was going on and yet no one had the decency to call me – I felt insulted and told them so.

I now know that an awful lot of effort had been put in by my ex-wife to ensure that the children couldn't get in contact with me. She had taken various steps to ensure that the children would be unable to recite any contact details with regard to me or any members of my immediate family. Her actions included the confiscation of the children's mobile phones that I had bought for them. The end result being that when they were asked at the hospital, they had no idea what my phone number was and therefore couldn't recount any contact information with regard to me at all. Apparently by lunchtime my daughter had managed to remember my e-mail address which is how the news was eventually broken to me. Without my daughters actions that day both her and her younger brother would undoubtedly have spent at least the weekend in foster care, and that would have been devastating for the pair of them. Thankfully that never materialized but events like that do hit a nerve within the soul, and it made me realize just how totally powerless I was to stop something like that from actually happening. With hindsight I now understand why I didn't receive a call earlier in the day and I except totally that no one at the hospital was responsible for the delay.

Having completed various pieces of paperwork, I was taken through to collect the children. It was very emotional as they ran over and hugged me for dear life; I looked down to see two little faces staring up at me in total bewilderment. Everyone in the room could see that those two children just wanted to be with their dad where they felt safe and secure, as despite the best efforts of the staff, the days events had obviously taken a lot out of them both. I was so relieved when we left the building and headed home to the flat, where we could just shut the door and spend some time together in each others arms.

As we left the hospital I was informed that the police were now going to head round to Kate and Richard's house, and that both of them would be arrested following the very clear allegations of physical abuse that had been uncovered during the day. As we drove home it suddenly dawned on me that I was all alone as my mother was actually on holiday in Scotland. It quickly became apparent that I was now on a massive learning curve with regard to the children, its one thing being a weekend dad as I had been for the last 6 years, but it's something else altogether to be a full time parent and raise 2 children on your own.

I was totally devastated by the news I received that day and I felt like my heart had been ripped out. What was I going to do? How was I going to cope? I settled the children down as best I could. On that first night all we had was the school uniform that the children were wearing at the time. I had a camp bed for when the children stayed over, and so I made that up in the spare room for my daughter. My son would have to share with me as there was nowhere else to put up a bed. Being the youngest this was affecting him quite deeply and it was obvious that he wanted to share with me, although I knew that in the long term the situation couldn't continue and I would have to get myself down to the housing department at the council as soon as possible to register for a 3-bedroom property, hopefully nearer the schools – I then realized that I didn't even know where the schools were. It didn't seem to matter what angle I used to asses the problems, as the situation just looked so hopeless.

I made myself a cup of tea and slumped into a chair in the lounge, a thousand memories flashed through my mind. I just sat there trying to absorb the day's events, it was very emotional and I can honestly say that having found myself in that unfortunate position, there is nothing on this earth that strikes a father harder than a threat to his children. Something had gone seriously wrong and I was determined to find out the truth, the whole truth and nothing but the truth.

The following morning I awoke to see the beaming smile of my son gazing down at me and I couldn't help noticing how happy he looked despite the events of yesterday, there was no doubt in my mind that I was doing the right thing but it helped so much just to see that little face, with eyes so full of trust, looking down at me.

Slowly the house awoke and the three of us gathered together for what was to be the first of many 'group hugs', we decided between us that morning, that from now on we must rely on each other completely. One of the children suggested that from now on each day we would get together and share a 'group hug' – strange isn't it how even when put under so much stress and apprehension, love always manages to shine through. Part of me was being torn apart, and yet at the same time I was routinely witnessing things around the home that made me feel 10 feet tall. I knew that if we could just hold things together and get through the next few months then the rewards I would reap would be of a much higher value than anything that we as a family had just lost.

The social worker who had taken care of us at the hospital called round later in the day to see how we were settling in. It was a very emotional time for all of us. How they manage to stay unaffected while being surrounded by so much sorrow is beyond me. She was really pleased to see that we were obviously meant to be together, and it was also very comforting to hear her positive comments at a time when I honestly didn't seem to be able to make much sense of anything. Although I had a couple of reservations about what was going on it my ex-wife's home, I can honestly say that I hadn't expected this at all.

While she was there I raised the point that all I had for the children was the one set of school uniform that each of them had been wearing when I collected them from the hospital. I asked if it would be possible for her to call round to Kate's and collect various items, including; duvets, bed linen, clothes for both children, and if possible some items that I had bought them over the years for their bedrooms like TV's, video players, DVD players, stereos, any cuddly toys that were available to comfort the children, passports, child benefit book, birth certificates – in fact we needed just about anything that would enrich the children's lives as it was clear that Kate would have no further use for them as hell would freeze over before my kids would ever spend another night unsupervised in that house.

Unfortunately nothing was forthcoming, as it transpired after their release from custody Kate and Richard had decided to go camping. As a family we were facing the biggest catastrophe that anyone could possibly imagine, I was sitting there distraught trying to make sense of it all and pick up the pieces, and my ex-wife and her husband had gone camping. I sat there and I really questioned the sanity of this world that we are living in.

Despite the best efforts of our social worker over the following weeks to retrieve items from my ex-wife's house, unfortunately all we actually got was promises, promises that everything would be boxed up and forwarded to us as soon as possible. I was therefore forced to except that as it was still early days, then there was still a lot of emotion in the air. I must admit that I had serious reservations as to whether or not we would ever see any of these items but at the time I was assured that it would happen, so we would just have to wait and see.

Although the social worker was doing her very best to retrieve some of the children's items from their old address, it was obvious that despite all her experience she hadn't realized exactly what type of control freak we were dealing with. I tried to explain at the time that in my opinion I thought that it would be very unlikely, to say the least, for the items to turn up, and that I felt Kate wouldn't do as requested as she simply wouldn't be told what to do by anyone.

I honestly felt that no social worker was ever going to be allowed to order her around. Out of pure spite she would probably destroy or dispose of the items, rather than hand them over to us. I was asked to try not to be so bitter about things and we agreed to wait and see what would happen. It was laughable really as I'd known Kate for years at this point and was very well aware of what she would do, and yet here I was in my hour of need, being advised to wait and see by someone who had only just met her.

I also found the time to call Tony during the day and tell him that I was going to have to take time out to deal with all of this. He was very understanding and agreed to carry on alone and complete the contracts that we already had booked for the coming year. When I put the phone down I felt so deflated, everything I had worked so hard to achieve was wiped out in one phone call, and it was all down to the actions of someone else. Now the virus was starting to spread and it had just affected the first of many people around me who, through no fault of their own, where just in the wrong place at the wrong time. I would need to get used to this feeling of dejection, as over time so many people close to me would also be affected either directly or indirectly by my ex-wife's actions that day.

Over the weekend I also started to make a list of all the things that would need to be done regarding the children. Things like calling the Inland Revenue to arrange for the child benefit to be paid to me from now on. I also had to speak to them regarding the closure of my business. This was difficult as I had worked so hard with Tony to be a success and now it was all being taken away from me - that was so very hard to take. The child Support Agency also had to be notified that the children were now living with me, as they now had to arrange for Kate to start paying maintenance to me. It was a nightmare to be honest and that was without our housing difficulties or my benefit claim. The phone calls and appointments were endless but there was no doubt that these things needed to be done to enable us to move on with our lives and to start repairing the damage that had been caused during the previous 5 or 6 years.

On Monday 14th July 2004, the three of us headed back to the child protection unit based at Basingstoke hospital, where my daughter's injuries were due to be photographed. One of the most distressing things that I have been unfortunate enough to have seen in the last 35 years was the blown up photograph of my daughters face taken that day – if you ever want to find out for sure that you indeed have a heart then that's a pretty good way of finding out, although I have to say that I truly hope that none of you ever have to witness such an event. I can assure you that it's the most devastating feeling in the world when you sit down afterwards and ask yourself why it was that you weren't there to protect your child in their hour of need.

We had also gone up there to do the police interviews which would be videoed in the child suite, so as to minimize the distress to the children. Again this was very traumatic and I don't believe that there is a parent in the land who would want to go through with such events. I had to be positive and continue with my search to find out the truth about what exactly had been going on, and videoing the interviews on a casual basis seemed to be the best, and pretty much the only solution to a bad situation.

In order for me to move forward and put our lives back together I felt that it was very important for me to fully understand what had been going on and although it was a very painful experience, there was little doubt in my mind that in the long term this would be a major factor in the healing process and therefore it needed to be done. The best I could hope for now was for everything to be done with the minimum of fuss, as it was very important to me that the children must not be put in a position where they started to feel that they had done something wrong. None of this was their fault and we would all have to be very careful to enforce that view whenever possible.

While I was there, I again asked social services to try and retrieve some of the items that could be of help to the general wellbeing of the children - again they followed it through but all I got was promises and no actual items from the house. It may not seem much but already the delay in delivering these various items was starting to put pressure on the children, as both had raised concerns as to why Kate wouldn't send their things over. I was very aware that they were slowly starting to think that they had done something wrong and I reassured them that they hadn't and explained that it was a delay at the other end – I crossed my fingers and hoped that something would turn up soon, as this would help build a bond of trust between me and the children if I could manage to retrieve some of their individual items.

The videos were completed and as we sat and discussed them, the full details of what had gone on started pouring out. There's little point in me going into much detail with regard to the actual events as I feel that the actions of the police and social services speak for themselves, in the sense that as a result of the investigation it was decided that a criminal prosecution would be sought by the police with regard to the assault on my daughter by her step father. Although we had very strong evidence to support the fact that Kate was far more of a threat to my children than her husband, she hadn't actually been involved in this particular incident and that made it almost impossible for the police to seek a criminal conviction against her. To go with the strong evidence against Kate we also had the added issue that she had stood by and watched our daughter being attacked and had failed to make any effort or attempt to stop the assault. I'm told that in British law this is in fact deemed to be an offence in its own right and yet the police insisted that it would be almost impossible to secure a conviction armed only with video evidence. It was therefore decided that the best we could do was to remove both children from their mothers care permanently and place them with me (although this decision had already been taken at 5.50pm on 11th July 03). At this point I was also advised to speak to a solicitor in order to start a civil case against my ex-wife that would deal with her part in the atrocities.

The following weeks were extremely hard emotionally; there was a lot of anger in the air as with all cases involving children and I had to make a great effort to subdue it as it wasn't helping any of us. I had enough to deal with without anyone associated with me causing any more problems; I therefore made it clear to anyone who asked that it was my intention to try and put everything behind us and to put all my efforts into my family.

I had sent a couple of e-mails to my ex-wife just to try and break the ice, although I had been advised against this, as from now on all applications regarding contact with the children must come in an official form from Kate to my solicitor. She had ignored my e-mails, even the one begging her just to e-mail the children to let them know that she was ok, I couldn't understand her actions at all. When this failed I arranged for my solicitor to contact her and arrange for me and the children to meet Kate in MacDonald's, in the town centre. I was over the moon when we received a reply saying that Kate would attend. She hadn't seen the children for 2 weeks now and at last I felt that we could defuse some of the emotion by getting together. I should have saved myself the worry. She did turn up, accompanied by her husband, which I felt was extremely insensitive under the circumstances to say the least. I knew at that point that we were still miles away from seeing these events through the same set of eyes. What happened next even amazed me. She came in, sat down and immediately criticized my daughter's new haircut (she had been for a makeover the day before to give her a new beginning). It may not seem much but when you realize that both children were extremely apprehensive about seeing their mum at this time as they were very unsure of what her reaction would be – it certainly didn't help that her first comment would be a direct criticism aimed at my daughter. I had also naively thought that Kate may take the opportunity to buy the children a MacDonald's meal while we were there – again I should have known better as she never even bothered to offer us a drink, let alone a meal. Eventually I got the hint and went to the counter to buy us some food, already I felt that she had let the children down. All they wanted was their mother to say sorry and to spend four pounds on them to buy them a MacDonald's, but it wasn't to be.

My son plucked up the courage to ask for the return of some birthday money he had been given. He explained that Kate and Richard had taken it from him and spent it, and now he wanted it back. Unfortunately again it wasn't to be and my ex-wife refused to give him the money unless he agreed to go out with her on a day trip. This unfortunately just wasn't possible for me to allow at the time. Again I felt that this was just another example of her distorted thinking. She honestly felt that trying to bribe my son was a healthy solution to the problem. I was pulling my hair out wondering why she just couldn't see how much harm her behaviour was doing, why didn't she just give him a ten pound note to keep the peace after what she had done – but no, her ignorance wouldn't allow her to see my point of view or comprehend what it meant to my son. She just sat there in the chair looking at the floor waiting for one of us to feel sorry for her. She had picked the wrong place to come for sympathy and the three of us spent 20 minutes chatting to ourselves, waiting for her to strike up a conversation. After half an hour it was obvious that she didn't have anything to say to us. What a shame, as that one magical word – sorry – would have been more that enough, I guess it was a step too far for her to even contemplate. She had shown absolutely no interest in her children at all and I therefore made our excuses and announced that it was time for us to head home. At this she turned on the water works as a last attempt at getting some sympathy from any of us. I didn't feel that she deserved my sympathy, all we wanted was an apology but we never got it. In fact to this day she has never apologized for her actions towards the children and personally I am now convinced that she never will. She totally will not except that she has done anything wrong and continues to tell anyone who will listen how this is all one big mistake, the point she missed is that no one is listening to her any more. Although I didn't know it at the time, this was to be the last time either myself or my children would see Kate for nearly 2 years.

Although I was an emotional wreak, I needed to get myself together and head into town down to the local social security office to complete some benefits forms, after all I had just lost my business due to all of this and I now had no weekly income to feed us. Completing my claim for income support and child tax credits in turn triggered a home visit by an officer attached to the child support agency, this was arranged for the following Friday afternoon at my home address. I had been paying my ex-wife regular maintenance for over 6 years at this point and so I therefore felt that this would be quickly resolved, and could probably be sorted out before any of my other benefit claims.

Having discussed the situation with my new 'lone parent advisor', it was suggested that due to the circumstances I may be legible for a 'crisis loan'. Having completed my application for benefit I made my way round to the counter that dealt with crisis loans, where I was given a form to complete and then asked to wait while they discussed it. They told me that I would receive a decision in about 10 minutes. I sat there and started thinking about what I would need on an urgent basis, after a couple of minutes I was called back to the middle aged lady on the counter. I thought it was a bit quick but also understood that it was an open and shut case. I had been given paperwork by the child protection team that fully explained the situation and informed anyone that read it that this was to be a permanent arrangement and the children would definitely be staying with me for the long term.

I approached the counter to collect my cash just thankful that my luck was beginning to improve, after all when I walked in the building I hadn't expected to leave with any money quite so soon. I shouldn't have been so confident, as to my amazement they turned me down – wait for it – their explanation was that 'I was in too much of a crisis to receive a crisis loan from their department', I nearly broke a rib laughing and I have to be honest and say that it did add a little humour to what was a difficult situation for me. They went on to explain that as I was in such a large crisis I would need immediate financial help, and because of this they would have to deal with it by post! I was learning very quickly that finding your way around the benefits system is an art in itself.

For a laugh I followed the application through by post and a couple of weeks later I was indeed offered a crisis loan of two hundred and eighty pounds. I was also informed that I would have to repay this amount at a rate of twenty five pounds per week. This would be taken from my benefit of one hundred and twenty seven pounds a week that they would give me in total for the three of us. Although the offer was very much appreciated, I turned them down on the basis that it was too little too late, as by the time they made their offer my mother had been out and replaced any items that we urgently needed. Again the whole situation was affecting someone else, why should the actions of the two sad individuals who had caused the mess have to cost my mother so much money, it all seemed so unfair.

I was then advised to go round to the housing department and complete an application form to claim housing benefit and also while I was there, council tax benefit. I then had a meeting with the housing manager to explain the full situation to her and I completed an application for a larger property as the flat was deemed to be too small for us, mainly due to the fact that the children were of opposite sex and couldn't therefore share a bedroom due to their age.

At the end of the week I had completed so many different benefit forms that I was sick of the sight of them all. Then it was time for my home visit to sort out the details regarding the child support agency, at last I felt I had something straight forward to deal with, after all it would be straight forward wouldn't it, as my situation was as black and white as you could ever want it. I honestly felt that someone would have to pull out all the stops to make a mess of this application. In my opinion there were no real decisions to make apart from how much my ex-wife would pay towards the upkeep of her children. That's how it had worked for me as a father and I could therefore see no reason why things shouldn't be the same for my ex-wife.

How very wrong I was as it turned out that although I wasn't aware of it, some years earlier during my divorce, Kate had told the Child Support Agency that I was a missing father and that she was therefore not receiving any help from me towards the upkeep of the children. All this had gone on despite the fact that I was going round there every week with money for her. I had also been buying the children's school uniform, school coats, school shoes, paying for school trips and various other expenses while this deceit was going on. Every member of my family had helped her over the years. I was told recently that she had turned up at my mother's place of work a couple of years ago asking for money and my mother had given her two hundred pounds in cash to help her out – that was the sort of people who were in my family and I'm very proud of them, and yet she repays them with such lies and deceit. I was so very disappointed as I never thought she could stoop so low as to cast doubt upon my commitment to my children. In time I learnt to except that it was just another devious act from within a sick mind, but at the time it hurt me deeply to find out what she had done.

Maybe the system is designed to kick you while you are down because I have spent the last 18 months trying to resolve the issue with the child support agency. In fact the file now lies in the hands of my local MP who is desperately trying to get this situation resolved for us. 18 months and we have not received a single pound from my ex-wife towards the upkeep of her children – she makes me feel sick. I don't feel that any individual should need the child support agency to tell them that they need to contribute to the welfare of their children and any individual that does must have some deep rooted issues that they may need to get help with. You tell me: How can a mother behave in such a way? Have you ever known a mother to show such a lack of respect for her offspring?

In short I feel that the facts speak for themselves. It's a very sad reflection upon our society that this is the case after all that I have been through – surely its not rocket science to solve the problem and I just hope that it gets resolved very soon, although I'm aware that I am not alone with my difficulties as some 4 million people are currently having difficulties with the child support agency – all you government dudes, if your reading this my friend, you need to get it sorted out - sharpish!

By this time the children only had a week left at school before the start of the summer holidays, I had no idea what I was going to do or how I was going to cope.

One morning I called into the reception of both schools and introduced myself to the school staff. It's interesting to note that the first time I walked into my sons reception area with him to introduce myself, the person I was speaking to announced that this was the first time in the 2 years that she had known my son, that he had appeared with a smile across his face – that just added to my belief that we were doing the right thing.

That evening my mother came round with a surprise for all three of us. She had decided that the best thing would be to book the children into a summer play scheme. She felt that this would give me 6 weeks to get some of the benefits and things sorted out, and it would also give me some spare time during the day to deal with solicitors and all the other important things that were ongoing at the time. She duly produced details of a local play scheme and also a cheque to cover the cost of it, I looked down and the cheque was for just under one thousand pounds, I remember thinking bloody hell childcare is expensive – I had such a lot to learn.

Sometime over the following week I received a school report for my son, I hadn't seen one in over 4 years as this type of information was denied to me by my ex-wife – it made very interesting reading. I also received the full case notes + report from the child protection team based within social services, this too made very interesting reading. Again I don't feel that there is much to be gained by spilling all the gory details, suffice to say that everyone involved believed that the action that we were all taking was correct and that both reports added significantly to the strength of those future objectives.

As we gathered more and more information together it quickly became clear that Kate was much more of a problem than I had at first thought. I just like everyone else, had presumed that most of the problems stemmed from their step father, this proved very much not to be the case. The problem I now had was that criminal law does not deal with what someone might do, rather what someone has already done. Richard had been caught out due to the injuries to my daughters face that day and the law was able to deal with it as an assault, but it couldn't deal with what the other reports were clearly saying about Kate's extremely controlling behaviour. In English law that would be classed as mere hearsay, irrelevant of how strong your evidence was. It started to become clear that I was going to need another solicitor and that I would have to pursue a civil case against Kate. It was explained to me that a civil court could look at the facts and make a judgment without actually having an injury to prove a case. If I could prove that Kate was likely to hit the children, as she had so clearly been doing, then this would be a strong enough case for the civil court to pass a judgement, we could all then begin to put these events behind us.

I made up my mind and headed off into town to find myself a solicitor, knowing that I would have to try and get this resolved quickly as I needed to return to work. I was amazed to be told that to go through with the whole legal process to gain legal custody of my children it was going to cost me an estimated five thousand pounds. I really couldn't understand this as I already had both children under my full time care – they had been released from the hospital on the condition that they stayed with me and I had the paperwork to prove it. Apparently I now needed to sort out all the legal paperwork that is so often caused by such events. It suddenly dawned on me that people were now going to actively try to make money out of our misery, and that my friend is a bloody disgrace.

Five thousand pounds, imagine how I felt. I hadn't done anything wrong in the eyes of the law, I had lost my business and now they wanted five thousand pounds from me because some jumped up prat had decided to have a pop at my daughter – what's this country coming to. It was then explained to me that while I was in receipt of benefits I would be entitled to free legal help. So the decision was made for me right there in the office, I was now not going to be able to return to work until all legal matters were resolved. This had major financial implications on my family and I have to say that it was very hard not to start feeling very bitter towards the people who had caused all this mess. I just sat their and cried, unable to comprehend why it was that everything around me was systematically being destroyed and yet my only crime was to try to help my children and build us a better future. The only positive thing for me was the fact that I felt that maybe now we may have a change of luck with regard to clothes and various other items that we had still not received from Kate's house.

My solicitor then went on to spend the next couple of months trying to solve various problems with my ex-wife. We again formally requested the list of items that we required and we also made various offers for Kate to see the children, but all to no avail. She continued to keep hold of all the children's belongings, although a while later my solicitor received a letter from her solicitor saying that all beds, bedding, clothes etc had either been destroyed or disposed of, due to the fact that they were moving house in the near future. She added in the letter that I had been offered all the items by her a couple of months earlier but had 'turned them down', for some strange reason. It amazed me how she could continue to lie when faced with such a serious situation, my advice would have been to face the facts and admit you had been wrong, but no, not her, she was in complete denial. At the time she thought that all the evidence we had was the fact that her husband had hit my daughter; she was in for one hell of a shock if we ever walked into a court to discuss custody of the children. In a way I was quite looking forward to seeing her face when she realized that she's been caught out, hook line and sinker, and that the majority of the allegations were against her.

The thing that I really had trouble understanding is that she turned down every opportunity that my solicitor gave her to see the children. In total we wrote and offered 5 times, and each time she wouldn't accept the condition that the children could not see her in the company of her husband. She wouldn't swallow her pride, even to spend time with her children. She had turned into a very sad individual and she was certainly not the person whom I had married all those years earlier.

By October 2003 my solicitor was at her wits end with the lack of response from the other side and so she suggested that we offer to go to 'Mediation' to try and resolve some of the issues. An appointment was made for both Kate and I to meet at an independent solicitor's office in the town centre for an hour to sort out when she could see the children, and under what conditions that meeting would take place. Unfortunately for whatever reason Kate failed to keep the appointment, and I was left to stare at the empty chair opposite for an hour, in the hope that she might turn up. Another three hundred pounds had just been wasted! As it turned out she never did attend the mediation sessions.

There wasn't much else we could do, she hadn't turned up for the 'mediation' and also hadn't answered the last couple of letters from my solicitor regarding access to the children. My daughter's birthday came and went at the end of October. It was so very disappointing that she never received a birthday card. Her mother had the address and again I really can't understand why a card wasn't sent.

Richards's case also appeared at the local magistrate's court in October 2003. He was fined and also ordered to pay my daughter fifty pounds compensation for her injuries and the distress that it had caused her. He was also put on the child offenders register for a period of ten years. Personally for the record I didn't feel that justice had been done. I would have preferred the old fashioned way of an eye for an eye. I would have been extremely happy to punch Richard in the right eye 3 times, and he could even have kept the fifty quid. If only I ruled the land!

By December my solicitor informed me that we could go no further, as my ex-wife had not objected to me having custody of the children but neither had she given her permission. Only English law could waste 6 months and a couple of thousand pounds and make absolutely no decision at all, I was left with no official legal solution and the case was closed.

I later learnt through friends that Kate and Richard had definitely moved house and left no forwarding address. I was a little disappointed but also felt that maybe that was for the best, between them they had shown absolutely no interest in trying to rectify the wrong that they had done – even the social services report says, and I quote; '*Kate and Richard clearly have many issues with which they are dealing with at this present time, unfortunately both seem rather more preoccupied with their own situation rather than that of the children*' – in my mind that just about sums them up, 2 extremely selfish individuals, who even under these extreme conditions were still failing to grasp the enormity of what they had done. They were so far up themselves that my children were just in their way and so I was glad that they had moved, glad to see the back of them and I hoped I wouldn't have to see either of them for as long as I lived. I fail to see how my future could ever possible be enriched by their presence, they are the lowest form of society in my book and I hope they can live with what they have done.

By Christmas this whole episode had cost members of my immediate family over five thousand pounds – and my legal bill had been free! The main cost had been kitting out the children with clothes, coats, shoes; in fact everything that they required for their day to day existence had be replaced and therefore bought by someone, that someone was all too often my mother. It's terrible to think what a drastic effect these events were having upon her life, at a time when she should be thinking about retirement and enjoying herself. Through no fault of her own she was being systematically relieved of thousands of pounds and all because of someone else's ignorance – how would you feel? Christmas came and went and although it was a very difficult time both emotionally and physically, we did actually manage to have the best Christmas that we'd had in years. I had previously not been allowed to see my children on Christmas day for 6 years, so personally the rewards were great.

As it seemed that Kate and Richard had simply disappeared

into thin air, I was getting a little concerned about whether or not the children would like to see their grand parents on their mother's side. I also had at the back of my mind the thought that somewhere there might be Christmas presents for the children from Kate and Richard or the grandparents. As no one had made any effort to get in contact to arrange delivery I thought that for the benefit of the children, I would try and make the first move.

After a brief family discussion, during which both children explained to me that they didn't feel as though they knew their grandparents that well - apparently Kate and her parents had fallen out 4 or 5 years ago. Kate had therefore not allowed her mother or father to see either of them for a considerable period of time. After careful thought I decided that it probably wouldn't hurt any of us if I invited her mother and father round to the flat for a cup of tea and just see how things went from there. I have to admit that I had serious reservations about some aspects of the visit, I personally hadn't spoken to Kate's parents for over 6 years now due to my divorce, and so I had no idea how the meeting would go; after all we hadn't been blessed with the best circumstances under which to renew our acquaintance had we. All I knew was what I had seen with my own eyes, and it was very obvious to me that Kate's mother was at least as controlling in her behaviour as her daughter, which is a fact that probably wouldn't surprise many geneticists around the world as I think its generally agreed that most of our behavioral patterns are either taught or simply just picked up from our parents during childhood. Never the less I decided that in the safety of my own home it was worth a risk, if for no other reason than to hear them try and explain this one to me. It did occur to me that they too may have information that may be of assistance to my cause, and I was therefore willing to listen to whatever it was that they had to say.

They duly turned up and to be honest everything seemed fine. We exchanged formalities and they did bring over a small pile of presents for the children, which not only surprised me but also gave my spirits a lift. They went on to explain that they hadn't seen their grandchildren for a few years after a family row between Kate and her mother – the story unfolded just as I had been told by the children.

During the visit I took the opportunity to observe the children's behaviour while they were in their grandmothers company. Generally things were ok apart from the fact that my son kept wandering off into our bedroom to play with some of his toys, whenever he got the opportunity. It was clear that for one reason or another he was uncomfortable in their presence. There was nothing in his behaviour that suggested that he didn't like either of them, maybe it was just a bit too early for him and it bought back negative thoughts relating to his time spent with his mother, we may never know for sure. I felt that there was no point in forcing him to do anything that he didn't want to do, so I just let him play in the bedroom.

At the end of the visit I explained that as yet we hadn't received any of the requested items from Kate's house and that if they could influence Kate in any way, it would be more than useful as we were struggling along with the very minimum of clothes etc. The children were also requesting cuddly toys and various other portable items, anything would help the situation. Kate's mother explained that she no longer spoke to Kate after a major row, although she would do her best to make contact and try to resolve some of the issues, but there could be no guarantees. She also explained that part of the reason for the argument between mother and daughter had been Kate's new husband, and the fact that she couldn't stand him. This she explained had also become of source of conflict between her and her daughter, she added that this would be a major stumbling block as she felt that Richard had far too much influence and control over her daughter. I have to say that I found this statement rather strange because as far as I was ever made aware, I had been led to believe that Kate's mother had felt that Richard was the perfect son in law. This was obviously the total opposite to what she was telling me now, and so with good reason questions started to form in my head. It's safe to say that at the time I was ultra cautious of whatever anyone told me, after all it had been difficult over the recent months to distinguish fact from fiction at times.

I listened intently to what she said but my own opinion was that she was now feeding me negative thoughts about Richard in order to try and show her daughter in a better light. She was obviously unaware of the full nature of the facts that were now in my possession. As far as either of them was aware the only accusation was that Richard had hit my daughter, and as Kate had not attended any of the solicitors meetings or replied to our letters, no one had been in a position to tell her that we had details of mental and physical abuse going back over 5 years, relating to the pair of them.

As they made there way down the stairs back to their car, I had already come to the conclusion that Kate's mother was not telling me the whole truth. I understood her reasons but would have preferred it if she had just been more direct. At the time I was probably beyond offence anyway so whatever she wanted to say would have been fine by me, but she chose to be deceitful – I should have expected it.

The visits continued and although it was difficult, we got through them. It wasn't rocket science to work out that we would have to take things slowly and take the time to build on the trust and confidence of the children. It is interesting to note that apart from saying hello and goodbye, Kate's father never spoke a word. He wasn't miserable or anti social in any way, you just got the feeling that his opinion didn't count in their house and he could speak only when spoken too. I was surprised by just how much mother and daughter had in common to be honest.

During one of these visits, Kate's grandparents arrived with three or four cardboard boxes that they had managed to retrieve from the children's old home. At long last we had managed to get 4 cardboard boxes of the children's belongings. It doesn't sound very much does it but to us it was a massive breakthrough - a major step forward. My joy was short lived as before we had unpacked the boxes Kate's mother casually asked me if it would be all right for her to take the children out for the day, maybe to the zoo or something similar.

Everything was absolutely fine until I turned and said no, immediately adding that in my opinion it was far too early for such an event. I added that as the invitation did not include me, then it would not be possible under any circumstances, as neither of the children were going to be let out of my sight until all matters regarding Kate and Richard had been legally resolved. I made it very clear that it was a major problem for us because Kate had not dealt at all with any of the issues, and I therefore wouldn't allow either of them out of my sight as I couldn't guarantee that they would not just head straight round to their daughters house to see Kate with my children. My ex mother in law totally failed to see my point of view, and then I witnessed something that had so far been unseen through my young eyes – I sat and watched as grown women of over 50 began to sulk, right in front of me in my lounge, like she was a teenager. Maybe in her household a quick sulk or tantrum might achieve positive results but here she had forgotten one minor point – she was in my house!

After 20 minutes or so, having realized that apart from looking totally ridiculous, she wasn't actually achieving the desired effect, she started to perk up a bit, maybe the realization had dawned on her that she wasn't in a position to get her own way for the first time in years and so she decided that she would bite her tongue for the time being. They finished their cup of tea, said their goodbyes and disappeared into the night. Another visit over thank god. Progress was painfully slow but there was just no other option available to any of us. I just wasn't prepared to let the children out of my site when it was clear that no one within Kate's family accepted that she had done anything wrong. As far as they were concerned it had all been Richards's fault – how wrong they all were.

It was starting to become clear that Kate's mother looked upon this whole affair as some sort of game. It seemed that to even strike up a sensible conversation with her, I would have to offer her some form of incentive. At times I felt like I was stuck in some form of hostage situation with regard to my children. She just wouldn't except that her grand children had been removed from her daughter's care due to overwhelming evidence of both violent and mental abuse – and I had masses of evidence to prove it.

Although things were tense during and after their visits, I was still hoping that one day we could solve all the problems and move forward. I was aware that my children would need their mother in some form for the rest of their lives, what I didn't know was how the hell were we going to achieve that. She also had to except that Richard would never be allowed near either of my children again for as long as I was alive – that point was not negotiable with anyone other than my children and I somehow couldn't see their view changing for a considerable length of time – if at all.

The next time they visited was on my son's birthday in January 2004. I knew I was taking a chance as the last thing that my son needed was a row on his birthday, but I also understood that his grandparents would want to see him on his special day. With hindsight I should have realized that we hadn't moved forward far enough in the relationship to have them round on such a personal event. I should point out at this point that Kate's parents were still very much strangers in our home. Both children now had so much more freedom in their lives that all they really wanted to do was spend all weekend doing the things that they hadn't been free to do before – like being children! In my view there were lots of reasons why both should show such a lack of interest in their grandparents but it seemed that I was the only one in the room who understood that simple fact, and any explanation that I tried to offer suddenly became treated as if it were a personal attack.

The other thing that was starting to really bug me about the visits was the fact that despite numerous polite requests that we should not talk about past events in front of the children, Kate's mother relentlessly tried to raise the subject whenever my children entered the room. I explained to her time and time again that not only did I feel that such talk was insensitive and inappropriate but that it was also my wish that the subject was not to be raised within earshot of my children. It was clear that Kate's mother was struggling to cope with the fact that I was now in charge of her grandchildren, and that from now on she would be doing exactly as she was told or nothing at all. She was struggling to cope with that simple fact, simple to me but I guess not so simple to a control freak that is used to throwing a tantrum and getting her own way. In their small heads they probably thought that I was on a power trip or something. I can almost hear her at breakfast time muttering to anyone who would bother to listen: *'How dare he speak to me like that, who does he think he is'*. Well guess what, I'm the keeper of the gate!

The final straw came during the visit on my son's 10th birthday. Kate's mother came in firing on all cylinders. It didn't take me long to figure out that the softly softly approach that I had been using had foolishly been mistaken for weakness on my part. She opened up with all the usual stuff about not ever seeing Kate and that in her opinion Richard was a total prat. Interesting, but I'd heard it all before. When she felt that I had been sufficiently softened up she threw in how nice it would be to take the children out for the day. Again despite my repeated requests not to discuss things while the children were in the room, she had done it again but this time she had put me on the spot. If I wasn't careful it would look like I wasn't allowing the children to see there mother. They had both been protected from all of the negative events of the last year or so and were unaware that their mother had abandoned them at this point. I was still stalling them just in case we could resolve the difficulties and get Kate to address the problem that she had caused and to take some responsibility for it. I was less than impressed with the way that I had now been placed in such a position by her parents, while they were guests in my home. Again I explained to Kate's mother that I couldn't be sure that she would not just head straight round to her daughters home with my children, as any normal mother would probably do. I explained that as her daughter did not except that her actions had been wrong then that caused me to believe that there was still a real threat to my children, should they come face to face with their natural mother. My ex mother in law was just raising her voice, telling me in no uncertain terms that she did not see her daughter and had no intention of doing so in the near future (I guess she had forgotten that only weeks earlier she had obviously seen Kate as she had delivered boxes from her to my house) when her mobile phone rang and distracted her from the verbal tirade she was hurling in my direction. You'll never guess what, but that day in my lounge I witnessed a miracle, because on my ex-mother in-law's mobile phone was the invisible women - yes the same women that my ex mother in law never saw, never spoke to and didn't know where she was. Well I now knew where Kate was - she was on the bloody phone in my lounge!

As you can probably imagine the walking strop machine now looked extremely stupid. All those lies about how she never saw her daughter, all those lies about how she hated Richard, all came back in her face – just like spitting in the wind. It was the most fun I'd had in ages. By this time I thought I'd heard it all over the years but what I was about to hear even took me by surprise. Kate's mother stood up in my lounge and had the audacity to demand to see the photograph of my daughter's facial injury, as she put it: *'To make sure all this actually happened'*. I couldn't believe what I was hearing, where on earth had someone got balls big enough to walk into my home under those circumstances and demand to see that photograph. I had seen it once and I never want to look at it again as long as I live. I don't ever want to see my daughter with another mark on her body that has been inflicted by someone else. My patience and understanding had now been stretched too far. The best bit is the vacant look I got when I turned to my ex mother in law and said that the whole fucking world can't be wrong can they. How dare they come into my home and demand to see that photo, I felt insulted and I told her so. Half of the Basingstoke child protection unit had been involved at some time or another and here was the local village idiot asking me if it was all a dream, a figment of my imagination. It's fair to say that they made a speedy exit from my flat that day.

The following day having spoken to family members for advice, I called Kate's mother and politely told her that in my opinion her visits were causing a little too much distress at the present time, and I therefore wanted to slow things down a little. There was too much tension in the air during their visits and also for a couple of hours afterwards. She asked me when she could see them again and I replied that I would call her and invite her over as soon as either of the children asked me to do so, and I genuinely meant it, if asked I would call her immediately.

She had obviously gone away and had a grizzle as an hour later I had Kate's sister on the phone asking me to explain why I had upset her mother. Unfortunately it quickly became clear that her poor sister had been fed a load of nonsense by her mother. To be honest I'm not quite sure why exactly she even bothered to call me, as the conversation I had with her didn't relate at all to the one I had earlier with her mother. Looking back I suppose it would have been hard for Kate's mother to go back home and admit to the others that she had managed to upset the whole house during a social visit on my son's birthday – that really would have been too much to expect from someone who had already been proved to be a stranger to the truth.

Over the coming months the children never mentioned their grandparents again, I guess they had seen enough on my son's birthday. Both children were now forming an extremely strong bond with me, their belief and trust was growing at an alarming rate. For the first time in their short lives they weren't constantly being criticized or controlled. At the time it was obvious to me that neither of them had taken kindly to their grand mother's actions in my home during my son's birthday. One thing was certain and that was they were both becoming very protective of me and wouldn't tolerate any nonsense from anyone, even

Kate's parents. This pleased me more that anything as their self confidence had been shot to pieces when they had first arrived and the fact that they now felt comfortable enough to express an opinion truly made me believe that I was doing the right thing. It gave me a very rewarding feeling deep inside when I saw that they were starting to show such belief in their father; after all I was on a major learning curve and had no idea how to be a full time parent. I was just muddling through trying to do my best as anyone would under the circumstances.

The rest of the year passed quite quickly. We didn't see or hear from Kate's parents for the next 6 months. Without the stress that their visits always bought with them, our home quickly settled into a nice calm routine.

As we entered 2004 we had still not heard from Kate, despite many letters from my solicitor trying to arrange for her to come and see the children. I have to say that I was still having difficulty understanding Kate's actions and it didn't take me long to come to the conclusion that she obviously still had a lot of adjusting to do with regard to the whole situation – on that basis I decided that I would make no further efforts to encourage her to visit us. It was perfectly clear that she wasn't bothered about any of us at all and the only conclusion left to any sane minded individual was that we would have to just except it and try to move forward.

Maybe it was for the best but only time would tell. I still firmly believed that at some point in time both children would need their mothers support and I was so very disappointed to realize that despite months of e-mails and solicitors letters, we had been unable to see any sorrow or remorse from my ex-wife or to make any positive moves towards bringing our two sides together. All of my efforts were met with the same response, which was that was Kate and Richard would simply not accept that they had done anything wrong. In fact both the police and the social services report clearly stated that both Kate and Richard had relentlessly complained to both parties during interview, saying that they were making a big mistake, adding that they felt that they were both innocent. I guess they had overlooked all the other parties involved like the schools and even their own family members who had raised serious concerns about the way in which they both treated the children. Maybe we were all wrong – but I don't believe so. As my good friend Tony would have said: *If it walks like a duck and it quacks like a duck, then it probably is a duck.* Wise words from him and I had to agree.

We had come to a point in time where I had to be real and just except that I couldn't make my ex-wife see my point of view. If she choose not to except the evidence put before her then I would just have to deal with that and continue to drive forward alone towards the long term solution.

I decided to turn my attention towards the financial situation, starting with my claim for child maintenance. I figured that maybe if I could get that sorted out it might make Kate stop and think about her actions. If she was contributing towards the upkeep of the children, then surely she would want to see them. I had no idea whether or not this would have the desired effect but I wanted to get it resolved anyway as it would be another major step forward for me, with the main aim being that I work myself into a position where I could return to full time employment, and in turn support myself and my family.

Even after all that had happened I was still having severe difficulties understanding why Kate had not automatically been made to contribute to the upbringing of our children. It was her choice to refuse to pay her maintenance but why hadn't the Child Support Agency forced her to pay with an attachment of earnings or something similar. Money was tight and so the delay was so very frustrating. It was clear that Kate was now extremely bitter and was just trying to cause us as a family as much discomfort as possible. There was no way that I was going to let her twisted actions affect us and I decided to put it at the back of my mind.

While I was waiting for a response from the CSA, I turned my attention to the housing situation. A year had now passed and we were still stuck in a small flat over 9 miles away from the schools. I was still sharing a bed with my son and I was also finding things extremely difficult financially. I still hadn't received any news from the housing department in Basingstoke, apart from one nomination that was for a new house that was to be built within 200 yards of my mother's house. This sounded ideal as my mother had been helping me so much both financially and with childcare. I was understandably very cautious as to where the children spent their time and had decided months earlier that if they were not with me then the only other suitable place for them to be was with my mother, whom they both had complete trust in.

Unfortunately having sent my completed application form to the housing association that was dealing with the new property, six weeks later I received a letter telling me that all 12 of the properties that had been built had already been allocated to people a couple of months previously, in early September 2003. It turned out that Basingstoke council's nomination on my behalf was actually worthless. Their offer to allocate me a house from this project had been written over two months after the homes were actually allocated to members of the public – their headed paperwork, sent to me officially offering me the house, was dated December 2003. It turned out that the nomination was used purely to stall my application for time and I have to say that under the circumstances to get our hopes up by implying that we had a very good chance of being allocated one of the properties was extremely hurtful to say the least. Once again I had to learn my lesson the hard way and except that working your way through the housing system in Basingstoke was not as straight forward as they would lead me to believe. I'd had to deal with so many lies over the last year but that one stands out in my memory as one of the worst, simply because I felt that they had no need to treat me like a fool and mislead me. It was the housing manager who I had been dealing with at the time who had misled me and in my opinion she should have known better. My advice would have to be that next time she may wish to think a little about the effects of her actions, before making promises that she knew full well she couldn't keep.

I was now extremely disappointed with the housing department to say the least and at that point I decided to make my complaint an official one. I took my complete case to my Local MP for assistance, after all I had the backing of social services saying that I needed to be re-housed urgently and due to that I was on the housing register listed under 'priority'. Now all I could do is sit tight and wait for a couple of weeks to see what type of response I was going to get now that I had bought my MP in the fray.

Financially things were also now extremely difficult. Christmas had just been and gone and the heavy winter bills were coming in. There was still no clear indication of when I would be able to return to full time employment and begin to receive an income upon which we could actually feed ourselves, due to the fact that I still hadn't resolved anything at all with Kate, housing or the Child Support Agency. In fact a few thousand pounds of tax payer's money had gone up in smoke over the last year and yet the grand summary of our complete achievements was absolutely nothing. The Child Support Agency hadn't even managed to type my name in to their computer system yet, so there was little chance of any maintenance turning up from my ex-wife and it was clear that she had no intention of supporting her two children of her own free will. I started to realize that if we didn't sort things out soon I would be in real financial trouble. When the events had first occurred my mother had written cheques to cover most household bills for a period of about 6 months, but now even that seemed light years behind us.

Maybe it was the general pressure of the whole situation, I don't know, but things were really starting to get me down. Whatever I chose to do, something always seemed to be in my way. All I wanted was to get back to work to support my family so that we could be self sufficient and in turn happy amongst ourselves – it just felt like I was always asking for too much.

Although my local MP did his best it was clear that the council were still just stalling for time. After a couple of months of writing and receiving letters, but not actually moving forward in the housing queue, I decided that it was time to take my complaint to the next level. In March 2004 I sent my complete file to the Government Ombudsman responsible for housing. I gave full details of my complaint and also details of the appalling way in which I felt I had been treated. Within 3 weeks of the file landing on the Ombudsman's desk I was offered a 3 bedroom property on another estate that lined the outskirts of Basingstoke – I was on the move again and this time my destination was Brighton Hill.

In many ways my dreams had come true. All I had wanted was a 3 bedroom house so that we could get settled and start to build a proper home, a home which was going to be ours, a home full of happiness and joy. All our thoughts and dreams were now going to become reality, getting this far had been so traumatic for all three of us but now we could officially say that we were going to make a fresh start. I still hadn't heard from Kate, and as difficult as it was for me to take in that she had just abandoned her children, now I honestly couldn't care less whether she was here or not. I was confident that we would now be ok, over the last year we had evolved into a close family and now we were going to get our new home.

I was informed that the house wouldn't be ready for us to move into until the last week of May. I started to clean the flat from top to bottom ready for the big move. The children were all excited and between the three of us we started to choose colour schemes for our individual rooms. It was now the end of March, the good weather was on its way and everything was hunky dory. Or at least that's what I thought, after all surely it wasn't possible after the year I'd just had for things to get any worse. I didn't know it at the time but I was now definitely heading for the hardest part of my life so far. I've thought long and hard as to the reasons why so many things were going wrong at the same time and to this day I haven't figured it out yet. My best guess is that it's all a dress rehearsal for something else, something bigger that's lying in wait for me in the future. If I'm right then it's going to be interesting to see, because this has been one hell of a dress rehearsal.

Despite my inner feelings I felt safe in the thought that no one could expect to lose as much both emotionally and financially as I had, and still expect more bad news - but that's exactly what I got; although it must be said that this time I had bought it upon myself.

CHAPTER 13

PERVERTING THE COURCE OF JUSTICE

On 6th April 2004, right out of the blue, I was arrested at the Royal Courts of Justice in the Strand/London, by the serious crime squad based in Southampton. This followed the failed appeal by the Aubrey brothers against their conviction for GBH, during which I had been a witness. In layman's terms what had happened was that the appeal had raised serious questions regarding the validity of the brother's original conviction. The end result being that either the police or the witnesses at the appeal were lying. If it could be proved that there had been a major miscarriage of justice then I expect that the doors to financial compensation would have been blown right open. I just couldn't see any scenario where either the police or the legal system in general was going to stand up and admit that it was all their fault, mainly due to the fact that both brother's had already served over two and a half years by the time that their appeal reached the high court in order to be heard in the first place. Obviously all of this was now placing me in a very precarious position. To be accused of lying on oath, in the high court, was something that needed to be address very carefully indeed.

Now we really did have a big problem to deal with as I was still left with no official closure to the civil case against Kate with regard to the children. From the first moment that I was arrested it suddenly dawned on me that I would now be facing the biggest legal battle that I could possibly imagine. I was under no elusions that this was my worst nightmare becoming reality right before my eyes.

Following my arrest I was released without charge, it seemed that the police had no actual evidence to support their claims. I was asked to report back to the police station in a couple of months, by which time the police hoped to complete their investigation.

I duly returned as requested only to be told that they hadn't actually made any progress since our last meeting. They went on to explain to me that I should expect things to take quite some time as they intended to have a thorough investigation into what had gone on. The stakes were starting to rise now and it was such a relief to be released once again without charge. Before I left I was told once again that I would be required to report back to the police station in a month's time.

The following month I made my way back to the station where again I was told that very little progress had been made. The stakes were getting higher by the day. If the police chose to do nothing then they would be as good as admitting that something was wrong. At this point the police had to make a decision as the whole situation was becoming laughable and my legal team was now demanding that I be either charged with an offence or released without charge. They then decided to raise the stakes even higher at this point and I was formally questioned about my involvement in the high court appeal. I was interviewed by 2 officers and after an hour of repeating 'no comment', I was formally charged with Perjury, although this would later change to 3 counts of attempting to pervert the course of justice. I was released on bail, due to the fact that I had 2 dependant children to look after and I was told to attend the local magistrate's court during September 2004.

I left the police station and I was totally devastated, the timing couldn't have been any worse, as I still had a missing ex-wife and a thousand other problems to deal with. Personally I had several genuine reasons for concern at this point. Firstly I was not in a position to get embroiled in any lengthy criminal proceedings. Secondly just about everyone I knew had serious reservations about the safety of the original conviction of the two brothers, mainly due to the following: The DNA tests from the alleged vehicle used in the attack had come back negative. Blood was found inside the vehicle but it didn't match the victim of the assault. The victim had also sworn on oath, in a court of law, that he had in fact miss-identified both brothers at the time of the original assault; due to the fact that he had believed that Ivor Aubrey had an Indian ink tattoo on the back of his head. Various witnesses stated that one of the original assailants had a very distinctive tattoo on the back of his head. When Ivor Aubrey stood in the dock of Winchester crown court and was asked to turn round to show the jury the back of his head – guess what, there was no tattoo! The only logical assumption that one could come to is that the victim had wrongly identified his attacker on the night of the assault. Whoever the elusive man was, then one thing was certain and that was that the man in the dock could not possibly have been the same man who had been seen at the burger bar. Mistaken identity or a set up? We may never know for sure.

Based purely on the facts before the court I found it impossible to comprehend why both brothers had been jailed for a total of over ten years, whichever way you choose to look at it, I think it's fair to say that at the very least something fishy was going on.

My concerns quickly became reality, when during my official interview; the police raised various points that were totally beyond my rational thinking. The first thing that they produced was a sworn statement from the principle of my old school John Hunt of Everest. This statement turned out to be very interesting indeed. It stated that I had attended the school between 1974 and 1977. The police therefore claimed that I had attended school with Ivor Aubrey and had therefore lied to try and help him. They claimed that we were old friends that dated back over 25 years. This statement was obviously causing me great concern as I wasn't even in the country between 1974 and 1977. To say that this statement caught me by surprise would be an understatement. How had the police got hold of a sworn statement from someone with such authority, that couldn't possibly be true?

Secondly I was faced with a statement from an old friend, who I cannot name for legal reasons. He had given evidence against the brother's at the original trial. In fact it could only have been his positive identification of the brothers (based on his sworn evidence that he had known the brothers for over 10 years) that had resulted in the police getting the conviction that they were after. Now suddenly I was facing a statement from the same man which stated that he didn't know me, or either of the brothers he had helped to convict a couple of years earlier. Again both statements couldn't possibly be true now could they? It seemed that our learned friend appeared to be saying exactly what the police wanted him to say, depending on the situation.

Thirdly, and the one which was causing me the greatest concern, was a statement from one of the police officers in the case who stated that he had never met me and didn't know me.

The problem was that we had met before and luckily it was at Winchester crown court, where our meeting would have been recorded on the C.C.T.V. that is always installed within such establishments today. In fact I had been discussing our earlier meeting with the same police officer only a couple of hours earlier and now there was a statement on the table before me which stated that we had categorically never met before. I have to say that it's a very strange feeling when you are sat in a police interview room and you know beyond any doubt at all that the evidence before you is false. I knew that I may have problems proving that the star witness ever knew me but I was positive that I could prove that I wasn't even in the country at the time I was supposed to be attending school with one of the accused. I also knew that I could prove beyond any doubt that the police officer was lying. In my mind all I had to do was formally request the footage taken at the court that day, and it would clearly show him and I sharing a very jovial chat and therefore prove that he was lying.

As I made my way home from the police station that day I was extremely concerned, as it was obvious to anyone who cared to read the original case notes that there now seemed to be a major contradiction in what the police were saying now, and what they had said at the original trial. The only conclusion that I could come to was that for some reason I was being set up as a scapegoat and all the lies were now going to be placed on my doorstep. All of this was putting me in a very precarious position as I was sandwiched between the defense and the prosecution, and believe me with so many people obviously lying, then this was not the best position for me to find myself in.

The only good news, if there was any, was the fact that my defense council actually had the evidence to back up what I was saying as everything was confirmed on the tape recording from my police interview. We also had the written statement from the school principal which was utter nonsense and could only have been written on the instruction of the police involved, as it was blatantly not true. It was a major mistake for them to make considering the fact that I had not even been in the country. In fact my alibi at the time would have been that I was in the British embassy in Jeddah, living next door to the British ambassador – not a bad alibi to have, even if I do say so myself!

I now had to make a straight choice. Do I plead guilty or not guilty? In order to prove myself innocent I would have to take on both the police and the establishment behind them. For some strange reason there are still people in this county who believe that all police officers tell the truth – god help them. Before you lock horns with the establishment my advice would be to think very very carefully before you do that. I was in no doubt that not only did I stand every chance of loosing custody of my children if I lost but I would also have the rest of my life turned into a living hell if I won – not much of a choice was it! Of course I knew that I could prove that someone was lying, but would it be worth the eventual cost that I may be asked to pay. I played each scenario over and over again in my head but no matter how hard I tried I couldn't make up my mind what to do. I was in a no win situation and the stakes were extremely high.

In order to try and make a final decision I asked my solicitor to try and retrieve the CCTV footage from the court cameras, to confirm what I was saying about the alleged meeting with the police officer. Unfortunately this footage was unavailable and no satisfactory explanation as to why was ever offered. It was becoming abundantly clear already that this was going to be a difficult point to prove. I quickly realized that I now had no choice in the matter as the best scenario for everyone involved would be for me to cop a guilty plea, despite the evidence to the contrary. It was crystal clear that it just wasn't going to be worth the argument with the establishment. My children came first no matter what and I had no doubt that my best option was to plead guilty and go for the suspended sentence, based on the child care issue. The problem I faced was that even that was no forgone conclusion due to the seriousness of the charges against me. In my heart I knew that they would never let me get away with perverting the course of justice, I knew I would go to prison for it but there just didn't seem to be any other logical choice available to me.

A couple of days after my release from police custody I went down to the local citizen's advice bureau for some help and advice, as things were now so bad. I needed some help and I needed it quickly. I explained to them that all this had started a year ago, through no fault of my own. I had been doing really well but due to the circumstances I had been forced to finish work and the bills had just mounted up. The Child Support Agency had let me down badly and there just wasn't enough money to go round. I'd been on income support now for 15 months and I had slowly made all sorts of cut backs during that time. Now there was nothing left to cut back.

After a brief discussion I was advised to file for bankruptcy. I explained that I had previously been declared bankrupt back in 1990 and therefore felt that I couldn't do it again. The old boy dealing with me toddled off muttering something about the rules being changed regarding bankruptcy. He came back holding his little booklet and we realized that although not recommended, it could be done twice. A few days later, on 16th April 2004 I was again declared bankrupt at Reading County Court. Now I really had lost everything and I knew that it would be very difficult to come back from this one, and I still had the police charges to deal with. It's very difficult to watch your whole life being destroyed in front of your eyes. Last time it had been hard but now I had 2 small faces that were so dependent upon me, and this time I was alone to cope with all of it.

As May approached we were looking forward to moving into our new home, although for me the novelty had worn off a little. In the back of my mind I knew that I stood every chance of loosing it if I ended up in prison.

On 10th May 2004 we moved in. Internally it was in a bit of a state but we were just grateful to be given the opportunity. We had also been given one hundred and eighty pounds by the housing association to help towards the cost of redecorating the place. The day after we moved in I started stripping off all the old wallpaper so that we could start afresh.

During the first few weeks we had a couple of minor teething problems with the local kids on the estate. Unfortunately this was just something that we would have to go through. The main problem was that as my ex-wife and her partner had been so controlling for so long, the end result was that both children were way behind with their social development. Neither had been allowed to play outside or have visitors inside the house and therefore they had a lot to learn. I figured that the best way to over come this difficulty was to encourage them to play as much as possible, while I was close by keeping an eye on things. I knew that there would be days when I would have to bite my tongue as a parent, I crossed everything and hoped for the best.

It wasn't long before my son came home one afternoon with his nose spread across his face and his bike so badly damaged that it had to be replaced. He had been attacked by 4 members of the same family, 2 boys and 2 girls. They had stamped on his face and set about his bike with a hammer. We had a family chat and I made both children aware of the dangers of living and playing on an estate – lesson one had been learnt!

The next few months passed quite quickly as I set about decorating the house and designing the back garden. Winter was fast approaching and that meant that both children's birthdays and also Christmas would soon be upon us.

In early October 2004 I was due to appear at Southwark Crown Court in London to answer the charges of attempting to pervert the course of justice. As I made my way there on the train it gave to time to think about many aspects of the case. One of the brothers who had been sentenced to four and a half years for the original assault had now been released, the other brother was due for release in 6 months time, and I now had 2 dependent children - it all seemed so pointless to me, but then I guess it would.

At the Crown Court, after an hour of legal arguments my case was adjourned until early December 2004, this next date was to be a plea and directions hearing. I could now see the light at the end of the tunnel and although I wasn't over keen for the date to arrive, it would be fair to say that by then I had had enough of the pressure that I was under and I just wanted to move towards a rapid conclusion – whatever the outcome I just wanted it all to end.

Following my court appearance in October the local newspaper had printed half a dozen lines about it. The article had just said that I had appeared at a crown court in London, charged with attempting to pervert the course of justice and that I was due to appear again in December for a plea and directions hearing. At this next hearing the court would either accept my guilty plea, if that is what I choose to do, or if I pleaded not guilty, then a date would be set for my trial to commence. You would be forgiven for thinking that the article in the paper would hardly have been enough to have even been noticed by most people, unfortunately there was one person out there who was looking and who was rubbing her hands with glee as she absorbed every word that had been written – my ex-wife! I didn't know at the time that she had seen it, but behind the scenes another storm was brewing and this time it was going to be the mother of all storms.

Within a week I was served with court papers at my front door by a private detective. The papers stated that my ex-wife was applying for full custody of both children on the grounds that I had been arrested on serious charges and that I was highly likely to be going to prison for a period of 3 or 4 years, sometime in the New Year. The letter stated that the date of the first hearing was to be on 9th December 2004, just 2 days after my appearance in London on the criminal charges. I guess it was going to be a busy week. I had been battling with her for over a year now, trying to get her into a court of law to sort out the mess that we were in. No matter what I tried she just ignored me. Now suddenly she was willing to walk into a court of her own free will and challenge my right to retain custody of our children. How sad it would be if this disturbed individual was to be allowed to regain custody of our children due solely to the nature and seriousness of the charges that I was now facing.

It turned out that when Kate and Richard had moved without leaving a forwarding address, they had in fact stayed in Basingstoke somewhere and that Kate had also kept her job at a local computer company. Personally that made things even harder for me to understand, if she no longer wanted to have anything to do with her children, then why hadn't she just moved miles away as I had at first presumed, it didn't make sense to me that she still lived locally.

The time soon passed and before I knew it December was

upon us and it was time for my court appearance in London. The whole situation just seemed so pointless to me. The event had turned into a complete mess and I was now stuck right in the middle of it. My head was telling me to fight it all the way but in my heart I knew that I would have to do everything in my power to bring things to a swift conclusion, so that I could concentrate fully on the civil case that was due a couple of days later. I came to the conclusion that I just had too much to loose. The only thing that I was certain about was the fact that I wanted to keep custody of my beloved children. After weeks of deliberation I decided to go for the safer option and plead guilty to the charges and go for the suspended sentence in order to try and get a speedy solution to the whole affair.

The main problem that I now faced was that all the legal people involved were telling me to expect between 4 and 5 years in prison for this type of offence. I also knew that even the highest courts in the land only had the power to suspend a sentence of up to 2 years, anything higher was deemed to be far too serious to warrant a suspended sentence. As I had already been told by the judge back in December that I should expect a lengthy custodial sentence, I quickly realized that I was in a very precarious position. In layman's terms it would only be possible to get my sentence suspended under the very rarest of rare circumstances. Maybe the situation looks very different to you sat there reading all this now, but I can assure you that when you find yourself stuck in such a predicament then all the choices suddenly dry up. This wasn't the stuff of story books – this was now the real world.

I entered the court room when called and confirmed my name and address. I then sat down for half an hour while the prosecution outlined the case. I was then asked to stand and also which plea I intended to enter, when asked I replied *'guilty'*. The case was adjourned so that the probation service could put together a social enquiry report for the benefit of the judge. A date was then set of 11ᵗʰ January 2005 for me to return to Southwark Crown Court to receive my punishment. I was given unconditional bail and allowed to return home to the children.

One of the worst things about this case was that it had been committed within London. This meant that it was what is known as a 'section 51' offence. This meant that it could only be dealt with by the metropolitan police in London and as a result, all my court appearances would have to be held within the jurisdiction of the metropolitan police. I therefore had to travel up on the train, sometimes for only a few minutes just to confirm my name and address. The reality of this is that I was having to pay out forty eight pounds for every court appearance, and as this had to come out of my income support each time, the end result was that we would often have no food in the house. I don't expect your sympathy but this was one of the most difficult periods in my life. I have to say that it was extremely difficult to sustain moral in my house while all the time the cupboards were bare. Surely that is not the way to raise 2 children under the circumstances and in my heart I felt that it was so unfair that all three of us should be punished in such a callous manner.

Two days later I was off to the county court to face my ex-wife for the first time in over 18 months. It's hard to explain how I felt on the inside as I drove to the court. She had mistreated both my children for a period of about 5 years, she had stood by and watched her husband assault both my son and daughter, and had done nothing to prevent the attack or to help our daughter receive treatment for her injuries, instead she chose to send her to school for the day. She had then failed to attend our arranged meeting at mediation and had also not responded to my solicitor's letters offering her, on many occasions, the chance to see her children. She had then abandoned them and cruelly moved home without informing her children as to where she was going. She had them systematically destroyed all my children's worldly possessions and she had deliberately missed my daughter's 13th birthday, although in a cruel twist she managed to send a card to my son on his birthday 2 months later. It was obvious that she was just trying to create a divide between the children. Under the circumstances how could she buy a card and present for one child and not do the same for the other, I found her actions extremely cruel and most unwelcome. I had enough on my plate at the time, without having to explain to my daughter why it was that she was being singled out. It didn't take much to work out that Kate was deliberately directing her anger towards my daughter and to be honest I felt that this was one of the cruelest things that Kate had done so far. She had also made various false accusations about me to various people over a long period of time. In short she caused them more heartache and stress that I could ever put into words and now I was expected to turn up and meet her with a smile on my face. Just to make matters worse, if that was possible; when I read her reasons for her court application I was even more concerned. The official papers stated that as I had been arrested on serious charges and was therefore facing a custodial sentence, she proposed to 'live apart' from her husband so that she could have her children back. Once she had achieved this objective then it was her clear intention to move back in with her husband and she wasn't even trying to conceal that fact. Maybe I was being naive, I was hoping to read something along the lines of *'I'm sorry'* or *'I've had a change of heart'* or maybe even *'I've missed you both'*; no such luck......... her reason was revenge, revenge on the two people who in her opinion had caused all this in the first place. I knew then that I would have to be extremely careful not to allow Kate to be alone with the children.

In order to make sure everything was water tight I had arrived at the court about an hour early. This meant that there was no chance of me bumping into either Kate or her mother before we were actually in the court room, just in case they caused a scene. I had already suffered extreme verbal abuse from Kate's mother while out shopping in our local supermarket by this point. Although it was obviously a little embarrassing at the time, part of me couldn't help laughing at her as she launched her verbal tirade, as she was so far off the mark with her comments. Isn't it strange how these people try to justify and perceive their actions. I was amazed to be told by her that all of this was my fault. In short I didn't fancy another verbal lashing from any of them as the experience was already going to be extremely difficult for me without having either of them shouting obscenities in my face.

I made my way upstairs and found my legal representative. We both then headed into a side room to discuss what we were going to do. It was strange really as I was so apprehensive about seeing Kate after all the aggravation she had caused and yet she wasn't there in the room to discuss things. I had naively presumed that she would have been there, how were we going to solve anything if the main offender wasn't even present? I couldn't help myself and after a brief discussion I had to ask where Kate was. Even after everything that I had been through the answer shocked me. I have to say that by this point I had believed that I would never be shocked again for as long as I lived, and yet there I was sat in the court house, in a state of total disbelief. I was told that she was 'too scared' to enter the room while I was there. So scared in fact that she didn't feel safe in a court house side room with 2 legal representatives present – if it wasn't so serious it would have been laughable. Here we had someone that was faced with visual and factual evidence that she had been less than ideal in her treatment of her children and somehow she had convinced herself that it was my fault. With hindsight I should have seen that one coming but I didn't.

It turned out that we were limited in what we could achieve during that first hearing as we weren't going to know what was happening on the criminal side of things until 11th January. What we did know was that I was due to appear again at Southwark Crown Court for sentencing but in the meantime we needed to sort out something between Kate and the children. Her court application stated that she was applying for full custody of both. I have to admit that both myself and my legal friend shared a chuckle as we read the papers. What planet was Kate living on – full custody, the feeling was that she had more chance of winning the national lottery and being shot on the same day, than getting custody of the children. It was almost sad to watch.

I had been sat with my legal eagle for about an hour when suddenly there was a knock at the door and in came a woman who introduced herself as Kate's legal representative. She sat down and announced that Kate wanted full custody of both children. She added that in the meantime she wanted to take them out for the day without me being present, and she wanted to be accompanied by her immediate family, including her husband – I nearly fell off my chair laughing until I realized that she was serious.

The women then left the room so that I could discuss things with my representative. I explained that my position hadn't changed from day one despite everything that had gone on over the last 18months, and that I had no objection at all to Kate seeing the children, my only stipulations were that I was personally going to be present until such time that I was satisfied that there was no longer a threat to either of them. I didn't care how long it took but I would be by their side until such time as I was totally and utterly satisfied that there was no longer a threat – that was non negotiable. I also demanded that Richard was never to be present during any of the visits. He was a nobody and I could see no way that he would be able to enrich our lives and so I had no wish to see him. All he would trigger in me would be anger, although I had realized a year earlier that on a personal level I had to be bigger than that and put my anger aside for the sake of the children. I wasn't here to get angry or even, I was here to sort out my family's future so at last we could start to put this mess behind us.No matter what anyone else thought at the time, I firmly believe that all children need their mother at some point in their lives and it was therefore my responsibility to ensure that happened, but I also had to ensure their safety and I still hadn't seen any signs of acceptance or remorse from Kate and that concerned me, although I was aware that we needed to do something and we needed to do it today while we had the chance.

My proposal was that she should telephone the children at 10.30am the following Saturday and every Saturday thereafter until such time as we were in a position where we could start to move forward and make some positive long term decisions. She could also visit them at my home address for a couple of hours to drop off the Christmas presents she claimed to have bought.

My proposals were put to her and her response was: Firstly she demanded to be allowed to take them out for the day. Secondly she felt that she was too scared to come to my home address, although it was obvious to everyone present that she was just using this as an excuse for her absence over the last couple of years. She didn't seem to realize that she was in no position to argue about anything. It suddenly dawned on me that as she had failed to address the problem last year, she still hadn't actually been told that we had over 4 hours of video evidence against her and also statements from various official bodies given quite interesting details. We also had photographs of my daughter's facial injuries, but Kate still wasn't aware of any of that. In her mind the last thing she had been told was that her husband had hit my daughter, in her head she had convinced herself that she had done nothing wrong and so I guess she felt that she would just be allowed to stroll in and demand to take her children out and no one would object – she needed to wake up big time, and quickly.

In response I proposed that she should make the phone calls and also that maybe she could meet us in MacDonald's for a meal. After 10 minutes she rejected that saying that most of it was ok, but she didn't feel safe in MacDonald's alone with us, so she wanted to bring her mother. Again I had a chuckle, there was more chance of me welcoming Richard with open arms than me sharing a MacDonald's with that twisted control freak. When I'd finished laughing I proposed that she could bring her sister with her as we had always got on with each other, it would also help my case to have a witness close by, as Kate had already proved that she was a stranger to the truth, the last thing I needed was to give her the opportunity to make any more false allegations. From now on I was determined that I should never be alone with Kate at any cost.

By this point I was just looking forward to getting home for a nice hot bath, we were almost there, a few more minutes and the short term problems would be solved – or so I thought. She rejected that offer as well saying that she wanted to sit alone with the children on another table and that she also wanted Richard to be in the near vicinity. I thought she'd gone mad for a moment but again I soon realized that she was serious.

By now she was starting to get on my nerves a little with her petty ways. I had spent 18 months trying to get her to speak to her children and now here she was in the same room as me and she was arguing about minor details. Had the tables been reversed I'm sure that I would have wanted to see my children under any circumstances. I said that I had had enough of her nonsense and that she could either take it or leave it as I wasn't prepared to offer any more at this stage. In my reply I also added a couple of issues that had been raised during the last year or so, to give her an indication that things weren't well, and that we had proof regarding a lot of the things that had gone on. I gather that there were raised eyebrows in the room as the details were discussed; apparently Kate had gone to her solicitors stating that I had refused to allow her access to the children and due to that her legal team wasn't actually aware of the social services or police involvement. It seems she had tried to mislead them and now she was slowly getting found out. Again it was almost pitiful to watch as she continued to proclaim her innocence even when faced with such overwhelming evidence against her; she just wasn't going to admit that she may be wrong. The problem was that I didn't feel that we were going to get anywhere if she didn't change her attitude, and begin to adjust to the fact that I was now in charge of the children, and that fact was very unlikely to change no matter how many times we sat down to discuss it.

It's fair to say that a lot of people were making money out of our misery and misfortune and yet there was no real effort being made to actually address the problem and tell Kate that her methods had been wrong. Unfortunately that might bring a speedy conclusion to the proceedings, and therefore all the legal people were saying that we couldn't tell her to change – how then were we meant to solve the problem? I didn't need to change anything as it was quite apparent that I was doing extremely well and so were the children, I was starting to get frustrated and confused. Why couldn't I just tell her some home truths face to face, I felt that within 10 minutes the problems would be solved if I could just get a couple of minor points across to her – it wasn't to be.

After another brief discussion with her legal team it was agreed that we would adjourn the case until after my sentencing in January. We would also allow Kate to telephone the children every Saturday from now up to January 11th 2005 and that we would also go and meet Kate at MacDonald's for a meal. Both myself and my legal team felt that it would be very unwise for me to put myself in a position alone with Kate. We therefore demanded that my brother be in attendance in MacDonald's with us, so that there would be no confusion as to what was said between both parties. Kate had already proved that she was a stranger to the truth and from now on I was determined to ensure that the little loophole was firmly closed. Slowly but surely we were making progress, although I have to say that it was painfully slow.

We could all go home now and start planning for Christmas, a big weight had been lifted from my mind and I knew in my heart that the correct way for us to proceed was to have the initial contact over the phone.

This was going to interesting as it was now the second time that I had arranged to meet Kate in MacDonald's. I waited with baited breath to find out if Kate might buy the children a meal or a milkshake, as the last time it hadn't occurred to her to offer. After 18 months away maybe this time she might actually spend some money on them, we would have to wait and see.

Just for the record we met her again and spent 2 hours with her in MacDonald's – at no time did she offer to buy either of the children a single item from the menu, it never occurred to her. How would you explain that to a 10 year old child? All my children wanted to do was go to school on the Monday and tell their friends that they had seen their mother and she had bought them a MacDonald's, just like every other child in the country - unfortunately it wasn't to be.

At least now we could settle down to celebrate our first Christmas in our new home. I wanted this Christmas to be so special for all of us, we had been through so much and it would be a nice break from all the legal stuff to spend some quality time with my children. After a visit into the loft to retrieve the tree and decorations, I sat back and I was almost overcome with emotion as I watched with pride as both children created our Christmas display in earnest. I was just so thankful that any mental damage now appeared to be a distant memory for both of them, they felt safe, secure and free to express themselves and that was so nice to see. On a positive note, buying presents was so easy as all of the children's toys had to be replaced anyway thanks to the previous actions of Kate and Richard.

I was also aware that I needed to make a decision about how to explain the legal mess that I was in, to the children. I came to the conclusion that I wasn't going to do anything about it just yet. I would wait until after the New Year so that we could just sit back and enjoy the festive season, and then we could deal with everything else in the New Year.

The best news I had was something that couldn't be bought and that was that somehow I had managed to overcome 95% of the psychological damage that had been caused. As with most things in life money couldn't cure that, it had to be done by hard work, love and understanding, that was what we needed and I seemed to have that in abundance.

Christmas came and went and the next challenge would be

to enjoy the New Year. I decided that the best thing to do would be to spend new years eve at home with the children and that we would get together an assortment of party treats and make it another special family occasion, and so we did just that. I have to say it was the best New Year that I'd had in years.

Just as in previous years, before we knew it Christmas had come and gone and it was back to the usual routine of the school run and everything else that came with it, only in this case it meant going back to the solicitors 3 or 4 times a week trying to sort out the legal mess that unfortunately hadn't gone away. The civil case was now on hold for the time being, the challenge now was to address the criminal proceedings and to try and make some sense of what had happened.

My first big test in the New Year would be on 7th January, as this was the day that I had an appointment with the Basingstoke Probation Service. The appointment was for 2 hours and the idea was that the probation service would produce a 'social enquiry report' that would be handed to the judge in my case. Hopefully he would then read it before passing sentence. Within it would be details regarding my personal background, my offence and also any recommendations regarding possible sentence. The problem was that at the hearing just before Christmas the judge had said that I should go home and sort things out because when I returned in the new year, it was *almost inevitable* that I would face a lengthy custodial sentence.

As the day approached I was obviously very apprehensive about the whole thing, a bad report would certainly mean prison, although it has to be said that I was facing exactly that anyway. A few years previously some mighty jobs worth somewhere had decided that it was time to stop handing out suspended sentences to criminals. The power to recommend such leniency had been removed from the probation service's agenda and it was now down to the sole discretion of the judge as to whether or not you would be a suitable candidate to be given what amounts to, a harsh telling off. I wasn't going to hold my breath for that one as I was facing charges of interfering with the law itself, ok if I had beaten up a defenseless member of the public they would probably let me off, but to have the audacity to question British law – I was hardly in a position to ask for mercy was I.

I had a 2 hour meeting with probation that day and I also returned 2 days later for a follow up visit to discuss the report in more detail, as my case officer was having difficulty getting to grips with the complexity of my case. I have to say that seeing her sat there in front of me, holding her head in her hands, didn't exactly fill me with confidence. All I want to say about that report is that despite speaking to my solicitor, social services and the child protection team within Basingstoke police, the writer of the report totally failed to grasp the severity of the situation. Knowing full well that I was facing about 4 years in prison, the summery at the end of the social enquiry report recommended a type of community punishment order. It only took me seconds to realize that when the judge read it, he would quickly come to the conclusion that whoever wrote it must have been half asleep at the time or at the very least, had shown little understanding of the law. What I was being accused of was legal sacrilege and there was little doubt that if it were legal they would hang me for it, as it was they couldn't but that didn't mean that they were going to let me off with a community punishment order, my only hope had always been a suspended prison term but unfortunately the report didn't mention that as an option.

As I left the building it was really starting to bother me that I needed to speak to the children about what was going on with regard to criminal proceedings against me. My son's birthday was coming up and I was due in court 4 days before hand, and I was highly likely to be going away for a considerable amount of time. Could you have told him after everything he had been through recently, remember he didn't start this; he was sat in his class working hard when these events first started. Sure he had seen his sister being hit but they all went off to school afterwards. The next thing he knew 2 uniformed police officers from the child protection team came to his classroom and told him to go with them to the hospital, where he found his big sister getting treatment. Imagine the fear in his eyes already, he lived in a very controlled environment and I bet that child was absolutely terrified about what would happen to him when he was eventually sent home. Thankfully he never was, but although I don't want to sound bitter, my view would be that it would have helped the initial situation if plain clothed police officers had attended the junior school – apparently there were none available on the day!

Over the last year or so my son has constantly looked to me for reassurance and support and now I had to sit him down and explain to him that I had messed up and was going to prison for a few years. Just sit there for a moment and try to imagine how I felt, inside I was distraught. You can flick to the next page and continue reading this book but I had to carry that thought around with me in the back of my mind for months, and as the time passed, the weight got heavier and heavier. In your heart do you really believe that I was such a bad individual that I should loose custody of my children, maybe you do and you have that individual right but I have to say that if we met on the street then I have no doubt that I would find you a very very sad individual.

For my defense to the criminal charges I knew that I would have to prove that I was an excellent father to the Judge who was due to sentence me for my crimes. I therefore decided to contact various official bodies regarding updated statements on the children's progress since they had been in my care. Letters were written to the child protection team at Basingstoke social services and to both of the children's schools. Although I knew we were trying our luck a bit, we also sent one to the case officer in charge of the children's case at Basingstoke police station. I knew that one section of the Thames valley police force was very unlikely to give any support to an individual when their criminal case was being dealt with by the serious crime squad based within the same force, but these were desperate times and in turn called for desperate measures – the letter was sent. I felt that if I could prove a significant improvement in the general wellbeing and social development of my children, then there was a small chance that I may escape my imminent imprisonment. When asked what the likelihood was of that happening, my barrister Mr. Robert Pulson informed me that I had a 2% or 3% chance of getting this thing suspended. My advice to you would be that when you get offered those types of odds, then don't play the game unless you have an extremely large set of bollox – you'll soon see that you'll need them.

While I waited for the replies to come in I spent my time doing various jobs about the house. I had explained the full situation to my immediate family and between us we started the process of sorting out what we would do with my house if I ended up in prison. It was so important that somehow we kept the house as we'd fought so hard to get it in the first place, to go and loose it now would be a crime in itself.

I also tidied the garden and did any last minute repair jobs that needed doing. I enjoyed pottering about but couldn't seem to shake of the depressive thoughts that followed me around every hour of every day, I'd really messed up and the pressure was starting to show. As a mature individual I didn't need telling, I was right in it up to my neck and I still hadn't explained it to the children, I just couldn't bring myself to do it no matter how hard I tried.

Another job that needed doing but thankfully I didn't have to do it, was the drawing up of 2 emergency care orders for the children. These were needed as both the Social Services and the Police were actively blocking Kate's application for custody of our children. Believe me if you don't think that what I'm trying to tell you is serious then you should now. I now had to watch as forms were completed to place my children into care, and I had to do it knowing that I faced 4 years in prison before I would ever get the chance to fully explain the things I was being accused of. It's on days like this that you really feel the pressure. That was one of the hardest days of my life so far, care orders my god what had I done.

Slowly the references that we had requested started to land on my desk and the pattern was clear. Everyone was so supportive of my cause. The schools were my best hope as they had been dealing with me on a day to day basis very closely now for quite a long period of time. What they had written turned out to be excellent news. They had the advantage of being in a position to see any improvement in the children on a daily basis, so I felt that it was imperative that their references were good. Anything negative at all would have been the end for me. Thank god they got it right. I have to say that both schools did me proud and I will owe them a dept of gratitude for a very long time. They were more aware than most about how difficult Kate and Richard were to deal with and were probably glad to see the back of them anyway.

Social services were in a difficult position and as they hadn't been involved with me for over a year now. They felt that they would be unable to give an updated report simply because they hadn't been involved with us as a family for so long. They added that in effect that was success in itself, as it meant that not only did they think that I was very capable of looking after my children but also in their opinion I was free to continue to do so. I wrote back to them trying to get something a little firmer to take to court with us. After all they were at the centre of the whole situation and it would be ridiculous to go to court facing such serious charges without getting the strongest possible statement from them.

A few days later they responded in writing by saying that they would definitely object to Kate ever having custody of her children again, in light of the evidence that they held on file. Under the circumstances I couldn't understand why hadn't they just said that when they were first asked. That question along with a few others will probably remain unanswered. They knew the truth about what had gone on but getting them to put in down in words was like trying to get blood from a stone.

I want to make it clear that on a personal level I had no problem with my allocated social worker; in fact she couldn't have done more for us as an individual. It was social services policy that was causing me great concern. In short they come in and tear families apart and then just disappear if you are deemed capable of looking after yourself. Due to the major changes in child law over the last 2 years, social services are absolutely buried in cases to deal with at the moment and can't possibly give all the help and support that families in this type of situation require. I needed a hell of a lot of emotional support as well as support with my housing application and various other problems caused by events such as these – unfortunately this wasn't forthcoming and that raises concerns for all the unfortunate individuals who are likely to find themselves in the same situation as me in the future.

It was around this time that I had my first piece of really good news. I received a reply from the police officer based in the child protection unit who had been involved in my case from the very beginning. It said that he too would object to Kate having custody of our children due to the evidence he was holding on the police videos. This was a major breakthrough as the child protection unit carried a lot of weight in a court room and the fact that they felt strongly enough as to put their feelings into words spoke not only very highly of me, but also of them as individuals. At last we had an official body saying what they thought and what they believed in their heart, instead of what they were allowed to say due to red tape. I knew in my heart that this statement would probably be a very powerful tool in my battle to retain my liberty. Once all the replies were back, all we could do was sit and wait. It's the loneliest feeling in the world when you have to wait like that. The judge had already told me that it was *'almost inevitable'* that I would face a lengthy custodial sentence, but having to wait what felt like an eternity to receive my punishment was a form of punishment in itself.

In the days leading up to my criminal case, my son was due a routine eye test. He had been issued with glasses while in the care of Kate and had been wearing them now for about 3 years. I had always been led to believe that he should wear them 24/7, as this is what I and everyone else had been told by Kate. I was therefore amazed when, during my first visit to the opticians, I was informed that he should only be wearing them for reading the board at school if he was too far away to see the writing without his glasses. I hadn't seen my son without them on for over 3 years. I'm not going to try and explain what sort of perverted gratification my ex-wife got from making a 9 year old boy wear glasses that he didn't need, to such an extent that it would probably permanently damage his eyesight. I've tried to understand her pattern of thought but I'm afraid that I just don't understand it at all; if you can then you're ahead of me already. In my opinion these are the things that cause the most psychological damage, unfortunately they are also the things that are the most difficult to convey across a court room to a judge.

While at the civil court at the earlier hearing, Kate had been made aware of the glasses issue for the first time and so this eye test was very important, as the first thing I had done when my son arrived was try to reduce the hours that he spent wearing his glasses. The problem was that he had been totally brainwashed, and even though Kate wasn't around he was still very fearful of being seen without them in case someone told his mum. The question now was that as he had spent some time following the recommended advice from the opticians, would there be any improvement in his eyesight? Had I done the right thing? I needed to know to put my mind at ease. I was very apprehensive on the way down there. What if they said his eyes had got worse? How would I feel then? In the end the eye test showed a major improvement in both eyes and not only was I overjoyed but so was my son. For years he had been fed negative thoughts and advice about how his eyes were getting worse and various other things and now we had someone who he trusted telling him that they had improved dramatically – he knew his dad was right, he knew his dad wouldn't let him down and he hadn't. Whenever our eyes met all I ever saw in my son was total belief in his father, that everything would be ok as long as his dad was there. At the back of my mind I was really starting to worry what the effect of my imprisonment would mean to him. I knew he would be absolutely devastated.

All I could do now was sit and wait for the moment of truth to arrive and as I did so, all I had for company was the same old thought flying through my mind every minute of every day, asking me when I intended to speak to the children. That was going to be so hard but it still needed to be done. How would I explain things? Where would I start and how the hell would I finish? I hope from the bottom of my heart that you never have to make such an important decision; no man should ever have to ponder such thoughts.

All in all I felt that we had done all that we could. We had received such a positive response from everyone involved that I must at least stand a chance of getting a suspended sentence; now all we needed was a fair and compassionate judge.

On Tuesday 11th January 2005 I was due to appear at Southwark Crown Court in London to be sentenced. In line with my never say die attitude, I bought myself a return ticket to London bridge on the train. I've no idea why as I was in no doubt that my chances of coming home were slim to say the least. Maybe it was one final act of defiance, maybe it was ignorance or maybe it was just foolish, whatever the reason as I approached the ticket payment office I had absolutely no doubt that I was going to buy a return ticket, even if it was just to show my children one day, that I never gave up on them, and that even at the bitter end – my heart had wanted to come home to them.

My solicitor, Graeme McPherson was unable to make it to court that day due to other commitments and so his wife attended on his behalf. I liked him, he was a good man. Also with me was my barrister Mr. Robert Pulson. He was young and up for it and again I liked him, he was my sort of guy, very direct but likeable. As I entered the court house and approached Rob the expression on his face said it all, he looked like he was going to his best friend's funeral. His first words were 'What the hell happened at probation', and he went on to explain that the social enquiry report was a disaster. We needed a break and a good report would have been just that. He was devastated that it was below par and again put my chances at about 2% for getting a suspended sentence. We had a full house of excellent references but would it be enough.

Also present at the court that day were 2 police officers. The first was my arresting officer; he was a decent guy and had treated me with respect throughout the ordeal. He was in no way involved with all the shenanigans that were going on at the time. In fact over time he managed to change my perception of the police force in general. He was as straight as an arrow and a decent bloke.

The second was the officer in charge of the original case that dealt with the attack at the burger bar. Part of the accusations against me were that my actions had caused him severe anxiety and distress over a period of about 2 years, resulting in him being unable to function in a normal manner either at work or at home. It's worth noting that one of the main reasons for me having to declare myself bankrupt in April 2004 was so that he would be unable to pursue me for financial compensation upon completion of the case. I felt sorry for him as I too had suffered severe emotional trauma during the last couple of years, but not so sorry that I was going to pay for his early retirement!

The case started with the prosecuting barrister standing up and outlining the crowns case against me. It was alleged that between 28/11/02 and 7/04/04, I had attempted to pervert the course of justice on 3 occasions. Firstly it was alleged that in November 2002 I had given a statement regarding events that had occurred at 1.30am one Saturday night in February 2001, at a burger van outside a nightclub in Basingstoke. It was also alleged that in March 2003 I amended that statement, and finally it was alleged that in April 2004 I had gone to the Royal Courts Of Justice in the Strand/London and given evidence at the high court appeal of Ivor and Brian Aubrey of Sherborne St John, Basingstoke, against their conviction for causing a section 18 GBH with Intent. This appeal was not against their respective sentences of four and a half years and six years but was to actually overturn their conviction and prove it unsafe.

As I had pleaded guilty at an earlier hearing, when the prosecutor had finished it was then the turn of my barrister to address the court. He explained my current situation as best he could and also that my situation had changed dramatically over the last couple of years. He added that I now had custody of my children. He went on to produce all the written evidence that we had gathered, along with school reports and various other items that we hoped would convince the judge to let me retain my liberty.

Once everything was handed in the judge announced that he would adjourn the case for a few hours while he read through all the case notes, it was approximately 11.50am. I was given bail by the court but not allowed to leave the court building. I went and sat in the restaurant to dwell alone with my thoughts. I had to be strong; today was going to be a massive test of character for me as I stood a very real chance of losing everything, both financially and emotionally.

At about 2.25pm I was informed by the court usher that the judge would be ready in 20 minutes. If you were religiously inclined then now was the time to pray, personally it was chin up, chest out, eyes straight ahead like a real man. Whatever was coming I was now ready for it – I knew I had to be so strong mentally, not only for myself but also for my immediate family.

We gathered all the paperwork together and then I took a

deep breath and followed Rob into the courtroom to hear my fate. The two police officers and the press followed behind us. As they all marched straight ahead I was guided round to the right and towards the side door of the dock. I was greeted at the door by a prison officer who was to stand guard during the proceedings. It had been a while since I had stood in the dock and maybe I had forgotten what would happen, but I have to say that it didn't fill me with confidence to see a prison officer sat 3 feet from me the whole time I was in there. No words can describe how a man feels when he is stood in the dock facing such serious charges so I'm not going to try. Everyone in the room knows that you're about to go to prison for a long time as they deal with this type of thing every day, in the end it becomes part of the job. My own thoughts searched back to when I was last in prison. The strip search on the way in and the cold shower before having to wear those starch filled clothes again. I sat down, crossed my fingers and hoped that I would get a compassionate judge today.

Over to my left sat the press officer who scribbled away for all he was worth for the next 50 minutes or so, desperately trying to keep up as he didn't want to miss any of the gory details. We all stood as the judge entered the room from a rear entrance, he walked to his desk and sat himself down. After a quick drink of water he looked towards me and launched his tirade.

Mr. Laurence, he said, *you have caused a hell of a lot of heartache and distress to a lot of people with the actions you carried out over a period of nearly 3 years. Along the way you have failed on every occasion to give any explanation at all for your actions. Despite twice being interviewed by the serious crime squad for a total of over 2 hours, the only words you have uttered are 'no comment'. You were then asked again by the probation service to give an explanation as to why you did the things you are accused of - and again you failed to give any satisfactory explanation of your deeds, in fact you attempted to mislead them. Along the way you have also caused a severe amount of stress, discomfort and anxiety to the police officer in charge of the case because as a result of your actions he was put in a position where his integrity had been impugned.*

You have also undermined the integrity of the main witness in the original case who has been proved to be an upstanding member of the community. In short you are a disgrace and you should be ashamed of yourself and your actions. In my view this was a professional attempt to strike an arrow at the heart of the British legal system. Had you not come up against such an experienced prosecutor as MR. Steven Parish, then it's my view that you may very well have succeeded in your quest.

I now have to decide what sentence to pass for your crimes. The problem that I have here is that I have been unable to find any similar case anywhere in the country with which to make a comparison. Not only did you give a statement, you then went on to amend it and then further still, you attended the Royal Court and lied, and you kept that up for 3 years – you should be ashamed of yourself. The only thing in your favour is the fact that you have saved a lot of the courts time with your guilty plea, although you still haven't given a satisfactory explanation to the events.

I actually felt that I had given a satisfactory explanation but as it wasn't what they wanted to hear - no one would listen. Whatever view you choose to take, the facts were that these 2 men were doing a job of work, they weren't a pair of thugs charging round the countryside beating people up. They were running a security business in the centre of Basingstoke and were being paid to help keep law and order.

It is a fact that there is a major drug culture in most towns across the country and believe me, when someone over 6 feet tall decides to drink large amounts of alcohol mixed with a cocktail of various drugs including cocaine, then they can become extremely violent. You've probably been affected in some way yourself by the level of violence that goes on in the centre of most towns today and where are the police when things like this get out of hand? Who is going to stop the violence at street level? It's all well and good to play the wise man after the event and to say that things should have been done differently, unfortunately when faced with such serious levels of violence a decision has to be made very quickly on the spot and so it's not surprising that occasionally things will go wrong.

It is a fact that the victim of the original assault is well known in the town and on this particular occasion had already attacked 4 innocent people that night that I am aware of, all of whom sustained some type of injury. Can you really put your hand on your heart and say that he was hard done by. Maybe he got his just deserts and maybe before he started complaining about how someone had come along and beaten him up, he should have thought a little more about what he was doing to those innocent members of the public who were just queuing up to buy a burger after a night out. I don't hear many complaints when a known trouble maker is physically removed from a pub by the very same men after ruining your mothers Christmas work do. Someone somewhere has to start putting some sanity back into our legal system. What happened may not be ideal but it is effective. Can you look me in the eye and convince me that the courts are dealing with the street violence effectively on your behalf?

The judge went on; *Mr. Laurence the conclusion that I have come to is that you should serve a punishment of 4 or 5 years in prison, having taken into account your guilty plea, for which I can give you a reduction of 1 year, I am still left with a sentence of between 3 and 4 years. As you are aware there are other factors in this case that require my attention. You will be aware that it is down to the sole discretion of the judge as* to whether or not it is suitable to impose a suspended sentence. I have looked at all the evidence and in particular the statement given by the child protection unit based within the Thames Valley force. It's ironic isn't it Mr. Laurence that over to my right is a police officer who you have caused such distress, and yet in my hand is a statement from one of his colleagues within the same force that supports you as a father and also raises serious concerns as to whether or not your ex-wife would be fit to care for the children in your absence, think about that Mr. Laurence, again you should be ashamed of yourself and your actions.

I have read all the documentation and it's clear that you are indeed a very good father who has been through so much over the last year or so. Having looked at all the information I have decided that if I put you into prison today then this will have a damaging effect on both your children who have come to be so dependant on you.

The problem that I have is that your offence is so serious that I am duty bound to impose a lengthy custodial sentence. Unfortunately the law only allows me to suspend a sentence of up to 2 years in prison and that would not reflect the true nature of your crimes. Even with your year off for pleading guilty I am struggling to justify a sentence of 2 years, but its clear that I have no choice in the matter as there is a clear threat to the wellbeing of your children should you loose your liberty today. Mr. Laurence you are a disgrace and I hope that you can take no satisfaction at all from the fact that you are walking out of here today. You will retain your liberty due solely to the fact that you are a single parent with 2 dependent children and it is clear that they have suffered enough recently. The biggest crime committed here today is the fact that I now have to watch you walk out of this room a free man after all the problems that you have caused – you really should be ashamed of yourself and your actions.

There was silence in the room as the oak door at the front of the dock was opened and it slowly dawned on me that I was now a free man, I was so relieved that at last it was all over. The pressure had been overwhelming to say the least but now it was over. I walked past the officer guarding the door and made my way out of the court.

Out in the corridor there was a lot of handshaking and general bullshit. I was in no mood to be humoured by a load of suits, I just wanted to get home and hug the children. This case had almost cost me more that I should ever have been asked to give, not financially but emotionally. For me, standing in the corridor that day there was no victory celebration as I felt I had nothing to celebrate. I still had to go home and face the civil case that had been triggered by my actions and so I didn't feel like laughing or jumping for joy, as the battle was only half won, if it had been won at all. In situations like these there are no winners or losers, so all I can say is that in my view the result was the right one and we will leave it at that.

Thankfully I already had my return ticket in my pocket so I didn't need to stop for anything on the way home. I was so relieved and I just wanted to get back home as soon as possible and shut the door, then I could run a nice hot bath and absorb the day's events.

I arrived home at about 5.30pm and I was totally exhausted from the day's events. I made my way upstairs and fulfilled the promise that I had made to myself earlier in the day. I ran a hot bath full of bubbles, climbed in and soaked for about an hour. As I sat there I could feel the tension filtering through my body and escaping into the steam filled air that surrounded me. All the pressure just seemed to disappear and a feeling of complete and utter calm came over me unlike anything I had experienced before. Tuesday 11th January 2005 is a day I shall remember for a very long time.

I awoke the following morning feeling invigorated. I honestly felt like I was floating on air as I moved around the house. During the night I'd dreamt that I was back in cell B16 on the 3's in Winchester Prison and it was such a relief to open my eyes and realize that it was just a dream; it could so very easily have been my reality for the next couple of years at least.

The day after, on the Thursday, I knew that I had to explain everything to the children. I knew I'd taken a big gamble by not telling them before I went off to court earlier in the week but if you had lived through all this with us day by day, then you would have seen what I had to see every single day, and that was that both children would be absolutely devastated if I hadn't come home. Now I'd run out of time and there was little doubt that I needed to sit them down and talk to them before the local paper printed a report on Friday morning.

Like everything in life it wasn't as difficult as I had at first imagined it would be. I went on to explain to them that everything was now ok. They were shocked but I believe that this was mainly due to the fact that I had made great efforts not to pollute their young minds with all the negative legal arguments that had been going on. I knew in the back of my mind that one day Kate would have to return and so I had decided at the beginning that my long term success depended a lot on what I did or didn't say to the children about their mother and various other things that had been going on over the last 2 years. As it turned out both children took it well and they were just relieved that I was still here. It's doubtful that the full consequences of my actions were understood by either of them due to their age but one day they would understand, and in my heart I think I did the right thing.

It's ironic but just for the record nothing was ever published in the local paper regarding my court appearance for perverting the course of justice on the following morning. In fact nothing appeared for about 3 weeks and then, just as I was about to breath a huge sigh of relief, there it was staring me right in the face on page 5 of the local gazette.

Over the following week I had to attend various appointments at the solicitors dealing with the civil issue, although now it felt like my problems had been more than halved. During one of these visits I realized that my life was definitely starting to change for the better. I'd battled against not only the system now for 2 years but also myself, slowly but surely we were starting to turn the corner and we were beginning to move forward. As I had been so preoccupied with all the legal details while I was in the criminal court I hadn't realized one very important fact, a fact that was to be pointed out to me by my solicitor. She explained that as I had been given a suspended sentence by the crown court solely on the basis that I was the full time career of the children and therefore needed to retain my liberty, coupled with the fact that we now had statements supporting my positive achievements with the children, then there wasn't a court in the land who would award custody of the children under those circumstances to my ex-wife.

Both the police and social services had made it clear in writing that they would appose any application from Kate to regain custody of the children and they had also confirmed their support for me as a suitable individual to take care of their emotional and educational needs. In effect we had won the civil case hands down and it would now be only a matter of time before Kate would be bought into line with what was to be expected of her. In short she could now take it or leave it as the arguments were well and truly over. I was so relieved to hear those words.

I believe that having read all of the above you would feel that the chances of Kate gaining any form of custody was minimal, but I have to say that the law works in mysterious ways and my advice to you would be never presume anything when it comes to the law. I say that from experience as I've been through it, and although what had happened had been a nightmare, believe it or not Kate still has a legal right to challenge the decisions made by all the bodies involved, either now or at any time in the future. My own personal opinion is that things need to change – how many chances should individuals get after such events, for me there is no grey area and everything should be kept black and white – she had been proved unfit to look after them and that should have been the end of it. Was it really necessary to put myself and my children through 2 years of heartache when she had made no effort at all to address the problems, in fact she had deliberately gone out of her way to make things more difficult for us. Why therefore does the law support such individuals in their application for custody? Forgive me for being cynical but it's simply because there is so much money to be made from other people's misery and that I'm afraid is a very sad state of affairs to end up in. My view is that this needs to change - it's a crazy world that we live in. Surely the law of the land should always be based upon common sense, and common sense was telling everyone involved that she was an unfit mother and there was absolutely no doubt about that.

Whilst at the solicitors I was also received confirmation that my civil case was due to be heard at the county court again, in Basingstoke on Thursday 3rd February at 11am. I was asked to go home and think about various issues including more phone calls and access to the children for Kate, if she still wanted it now that she knew I was a free man. Generally I had to sit down and draw up a plan that would be put to her at the next meeting. She could then either except what I was proposing and we could all begin to move forward or she could dismiss all of it and go ahead with her application for full custody, which was now generally regarded as being a bit of a none starter for her – I presumed she would probably choose to pursue her application for full custody just to cause us more discomfort but for now we would just have to wait and see.

The case was now 2 weeks away and as I sat down to make my list I knew that it would be very straight forward. I'd known since day one what I intended to do and in my view nothing had changed. My proposals were as follows 1) Richard was not to come anywhere near either myself or my 2 children. Kate and Richard both drive and they have 4 cars between them due to Richard's interest in mechanics. I therefore felt that there was no need for him to drop Kate off at my house either now or at any time in the future. Both children had said from day one up to the present day that they had no wish to see him again. 2) Kate's mother was not to be alone with either of my children until such time that I was completely satisfied that she was no longer a threat to my children. I proposed to ask the court to review this issue in 6 months time. 3) Kate could telephone the children at any reasonable time as long as the call was made to my mobile so that I could monitor what was being said. I proposed to ask the court to review this issue in 6 months. 4) All access visits by Kate would be personally supervised by me until such time as I was convinced that there was no longer a threat to either of them. These visits would be every other week for a period of 2 hours and would generally be held at my home address or at another venue with my consent. None of the above was now going to be negotiable, she could take it and we could move on or she could leave it and we could set a court date to get the matter sorted out once and for all – either way I couldn't care less now as I was looking forward to the future for the first time in a long time. The journey to get here had been hell but I was so glad that I'd hung in there on all those dark days because now it was looking more and more like a one way argument.

During the last court hearing we had agreed that Kate could call the children every Saturday at 10.30am. The court had ordered that these calls had to be made to my mobile phone so that I could use the loud speaker setting to enable the calls to be monitored. It's a very sad situation where an individual is in a position where they have to monitor phone calls between mother and children and yet that's exactly the position that I found myself in. It's interesting to note that at this point in time we had received about 7 phone calls from Kate to speak to both children and although she spoke to the children relatively nicely, she still wouldn't utter the word sorry. It was clear that she still didn't except that she had done anything wrong.

During the calls despite being clearly told by the court not to make direct invitations or promises of days out to the children, she repeatedly asked them to go out for the day with her. It doesn't seem much but you have to remember this is a very aggressive and controlling women who was capable of just about anything if she didn't get her own way, and so I didn't want her pressuring the children to go somewhere that they didn't really want to go.

It was during one of these calls that my son invited his mother to his 11th birthday party that was to be held at our home address. At first I was so very surprised that she had excepted the invitation because it was only a couple of weeks previously that the same women had sat in a county court saying that she didn't feel safe visiting my home address. She even stated that she didn't feel safe in the court house or even in MacDonald's and yet now somehow she had mysteriously conquered her fears and suddenly felt like turning up at my place for ice cream and jelly. It's hard not to think that at the very least she was unbalanced in some way or maybe she just suffered from a form of distorted thinking. Whatever, she was coming to my son's birthday party and if that's what he wanted then it was fine by me.

She turned up bold as brass and sat there in my dining room as though nothing had happened. Had it been any other individual I would have struggled to have believed their cheek but as it was Kate, I knew that I would have to just accept her ignorance. It's fair to say that there was an uncomfortable feeling in the house for the two and a half hours that she was there, but at least a face to face meeting had taken place between all of us and no one had been injured – to me this was success.

I have to say that in all honestly I could see that Kate's visit had been a positive experience for both children and that was all I was interested in. I'd left behind any negative thoughts months ago and now just wanted to improve our general situation as a family. It wasn't going to be easy putting things back together but it was something that was going to have to be done. Whichever way you look at the problem we were always going to have to put mother and children together at some point, my job was to ensure that for the time being I was going to be present when that happened. Now we had got the first meeting over with I hoped it would become easier for us to start moving forward and make some real progress over the coming months.

The days quickly passed and before I knew it Thursday 3rd February was upon us and the time had come for me to attend the local County Court to sort out the civil case. Before my sentencing for perverting the course of justice, Kate had made a court application for 'full custody' of both children. It would be interesting now to see how things turned out, as I was still here and a free man. I had a feeling that this minor detail had thrown a major spanner into the works for Kate. I don't think for one minute that she expected to be dealing with me personally from now on, she must have thought that I would be long gone down the slippery slope of life. Well she was now in for one hell of a shock as I was most definitely still here.

I arrived at the court at about 10am and met up with my legal representative once again. We went straight into the side room just as we had done before. We sat down and went through my list of proposals. That was it, job done. Now all we needed was for Kate to arrive so we could get this sorted. I had a feeling that I was in for a short day at the court this time. I didn't have much to say and I certainly had no intention of negotiating over it – now it was my way or the high way, the choice was hers.

She arrived and to my surprise we had a different Kate on our hands. Gone was the silly little schoolgirl who at the previous hearing had claimed to be too scared to even sit in a room with me, and in her place we had a very cooperative Kate – she was even smiling at one point in the conversation. I guess having suddenly been brave enough to attend my son's 11th birthday party at my home address 10 days earlier had removed the effectiveness of that excuse and so she would now have to come up with something new. I got the impression that it really didn't matter what she came up with as there didn't seem to be anyone apart from her immediate family that was either listening or interested anymore in anything that she had to say. This time everyone could see straight through her and no one was interested anymore about how she felt. The truth was starting to come out at long last, as it always does.

She was now faced with extremely strong evidence to support my actions over the last 2 years. Both schools had given very strong statements regarding my ability to care for the children, so had the social services and also the police. The simple fact that I was not in prison had proved beyond any doubt that my credentials had been proven over a period of nearly 2 years, and that was a fact whether Kate liked it or not. Everyone agreed that I had been a very positive influence on both children. They also agreed that both Kate and Richard had been a very negative influence on them, now there was nowhere left for her to turn and she would have to accept that I was now going to be responsible for the children and very capable of doing so for the rest of their lives. At last we had things the way I like them – in black and white!

We went through the motions while Kate tried to argue about every detail, saying how unfair all of this was on her as she hadn't done anything wrong and how it was all some big mistake. To be honest I felt like giving her a copy of the Kenny Rogers song 'The Gambler', in which he sings the following lines – *'You got to know when to hold em, you got to know when to fold em, you've got to know when to walk away and know when to run'*. My opinion was that she would do well to listen to the words and take heed, good old Kenny knew what he was talking about when he sang those words. As an individual it's so very important to know when we are wrong and to admit it. I have learnt the hard way that if you admit you're mistakes there will always be a queue of people willing to help you, but if you just sit there in denial, blaming everyone around you then you will end up sad, lonely and alone – maybe that's just what she deserved.

As the time passed Kate continued to proclaim her innocence and to imply that that the reason for her absence over the past 2 years had been *'bad legal advice'*. She claimed that when she had been to visit a solicitor at the time and that he had advised her not to make an application for either custody or access for either of her children – on the grounds that *'The children probably didn't love her anymore'*. It was laughable really as we were sitting in a room full of legal executives at the time and yet Kate seemed to think that they might believe the nonsense she was now coming out with. My old friend Tony had once told me that it was often better to keep your mouth shut and let the world think that you are a fool, rather that to open your mouth and prove it. Poor Kate, she obviously hadn't heard that expression before – still, it was amusing watching her make such a complete fool of herself.

By this point even the legal people had heard enough and so the decision was taken to show Kate some of the allegations against her. It had taken me 18 months of legal wrangling to get all of us into this position and now for the first time, I was going to get a chance to tell her first hand what I believed had actually gone on, and I was in a position to hear any reply that she might make. I'd waited a long time for this but in all honesty it was an anti climax. She was shown various statements from people who directly criticized the *'controlling and aggressive manner in which she treated her children'*. For the first time she now had it in black and white, even she should be able to understand the situation now that it was right before her very eyes. She was then left alone with her legal team to discuss the offer that had been put to them. I've no idea what was said in that room but by the time they returned we now had a slightly subdued Kate on our hands. Her representative went on to explain that she was willing to drop her court application for full custody and replace it with an application for access only – based on the condition that I would allow her to take the children out for the day. Needless to say I turned down her offer immediately – these weren't family pets that we were dealing with, these were my children and there was going to be absolutely no negotiating from me what so ever.

I then went on to make Kate an offer which she could either take or leave. Firstly she could call the children on alternative Saturdays at 10.30am with immediate effect. Secondly she could visit our home address on alternate Saturdays between 11am and 1pm to see the children. This was to be supervised by me personally for a period of 6 months, at which time we would return to court to review the situation. On these visits she could bring either her sister, brother, mother and father. At this point I was informed that legally I couldn't single out Kate's mother despite the fact that there was obviously a problem between the three of us and her. This was just another legal decision that was beyond belief. In legal terms she hadn't committed any offence by shouting obscenities at me in the supermarket or indeed by upsetting the whole house on my son's 10th birthday party at my home address. The best that I could do was to make it very clear that if any of her family wished to visit the children with Kate, then she would first need to obtain my permission over the phone.

Despite the fact that the law wouldn't let me block access to my children by Kate's mother, I held my ground and informed everyone at the court that she would not be welcome at my home address for the foreseeable future and that I couldn't care less who told me otherwise. I knew that she posed a direct threat to the welfare of my children and I had no intention of letting her undermine the solid foundations that I was trying to build within my home. It was going to be a long time before I could forget what she had done on my son's 10th birthday in my old flat in Tadley, plus neither of the children ever gave her much thought anyway. Thirdly I demanded that Richard was not be come anywhere near either myself or either of my children as none of us wished to see him.

I refused to negotiate on any of the points that I had raised and so after an hour we found ourselves sat before the judge once again, this time to get the court order drawn up. We went through the motions and this time the judge ordered that all my requests were reasonable and were backed up with hard proof, there could therefore be no argument as to who was right and who was wrong. He went on to draw up the order that covered all of my requests, adding that we would meet again in 6 months to review the situation regarding Kate and her mother. The judge also demanded that Kate sign a court declaration there and then, which stated that she would not allow either of my children to come into any form of contact with Richard for any reason. The order also stated that he was not to attend my home address for any reason, not even to drop off or collect Kate from my house. The judge explained clearly to her that if either child did come into direct contact with her husband then she was liable to imprisonment. He added that if things didn't improve in 6 months then he would order that the initial conditions would stand again for a further 6 months or until such time as Kate opened her eyes and accepted that what she had done was wrong. He went on to make it clear that her actions would not be, and could not be tolerated within our society.

Its worth noting that although the court order stated that Kate must prevent Richard from approaching the children, I was very well aware that English law could not and would not be able to hold one individual responsible for the actions of another. In reality this meant that should Richard choose to ignore the instructions of the court then the law would be powerless to enforce its own court order due to the simple fact that he personally had not been asked to sign it – despite the fact that he had been present when it had been drawn up and signed. Once again I was left with that familiar feeling that I was being humoured a little by those in authority. It is a fact that the court order was completely worthless and I therefore see no point in wrapping it up any other way. Once again those making the decisions should be very thankful that we haven't found ourselves in the position where we would have to enforce it. In my opinion this had been more luck than judgment as there had definitely been days when I felt that this order was going to be needed.

In essence I guess that a major victory had been won and I left the building feeling like we had at last reached some sort of closure. It really didn't matter to me now whether or not Kate made the effort to change, as now it was clear that she would find herself isolated from her children permanently if she didn't make some serious changes to her attitude and opinion during the next few months.

Personally this has never been about revenge, as I was well above all that. This had been about what is morally right for my children and the most frustrating bit about everything was the fact that Kate couldn't see how well we were doing. Had she bothered to stop and look she would see that between us we had 2 beautiful children who were evolving into their own individual characters and I couldn't help thinking how sad it was that she was missing so much of their young lives due solely to her own ignorance. My father had always said that there are some people that you just can't help in this world, and I had accepted long ago that Kate was just one of those people.

It was now the first week of February in 2005 and the Child Support Agency had still not finalized my claim, although they had assured me that they were dealing with it on an urgent basis. I have to say that personally I don't believe that any responsible individual should need any third party to tell them to pay towards the upkeep of their children. If a contribution is not being made by either party then I feel that this in itself should raise serious questions as to whether or not such individuals should be allowed care and control of any child. Children are our future and should be loved and nurtured for the whole of their lives and yet so many adults just seem to use them as pawns in a bigger game for their own personal gratification, and that my friend is the saddest thing of all.

At this point, following my courtroom success, I decided to put all my efforts into trying to resolve the problems that I was still having with the Child Support Agency. I'd written and phoned so many times that I had eventually lost count, and so I sent the complete file to my local MP for him to try and resolve. Finally maybe all the pressure would start to have the desired effect. Sure they promised to sort it out on an urgent basis, sure they promised to retrieve the maintenance from Kate on my behalf but the fact remains that this is the 3rd time now that I've heard these promises down my phone, and so due to that it's fair to say that I'm not going to hold my breath until I am actually holding the cheque from them in my hand. I have to say that in my opinion the CSA is a complete shambles and in short whichever way you look at it, they have let me down big time. Even with my MP on board things were still moving at a snail's pace.

During the next week I did receive a courtesy call from the CSA, but unfortunately the only news they had for me was the fact that they 'hadn't received the paperwork yet'. It was now getting beyond belief, it really was. Another seven weeks then passed while I waited for confirmation that my claim had actually been started. It then became clear that nothing had been done and so at this point I decided to write again to my local MP in order to keep the pressure on. I duly posted the letter and sat back to await the response – surely if I put enough pressure on my MP then they would at the very least feel obliged to start my application!

While I was waiting for a response from the CSA it was time for the first visit from Kate to my home address. She turned up with her sister. Immediately we got off to a bad start as Kate had already failed to follow the court's instruction as she had failed to phone me to inform me of whom, if anyone would be coming with her during the visit. She hadn't even walked through the door yet and she had failed to do what the court had requested of her. You tell me: How do you deal with someone with such ignorance? The courts allow these fools to be granted access to their children and yet here we were again in a situation where she was showing total disregard to all of their instructions and yet it didn't seem to matter.

Once again I was left to deal with the problem at ground level and once again it crossed my mind that we weren't achieving much in the courtroom, apart from making the solicitors slightly richer as we went along. I was now well past the point of complaining about it and so I let them both in and bit my tongue. Generally things went ok and I was just glad to get it out of the way. I now wanted a speedy solution so that I could return to full time employment in the near future. There was nothing else I could do legally now, so it was time to just get on with it. All I could really do is make sure that I was present with the children whenever Kate came over and anything else would have to work itself out. In my heart I knew that the situation would probably take years to settle in reality

Eventually even the Child Support Agency started to get their house in order, and on the 22nd February 2005 I received a letter confirming that at last they had managed to pick up the phone and finally make official contact with Kate. At least now the clock was ticking and Kate would be responsible for any maintenance due from this date forward. As I was still not working at this point, the letter explained that I would only be entitled to keep ten pounds per week from any monies collected. It also explained that as soon as I returned to full time employment I would then be entitled to keep all of the money due. The priority now was obviously going to be getting myself into a position where I could return to full time employment; at least then between us we could start to enjoy the benefit of my ex-wife's funds.

Words fail me when it comes to writing about the Child Support Agency, so in this case I will let the facts speak for themselves. So far it has taken them over 22 months to even begin my claim from my ex-wife. In that time seven and a half thousand pounds of outstanding maintenance had been written off, as it was confirmed to me in writing that the CSA were not going to pursue my ex-wife for any of the money owed. Just sit there for a moment and try to imagine how I felt considering the financial difficulties that were forced upon me by the tragic events of July 2003, and now I had to except that none of those funds were important enough to warrant collection.

Just for the record, in the beginning Kate had continued to cash the child benefit book while it was in her possession and I was powerless to stop it from happening. I know it sounds ridiculous under the circumstances but the Inland Revenue had written to me to confirm that in their opinion this money was also not worth pursuing, and so again I had lost out on more money due to me, due to the actions of my ex-wife. I have to say that I found this to be an absolute disgrace under the circumstances. That was very hard to take and I don't think I will ever except those decisions, or understand why it was that Kate was allowed to simply walk away from her financial obligations.

In my opinion she was the last person who deserved to be

shown such compassion. Wouldn't it be nice if I had a car loan totaling that amount and someone called me and said that I didn't have to repay any of the money – alas I can't see that happening can you? Decisions like that really do force me to wonder where the justice is in all of this, and I say that as a father who paid his maintenance and various other obligations for over 6 years without complaint.

At this point I realized that we had in fact reached some form of closure to another small part of the problem. The court case had been won and the CSA were now sorting out the financial side of things. Admittedly we had to go back for a review in the summer, but that was only to decide whether or not we could lift any of the restrictions that had been imposed.

In reality I was left with a feeling of total emptiness inside. I'm not sure what I had expected, but now everything felt like an anti climax. Nothing had been won at all, in fact however I looked at the situation the only conclusion I could come to is that as a family we had lost so much. The test now would be to maintain a positive attitude to enable us to sustain our growth in the long term. At least now I didn't have to go down to the solicitors three or four times a week, so hopefully I would also see a massive reduction in the number of stress related headaches that I had endured in recent months.

As planned the phone calls from Kate to the children and also the bi-weekly visits to our home address commenced. Although we were now moving forward at long last, we still had the same old problems, for example: Kate would continually try to bride the children into going out with her for the day, despite my repeated requests not to do so. The effects of this weren't drastic, as I was in complete control during all the access visits; it's just that it was becoming so very frustrating.

Over the previous months I had started to realize that unless I tried to build a bridge to the other side, then it was looking more and more unlikely that anyone else was going to bother. In the beginning I had naively believed that the whole point of the legal process was to enforce the law and to bring Kate into line. I was therefore having difficulty working out exactly what the legal teams had actually achieved on my behalf. All we had effectively done over the last couple of years was to meet up, and each time various questions had been put to me, which I in turn answered. A letter would then be written and posted on my behalf. With little more effort I could have picked the phone up and told Kate most of this in under an hour, had I been allowed to do so! It is a fact that most of the progress was actually made during one court attendance in February 2005, at which I had personally spoken to Kate and agreed to let her visit our home address. Everything else had, in one way or another, been a total waste of tax payer's money.

As I sit here today it is a fact that despite all that money being spent over a period of 2 years – they never even managed to retrieve something as simple as the children's passports for me. Forgive me for being cynical but surely under such circumstances where you have 2 adults with such serious accusations against them, who from day one had showed total disrespect for the law, then surely the first thing that needs to be retrieved are the children's passports – and lets not forget that Kate had been actively trying to get both children out of the country in the months leading up to these tragic events. I had been telling every one for over a year that I needed the passports, but all to no avail. You tell me, where's the common sense in all this?

Something else that I really couldn't understand was the fact that civil law seemed to be unable or simply unwilling to deal with any disclosures that arose from the video evidence that we had filmed back in July 2003. At the time they clearly added to the traumatic experience that both of my children were going through and yet to this day they have never been aired in any court of law. In fact they still sit in the storage files of the child protection team at Basingstoke police station. They have never been released despite a written request from myself via my solicitor, asking for the videos to be handed over. The official police reply was that it was not within their procedure to release them for private individuals and that they could only be released if requested for use in a court of law. As we had been unable to get Kate to deal with the problems in any official form, this meant that all the decisions being made by the so called 'experts', were being made with total disregard to the most important point in the whole case – and that was the actual opinion of my children. Surely those videos should be the starting point for any 3rd party who found themselves involved in the case. I have to say that I found the fact that they were trying to make such critical decisions which affected the welfare of my children, without first viewing the video account of these tragic events, beyond belief. How could anyone be expected to make a sound judgment without first having the details upon which the whole scenario had been based? The strange thing was that over the previous year I had requested these videos on various occasions, only to be told that we wouldn't be able to see them until the court case actually started. Well I've now completed everything that the law allowed me to do with regard to the whole issue and yet it is a fact that I have yet to see exactly what is on those videos. Yes I have a very good idea what is on them, but as their biological father and the person who holds full custody and therefore parental responsibility for my children in law, then I feel that if anyone should view them, then that person should be me.

In short it's disgraceful that as I sit here today I am still unable to access these very important pieces of the jigsaw puzzle.

Again my opinion is that various individuals were simply satisfied with making money out of our misery and not addressing the actual problem at all. I had now started to realized that unless I made the effort myself to resolve this, then we could in effect be stuck in this position for months, or maybe even years. The biggest single problem that I now faced was that so many people were profiting from this tragedy, and none of them had any intention of bringing it to a swift end.

Following our court appearance, Kate came to our house with her sister on 3 occasions before her sister plucked up the courage to ask me if it would be possible for her mother to attend with them on the next home visit. We had a court order that stated all visits were to be held at my home address and supervised by me for a period of six months, at which time I was well aware that it was extremely likely that the court would then allow Kate to take the children out for the day. The visits were going as well as could be expected, although they did cause some minor mood changes in both children which in turn resulted in a drop in form at both schools. I had conversations with staff at both of the children's schools during this period, as both had noticed that the children just weren't themselves. Amongst other things my son's concentration during the day was being distracted by the events at home. It may have just been a coincidence, although personally I don't think so. My view was that the visits were causing stress and apprehension to my children, and as they were both due to do their 'SATS' at school in the coming months, this was obviously causing me great concern.

After careful thought I decided that we were going to get absolutely nowhere until the day came that Kate and the children could safely carry out such a simple task as going shopping together. I therefore came to the conclusion that the ideal solution was for Kate and her sister to take the children shopping, accompanied by Kate's parents. I knew that I was taking a gamble but we simply weren't getting anywhere fast. In my opinion Kate was simply going through the motions until such time as the court would override me and grant her an unsupervised visit with the children, at least if I made the decision now I still had enough control over the situation to withdraw all access visits, thus forcing the issue back into the courts. My heart was telling me to over rule my head, but in reality I knew that I had very few choices left and that the sands of time were running out. With great trepidation I made the decision to allow the children to go shopping with their mother, sister and grandparents, for a period of 2 hours, one Saturday morning in March 2005.

The day arrived and I have to be honest and say that I had serious doubts as to whether or not I was doing the right thing – what if I got it wrong?..... What would happen then...? There were so many questions flying through my mind. Kate arrived with her sister and collected the children; the plan was to meet her parents in town at a coffee shop. I was worried but tried not to show it. As I collected the children's coats from the peg in the hall, my son approached me and quietly asked if I could come with him. I now had to make a very difficult decision and I had to make it there and then. Should I go with him? Or should I cancel the whole event? I had already prepared myself mentally for what I realized would be a difficult day. Whatever I felt, in my heart I knew that I had to be strong, as the slightest worrying glance or self doubt from me and both children would quickly loose confidence and refuse to go. I reassured my son and once again all I could see in his eyes was total belief, total belief in me and the fact that if I said it would be ok for him to go shopping with his mum, then that was good enough for him – he trusted me completely. With his chin held high he turned and walked out of the door, giving me a beaming smile and a quick wave as he went. Earlier in the day I had asked my daughter to keep an eye on him while they were out and to reassure him if she felt that he needed it.

This was a massive step for all three of us and so I crossed everything and prayed that it would all turn out fine in the end. I closed the door and was left with a feeling of total emptiness inside, as I still wasn't totally convinced that I was doing the right thing. I felt that I had been forced into this position by the lack of progress through the legal channels. I was still having great difficulty in understanding how we had got into this position despite spending thousands of pounds, and yet we still hadn't seen any sorrow or remorse from my ex wife. In fact she had shown, and was still showing, total disregard for the law all the way through the process, and yet I was still slowly being pushed into a position where I would eventually have to release both children into her care, unaccompanied, some time in the very near future. I felt that I was left with no choice other than to allow the shopping trip to go ahead now, while I still had some legal control over the situation. There was absolutely no doubt in my mind that when we returned to court for the follow up analysis in August, then the court would definitely allow my ex wife to take the children out for the day – the difference being that if I left things until then I would have absolutely no legal control over the situation, and that I'm afraid I find very disturbing indeed.

In my opinion if you have a bomb in your hands, then you have 2 simple choices. You can either disarm the bomb or you can blow it up – either way you will permanently fix the problem. But if you decide to do neither of the above but instead you decide to take a soft approach and caress the bomb, gently rolling it along beside you – then guess what, surprise surprise eventually the bloody thing will blow up in your face. There was absolutely no doubt in my mind that in my case the 'bomb' hadn't actually been defused or blown up, in fact the legal system had decided to caress my bomb – the problem was that they left me standing next to it, and not only that but to make things slightly more interesting they were tying my hands together so that I couldn't defend myself when it eventually went bang. I felt that it was surely only a matter of time before the 'bomb' went off, and I lost count of the days I woke up wondering if today would be the day when it all went wrong. I'm very thankful that so far it hasn't, but I do feel that various individuals that were involved with my case should have a long hard look at themselves for some of the decisions that they made with regard to my children.

They eventually returned from their shopping trip and to my delight they were both carrying a few items that had obviously been bought for them in town. At long last I thought we were now making progress as they approached me with big smiles and a bag full of presents. My joy was short lived however as it turned out that their mother had bought none of the items, and that they had in fact been paid for by the children's grand parents. Even after all this Kate still flatly refused to spend a single penny on her children – it was almost beyond belief.

I had made serious concessions in order for the shopping trip to take place and yet it seemed that my generosity had been ignored by Kate, as had all my other gratuitous acts over the last couple of years. As an individual you get to a point where you really have to switch off to some of the things that are going on around you. I felt that if I was going to let these things get to me then there would only be one outcome, and that was that these events would eventually destroy me. I had no doubt that in the end they would slowly grind me down until such time as there was no fight left in me, and I was determined not to let that happen. I was aware that I needed a positive attitude at all times as I knew I couldn't let it get to me.No matter how I looked at the situation, the only conclusion I came to was that the whole process had been a total waste of time and money, as here we were 2 years down the line and still, despite all my best efforts, we had no satisfactory solution to the problems. Kate was still showing total disregard for the law and they were doing absolutely nothing to change that, as a result despite the efforts of the best legal brains available, she had got herself in a position where she had access to the children, and yet in legal terms she had never once accepted or followed any of the conditions imposed upon her by the court. So why then was I made to suffer such emotional trauma for such a long period of time in the first place? It really is a sorry state of affairs to end up in. I honestly felt that I could do no more, I'd given it my best shot and it was clear that my reward was going to be absolutely nothing. I firmly believed that what I was doing was right but it was apparent that all the official bodies were so fragmented that at times it felt that we were all going in different directions. I truly hope that you don't ever find yourself in such an isolated position with regard to your own children, but if you do then the best advice I can give is to follow your heart. Whatever happens, and there will be dark days waiting on the horizon for you, don't ever doubt yourself or your actions – to do that will result in total failure of your objectives, believe in yourself no matter what anyone else says to you.

Even though I was at my wits end with the whole situation, I am still big enough to admit that Kate's visit into town seemed to have a positive effect on both children, and that was my only wish. The children seemed happy and that's all that mattered to me. One day they would realize exactly what their mother had been doing and how difficult she had made the whole situation, but for now I felt that it wasn't my place to tell them. I felt that in time they would see her for what she was through their own eyes, my job was to love and protect them and I had every intention of doing that.

The bi-weekly phone calls continued and so did the visits, slowly things started to settle. The circumstances were far from ideal as I realized that until Kate accepted that the children were now my responsibility, and in turn started to take some simple instructions from me regarding the children, then we were always going to be left without a solution. It was blatantly obvious that everyone involved was hoping that Kate and I would eventually resolve this major issue. But how can you even begin to contemplate any of that when you are dealing with such an arrogant, manipulative and disturbed individual. If they ever thought that I would eventually come round to Kate's way of thinking then I'm afraid they were in for a very long wait. On the other hand, as no effort was being made to get Kate to understand my views, then I guess it would be fair to say that I too was in for a very long wait – and childcare law in this country endorses that as a satisfactory solution!

In short I had very little choice but to let things figure themselves out now, as I'd done all I could for the children, both legally and emotionally. They say that time is a great healer, well that was all I was left with now - time. You tell me: would you be happy to have time as your only defense under the same circumstances?

Each new day bought more relief as it slowly started to dawn upon me that the nightmare was finally over. From now on the world was going to be our oyster and I was determined to make a success of things. As the weeks passed a feeling of calm filled my body and I started to dream about the future. I'd waited a long time to have thoughts like these and it was such a good feeling to welcome them into my life, the road had been hard but we'd made it – armed only with grit, determination and the belief that we were right, we'd made it through to the end and the initial challenge was now over.

CHAPTER 14

MY HOPES FOR THE FUTURE

I returned to the civil court as requested in August 2005, when the restrictions were lifted and I decided to bring the legal proceedings to a close. At the time I could see absolutely no way in which they legal system could benefit either myself or my children any more. After 2 years of legal arguments all I was left with was the court order that was still in force to block any approach from Richard with regard to both children. I realize that my views will undoubtedly come across in a very cynical way but I'm just trying to be honest and I say these things, having had the experience of living through this nightmare and the frustrations that came with it.

In short I feel that between all of us we have totally failed in all of my main objectives. We have failed to retrieve any of the items from my ex-wife's home and we have also failed to retrieve many important items including the children's passports and birth certificates. We have also failed in all our attempts to retrieve any child maintenance for the children and we have failed to retrieve the missing child benefit. Last but not least, and the thing that has left me the most bewildered is the fact that absolutely no attempt had been made to change the views of my ex-wife or to alter the way in which she addressed and dealt with my children. You tell me then if that's what you would call a satisfactory solution to my problems. Unfortunately the way the law stands, we as individuals needed to go through all of the above as it was a legal requirement. To be honest I have to say that from the bottom of my heart I feel totally let down by many of the people involved and some of their opinions and decisions will continue to amaze me for the rest of my life.

At the time of going to press, the CSA have still not managed to get their house in order despite my official complaint, followed by a generous portion of help from my local MP. It had always been my intention to bring all matters regarding my children to a close before I published this book, unfortunately due to various government bodies that has proved to be impossible. A couple of weeks before this manuscript was due to be sent for publication, I received a phone call from the office of my local MP who had been helping me to resolve the issue with the CSA. The call was to inform me that the MP in question was now due to retire after 22 years of loyal service to his constituents. The caller also confirmed that my MP's parting shot was that he was going to send my file on to the government ombudsman responsible for overseeing this shambles, as he felt that he had done all he could for me and yet we were still a million miles away from a long term solution.

Unfortunately last week Tony Blair announced that he is to call a general election on May 5th 2005 – in 3 weeks time. This is to have a major effect on my claim as part of the process for the up and coming election is the dissolution of parliament for a month. In effect this means that although my MP was good enough to forward my file, there is in fact no-one there for the next month to receive it and to deal with the problem – you honestly couldn't make it up could you?

In one last ditch attempt to resolve the issue I wrote to my MP's office asking if they could make one final call to the CSA on my behalf, due to the fact that my case officer based in Bristol now flatly refuses to speak to me personally on the phone. I have suggested that we cancel the collection service that I had requested from the CSA, which in my opinion is now responsible for the delay, and replace it with a request that my ex-wife now starts to pay me directly, thus removing the obstacle of the CSA's dreaded computer system.

A week later I received a reply to my request which confirmed that my offer was an excellent idea and that indeed this would be a viable solution to the problem. I was informed that the CSA were going to contact Kate during the coming week to arrange for the payments to start being paid direct to me from now on. We could then address the back payment problem as a separate issue and get the whole thing sorted out once and for all. All in all it sounded too good to be true, although it didn't take me long to realize that as Kate was going to play such an important part in the proceedings, then nothing would be as straight forward as it seemed at first glance.

Unfortunately when the CSA contacted Kate by phone to explain the situation in full, she flatly refused to start making the payments. Even when told that she was now required by law to pay this money to me she still flatly refused. The case officer then went on to explain to Kate that her actions were not helping the situation at all and that she would immediately seek an attachment of earning order against her – I'm told that Kate's response was to suggest that the CSA should go ahead and do just that. She confirmed that although she acknowledged the fact that she must pay her child maintenance, she had no intention of doing it of her own free will, and that if the CSA wanted the money then they would have to come and get it.

My case officer was absolutely astounded to get this reaction from a mother, she had come across it frequently from absent fathers but never in all her years had she come across a mother with such a cold and callous heart. During my conversation with the CSA I explained some of the background to my case and in particular some of the other problems that Kate was actively trying to cause both myself and my children. It's interesting to note that no matter who I spoke to on the phone about childcare issues, all were in agreement that none of this should be allowed to happen in today's society, and yet here I am and things like this have been happening to me almost everyday over recent months. The part I was having the most difficulty with is the fact that Kate has a very good job and an above average income, the bottom line is that she is so selfish that she just will not spend a penny of it on our children. To me that sums up the basis of the problem and in my opinion that is the root of all the problems in this case – until we change my ex-wife's perception of life so that she starts to put both of our children above her own personal gratification, then I'm afraid that we are going to get absolutely nowhere with regard to what I would call a satisfactory long term solution. I already know that I will never be able to change her opinion and that has been the most frustrating thing of all. It is a fact that Kate turns up for her supervised visits at my home address every fortnight, dressed immaculately and driving a brand new car, and yet she won't put food in her own children's mouths – I would generally say that things like this are beyond belief, and yet I sit here and its happening to me despite all the legal action that I've been involved in over the last 2 years – can you make any sense of it all because

I can't.

As a direct result of Kate's actions my file is now in the hands of the government ombudsman responsible for the CSA, although at the time of going to press he has yet to make official contact with me regarding the issue. I have now started the lengthy legal process of trying to retrieve the substantial back payment that I am owed. I actually have in my possession a letter from the chief executive of the CSA which had promised me the following: Firstly I was to get an official apology for the unnecessary delay that they had caused in processing my application. I was also promised an apology for the severe trauma and stress that their actions had put me through. The letter also stated that once completed, my application would be forwarded to the 'special payments unit' within the CSA in order for them to reimburse me the monies owed. None of the above has been forthcoming and I'm so very disappointed, I really am. It is fair to say that it is my intention to persevere with my claim for child maintenance and that I have no intention of allowing them to get away with treating myself and my family with such contempt. You judge for yourself, whether or not you would be happy with their performance had you been unlucky enough to find yourself in my predicament.

My opinion is that they are an absolute disgrace. We are not talking about a tin pot outfit here; we are talking about an official government department, responsible for childcare. These people are dealing with some of the most financially desperate people within our society and they deserve better, it's as simple as that – they should be deeply ashamed of themselves and their actions. Someone once said that a nation is judged on how it deals with its most needy individuals. Well all I can say is, that fact does not bode well for the United Kingdom as I sit here today. In this day and age, we as a nation must do much more to help the thousands of single parents that are within our society. Most of them are desperate for any type of financial help and to treat childcare claims with such contempt is nothing short of disgraceful – there is no other word. If I was the individual responsible for the CSA, I would hang my head in shame as I walked down the street past each and every one of them.

In summary I would have to say that there is absolutely no doubt in my mind that I suffered more anxiety, stress and emotional turmoil due to the incompetence of government departments such as the Housing department and the Child Support Agency, than I did from the actual events that started all this in the first place on 11th July 2003 – and when you stop to think about everything that I have written in this book, then surely that in itself must raise serious concerns as to how we as a nation are dealing with the future of our children.

The journey that we have just travelled has been a long and difficult one. In recent times I have seen 2 sides to this country that we are all living in. It was only a couple of years ago that I had believed that our country was second to none when it came to enterprise and opportunity. I had my own successful business, my own flat, car and all the trappings that came with them. I was also holidaying to some of the most exotic locations in the world. How easy it all seemed back then as I wandered through life in my own little bubble. I too had become part of the human rat race that I loath so much.

Over the last 2 years all of those material things have slowly slipped through my fingers as I drifted back down into a world that I had no longer believed existed within our society. Somehow I had long forgotten about all the hurt and suffering that I had witnessed while in prison in 1990. I'm slightly embarrassed to admit that, as I had promised myself that upon my release I would try to look out for people less fortunate that myself and try to help them if I possibly could. With hindsight I just wish that I hadn't had to go to such extremes in order to be reminded of our human obligation to help one another. There is no doubt that there is a whole group of people within our society who still need our help and assistance on a regular basis.

What I am trying to say is that amongst other things, over the last 2 years I have learnt the power of compassion. Without this I wouldn't have made it through to the end and would no doubt have been destroyed from within by all the anger and aggression that these tragic events originally caused me. It's so very important to us as individuals that we channel our energy in a positive direction – no matter what trauma we are faced with. Anything other than that will in my opinion result in total failure. I believe that I owe it to myself and also to both of my children to learn from past experiences.

Something else that I have learnt is that you can change the size of a problem simply by changing the angle from which you perceive it. In layman's terms what I mean is that if you have a puncture on your car, you can either; sit there all day and moan about it, curse the manufacturer and utter a thousand obscenities, or you can simply get out of the car and fix it. Not only is it better for your car if you choose the latter but it is also much better for you as an individual. We as humans can deal with the largest physical, emotional and physiological problems but what actually matters is how we look at them and how we deal with them.

Everything that I have been through has in some way helped to shape me and make me the man I am today. Without all those experiences I may not have coped with recent events. For years I resented the fact that I didn't have a normal upbringing like all my friends, due to the fact that at such a young age I was sent off to boarding school. Now in later life I'm convinced that my own family is so very important to me due solely to the fact that when I was a young boy I spent a great deal of my time away from my own family, which in turn has made me appreciate just how special my siblings are to me. There can be little doubt that the family structure is so important to set guidelines for the next generation of young adults. If you interfere with the family structure then you are interfering with your own future, so be warned, and always try to remember that children need a safe and settled environment in which to grow and develop. For the past two years I have done my very best to provide exactly that for my offspring.

I feel that without doubt one of the of the main things that made me a man in the first place was the fact that from the age of about 8 years old I had to stand up for myself, as my parents were over 7000 miles away on a distant shore. There was no running home and telling tales in my childhood, either I let someone take my things or I stood up and fought for them – I chose to fight and I have no regrets.

Now in my later years all those experiences have made me a very understanding and I hope compassionate man. Maybe its life's experiences or maybe its just age, what ever it is, I am now definitely more patient and controlled than I have been in previous years. A large part of that has to be down to the companionship of my two children, who since they arrived have breathed fresh air into my life and given me a reason to wake up each day. My newfound caring approach has to be down to them, as without knowing it, they have taught me so many valuable lessons during a short period of time.

Whatever I thought about my upbringing, one thing was certain and that was that I should be thankful that I had been given the opportunity to acquire a decent education that at the very least has enabled me to write the letters and to make the phone calls that were needed to defend my corner. During my recent trial I personally had to collect all of the relevant information together and ensure that it found its way to its rightful destination so that it could be used to its full potential. Believe me it was that fact and that fact alone that kept me out of prison in January 2005.

As I sit here a free man I want to spare a thought for those people who find themselves in a similar position to mine but who are unable to express themselves. Many fail the task and fall by the wayside and personally I look upon myself as a minor victory for each and every one of them. Those that didn't make it through to the end, those that never got the chance to see that they were right all along, and those who never got the chance to see their dreams fulfilled.

On a personal level I guess the road that I have travelled has been a hard one but I don't sit here with a feeling of sadness or regret about anything that has happened in the last 37 years, for me it's quite the opposite, as I feel like I have been blessed in so many ways. Amongst other things I've been to some of the most beautiful places in the world and I've got two healthy children who adore me – what more could I possibly want from life.

I came through the difficult challenges in my life and luckily I managed to sweep my children along with me and turn them both into a success, but it is fair to say that I could have been helped so much more along the way. The crazy thing is that it wouldn't have taken much. All I needed was a little care and common sense from various individuals, but alas we have all become so material that many of them had neither the time nor the enthusiasm to care about anyone else. How very sad that is because I believe that my children are worth so much more than that, and they will continue to be worth so much more than that until their dying day. I am so proud of them both for the way they have adapted over a very difficult period in their lives and I've been so fulfilled just by watching them grow and develop. Surely our children are worth fighting for and there can't be any doubt about that. Mine gave me some direction in my life at a time when I had none. Having both of them around has made me realize that there are emotions deep within me that I never knew I had. Nothing can compare to the look I get from those little round eyes as they turn and look to me for reassurance and safety on a daily basis.

Something else worth a mention is the sad fact regarding the way that we as a society look down upon single parents. I've fought my way through some interesting situations over the last couple of years and yet despite all the distractions the one thing that stands out the most is just how low in the food chain most people perceive single parents to be. If you get 5 minutes try and sit down with a cup of tea and just imagine what it's like to bring up young children alone today. Most single parents are in that position through no fault of their own and deserve more respect for their efforts. Those that whisper the word 'sponger' in their little groups as we walk past make me laugh with their ignorance.

What I have been through is almost beyond belief in a time when we as a nation think we can send rockets to the moon and maybe even one day live on Mars. Who's trying to kid who then? We as a nation can't even manage to tell a 35 year old psychotic mother that what she is doing is wrong. Our politicians talk routinely about helping people to overcome their difficulties all over the world and yet they struggled to help an average bloke living in Basingstoke, when he needed it most. I've had to sit by almost helpless on many occasions, due to red tape, while an individual was allowed to almost destroy 3 lives. I don't care how much 'spin' you put on that – it's wrong and it needs to change.

My whole life has changed in recent years. I've been through so much in such a short space of time and now I'm tired and weary from the journey. My dreams and hopes are probably very similar to yours; it's just that the path we both chose to tread was a different one. Just like the motorways that all end up in London, we as individuals all end up in the same place in the end. It's up to us what we do with our lives in between. I no longer worry about who said what and why they said it. Now I worry about how I'm going to pay for my daughter's driving lessons and then her first car. I worry about how my son is getting along at school and who he's playing with. All these things make being a parent a full time job, but like most things in life you will only reap what you sow. My advice to you would therefore have to be: Try and put in the hours while your children are still young, enjoy every minute of your time together because you never know what's round the corner and very quickly things can change, one silly mistake could cost you everything, as I so nearly found out.

This book has been all about therapy for me. It has kept me going through the darkest and loneliest of days, when at times I didn't know my arse from my elbow. It has been a very emotional and sometimes painful journey, yet I have no room for regrets. There were certainly days when I had to control my anger and aggression, but in time I realized that those negative emotions are no good for the soul, as all they do is eat away at you from the inside.

In this instance, if you were to ask me for advice I would have to say; whatever you choose to do always remember that you must keep a very firm control of your temper and also any other negative emotions. You must also keep a positive attitude at all times. Finally, believe in yourself and follow your heart. If you are able to do that then the rewards that you will eventually reap will be of far greater value than anything that you have lost along the way.

The hardest part for me was always going to be discussing what had happened with my children in recent years. General opinion was that one should never do their dirty washing in public but in my heart I knew that the story needed to be told. I don't feel like I'm washing anything dirty in public, as I don't feel that the three of us have done anything wrong. I've not made mistakes that others haven't made and I'm no worse than your average man on the street. Yes I made some bad decisions but we all have to live with that. I'm not ashamed of anything that I've had to write in this book and I'm not ashamed of my children, in fact the opposite - I'm proud of them, I'm so very proud of them.

Today my days are filled with joy and happiness. At last I've managed to find some of the things that I've been looking for in life. My two children are happy and settled. With love and hard work, between us we have achieved the impossible and made a success out of what could have become a living nightmare had we allowed it to do so.

I have just started the process of returning to work as one of Tony Blaire's young mums, under the new government initiative that they call 'A new deal for lone parents' – lets just hope it's a big improvement on the 'Raw deal for lone parents' that I have recently had to endure! Personally I'm really looking forward to going back to work as it's something I've missed so much during recent times. It's going to be so nice to get back out onto a scaffold during the coming summer months, with the sun beating down and big Tony giving his daily sermon on various events that are going on around us – it will be just like old times!

Despite all the failings of the various professional bodies to retrieve or achieve anything on my behalf, I still sit here with a feeling of joy and success. I can't hide the fact that I am so very disappointed by many of the decisions that have been taken with regard to my children, and yet through it all I have learnt that success and failure can be interpreted in so many ways. For me I only have to look at both my son and daughter today, to see that on a personal level all of my actions have been a resounding success. Should you pass them in the street you would be hard pushed to pick them out, and that gives me so much satisfaction that I cannot put it into words – 2 normal children, that's all I wanted when I started all of this and I'm so happy and proud to announce that looking around me today – that's exactly what I've got. In would also be true to say that a lot of the success has been due to the fact that I was surrounded by people who had the best interests of my family at heart, people who believed that I could achieve happiness for the three of us. If I'm totally honest I would have to agree that the odds of getting here today were slim to say the least at the beginning.

I believe that I've proved beyond any doubt that it doesn't matter what you do as you are growing up, just as long as you remember that it's never too late to admit that you've made mistakes. Put your hands up and be big enough to admit that you were at fault and you'll be surprised how many people step forward to help you in your hour of need.

Although I have always believed in myself, especially when it came to loving and protecting my children, as I found that the most natural instinct in my body, I will always owe a debt of gratitude to those around me who were brave enough to support me in the beginning. Those who stuck their necks out for me when all the odds were against us – well I told you I wouldn't let you down and

I haven't. Now that we have survived the ordeal its time for each and every one of you to give yourselves a big pat on the back for your efforts. Many of you I had never met before, and probably never would have met had it not been for the children and I want to take this opportunity to thank each and every one of you for all the help and advice that you gave me, just when I needed it most. It was so nice to see such compassion, tolerance and general caring from my fellow beings as I'd spent most of my life seeing only anger and aggression. It's nice to know that people still care about one another in this material world in which we live.

For the future my personal hopes are that things continue pretty much as they are, never have I felt more fulfilled than I do at this present time. The joys of parenthood have given me more than I could ever wish for, yes it can be hard and yes it can be demanding, but the rewards are so great that given the chance I wouldn't change a thing and I have no regrets. I have stood up to be counted when my family needed me most and that my friend makes me very proud to have achieved the things I have in recent times. Surely there is nothing on this earth that is more powerful than the bond between parent and child.

All there is left for me to say is that I'm proud of what I have become and I'm proud of both my son and my daughter, but above all else I'm proud to be a man. I believe that I now know the truth and I also believe that I now know where I'm heading. I know in my heart that I may never be what you want me to be and that's because I'm free to be what I want.

ISBN 1-41205513-X